Prophets
of the
LATTER
DAYS

RICHARD NEITZEL HOLZAPFEL

WILLIAM W. SLAUGHTER

Sources for Photographs and Illustrations

Abbreviations

BYU: L. Tom Perry Special Collections, Harold B. Lee Library, Brigham Young University, Provo, Utah

Church Archives: Church Archives, The Church of Jesus Christ of Latter-day Saints, Salt Lake City, Utah

DUP: Pioneer Memorial Museum, International Society, Daughters of Utah Pioneers, Salt Lake City, Utah

MCHA: Museum of Church History and Art, The Church of Jesus Christ of Latter-day Saints, Salt Lake City, Utah

MLUU: J. Willard Marriott Library, University of Utah, Salt Lake City, Utah

USHS: Utah State Historical Society, Salt Lake City, Utah

USU: Special Collections and Archives, Merrill Library, Utah State University, Logan, Utah

VRL: Visual Resource Library, The Church of Jesus Christ of Latter-day Saints, Salt Lake City, Utah

Quotations have sometimes been edited for clarity and consistency.

Endsheet images courtesy MCHA, Church Archives, Office of the President, Edward L. Kimball, H. Brent Goates, Mark Philbrick, Joseph Fielding and Brenda McConkie, and Manuscripts Division, MLUU, University of Utah.

Library of Congress Cataloging-in-Publication Data

Holzapfel, Richard Neitzel.
    Prophets of the Latter Days / Richard Neitzel Holzapfel, William W. Slaughter.
      p.   cm.
    Includes bibliographical references and index.
    ISBN 1-57345-902-X (alk. paper)
    1. Church of Jesus Christ of Latter-day Saints—Presidents—Biography.   I. Slaughter, William W., 1952–   II. Title.
BX8693.H55 2003
289.3'092'2—dc22
                         2003014687

Phoenix Color   70582-6774
Printed in the United States of America

10 9 8 7 6 5 4 3 2

CONTENTS

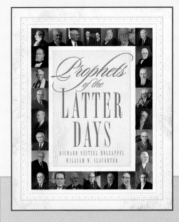

FOR MY
INQUISITIVE
AND THOUGHTFUL
DAUGHTER
ZANNA LESE
HOLZAPFEL

Richard Neitzel Holzapfel

IN MEMORY
OF MY FATHER,
SOLOMON WESLEY
SLAUGHTER,
WHO WAS WISE
BEYOND THE
UNDERSTANDING
OF HIS SON

William W. Slaughter

INTRODUCTION

Latter-day Saints sing a lively hymn, "We Thank Thee, O God, for a Prophet," written by William Fowler in 1863. An Australian convert to the church, William made his way to Utah in 1849. Composed just a few years before his death, the hymn became an instant classic, and is sung often at the Church's general conference and in other settings. Each person's voice raised in song is an expression of his or her unique feelings regarding the prophet. For some it is an expression of gratitude for two specific individuals: Joseph Smith and the current living prophet. Others think of the president of the Church who was living at the time of their baptism or some other important event in their lives. Each person has a unique interpretation of the meaning of the words of this hymn as well as of the lives and ministry of those who have been called to serve as the prophet, seer, and revelator for the Church of Jesus Christ. For all members singing the hymn, it represents a token of appreciation for those who have helped the kingdom of God roll forth, preparing the world for the Second Coming of Jesus Christ.

Like individual members of the Church who sing this hymn with personal feelings and thoughts, this book is our effort to capture what we experience when we sing these words penned by William Fowler so many years ago. Since neither of us has ever been invited to sing with the Mormon Tabernacle Choir, you may presume that singing is not one of our God-given talents. However, we hope you will hear our voices resound through the words and images collected herein:

> We thank thee, O God, for a prophet
> To guide us in these latter days.
> We thank thee for sending the gospel
> To lighten our minds with its rays.
> We thank thee for every blessing
> Bestowed by thy bounteous hand.
> We feel it a pleasure to serve thee,
> And love to obey thy command.

This book is also an outgrowth of our continuing interest in the visual history of the Latter-day Saints. Word pictures, drawings, engravings, paintings, early daguerreotypes, stereographs, modern photographs—each has a way of capturing aspects of life. In an effort to provide basic information about the presidents of The Church of Jesus Christ of Latter-day Saints, we have prepared a time line for each of their lives. To help us view the context of their lives, we have augmented these chronologies with the dates of national and international events. Each of the essays in this volume is an attempt to provide an interpretation of the unique life of these church leaders. These essays are not intended to be a comprehensive examination of their lives or of their ministry as Church president. We have purposely avoided taking a boilerplate approach; however, a few features in each chapter are constant, such as a time line, a discussion of the president's family, some statistical information about his life, and the status of the Church at the time of his death. These constants aside, each chapter is an independent creation suited for the individual ministry of a president. The images, many of which have never before been published, contribute a distinctive understanding to the ministry of each prophet. Additionally, we have produced several thematic sections that we hope will give further context to the lives and ministries of these great men.

President Harold B. Lee once said, "I think it is folly for one to compare one president of the Church with another. No one takes the place of another president of the Church. Each President has his own place. . . . And so, when you think of one president taking the place of another, he doesn't. That president maintains his own place. We shouldn't try to compare one as being greater than this one or greater than the other, because each one is, in the eyes of the Lord, in his own time the one most needed for that particular time. You may be sure of that." Believing this to be wise counsel, we have not attempted to compare, contrast, or evaluate the lives of the presidents of the Church in relationship to each other. The natural result of this decision is seen in the independent nature of the individual essays. We do, however, hope that the contextual information provided in charts and in the time lines will provide a basis to help readers see the unfolding wonder of the work of the Lord in the lives of those chosen "before the foundation of the world" to stand as prophets, seers, and revelators under Christ during the last dispensation.

TESTIMONIES OF CHRIST

The First Presidency and the Quorum of the Twelve standing in front of the Christus on Temple Square, 1999 (Church Archives)

JOSEPH SMITH

"The fundamental principles of our religion are the testimony of the apostles and prophets, concerning Jesus Christ, that He died, was buried, and rose again the third day, and ascended into heaven; and all other things which pertain to our religion are only appendages to it."

BRIGHAM YOUNG

"I testify that Jesus is the Christ, the Savior and Redeemer of the world; I have obeyed His sayings, and realized His promise, and the knowledge I have of Him, the wisdom of this world cannot give, neither can it take away. My faith is placed upon the Lord Jesus Christ, and my knowledge I have received from Him."

JOHN TAYLOR

"The Atonement made by Jesus Christ brought about the resurrection from the dead, and restored life. And hence Jesus said: 'I am the resurrection, and the life; he that believeth in me, though he were dead, yet shall he live' (John 11:25). . . . How far does that principle extend and to whom is it applicable? It extends to all the human family; to all men of every nation."

WILFORD WOODRUFF

"The Savior came . . . and entered upon the duties of the priesthood at thirty years of age. After laboring three and a half years he was crucified and put to death in fulfillment of certain predictions concerning him. He laid down his life as a sacrifice for sin, to redeem the world."

LORENZO SNOW

"The spirit of God descended upon me, completely enveloping my whole person, filling me from the crown of my head to the soles of my feet, and O the joy and happiness I felt! No language can describe the almost instantaneous transition from a dense cloud of mental and spiritual darkness into a refulgence of light and knowledge that God lives, that Jesus Christ is the Son of God."

JOSEPH F. SMITH

"Christ is indeed the Savior of my soul, the Savior of mankind. He has sacrificed his life for us that we might be saved, he has broken the bands of death, . . . he has declared himself to be the way of salvation, the light and the life of the world, and I believe it with all my heart."

HEBER J. GRANT

"I know as well as I know anything in this life that Jesus Christ is in very deed the Savior of mankind, and that God has seen fit to establish the Church of Jesus Christ upon the earth. I thank the Lord that I have an abiding knowledge of God, our Father, and Jesus Christ, his Son, and that I have pleasure in bearing witness to all the world of this knowledge that I possess."

GEORGE ALBERT SMITH

"I know that my Redeemer lives and gladly yield my humble efforts to establish His teachings. . . . Every fiber of my being vibrates with the knowledge that He lives and some day all men will know it. The Savior died that we might live. He overcame death and the grave and holds out to all who obey His teachings the hope of a glorious resurrection."

DAVID O. MCKAY

"The reality of Jesus the Christ must be sensed by you and by me, and the reality of his message must be mine and yours if we hope to advance spiritually. . . . He is the Son of God, who took upon himself mortality even as you and I, yet divine, even as you and I may become.

JOSEPH FIELDING SMITH

"I know that Jesus of Nazareth was the Only Begotten Son of God in the flesh, with life in Himself. Because of this wonderful truth, it was possible for Him to redeem us from death and the grave, and, on condition of our repentance, from our individual sins."

HAROLD B. LEE

"By the power of the Holy Ghost and in deep humility I solemnly bear testimony to the world that God lives and that His Son, Jesus Christ, was born in the flesh; that He was crucified and was raised from the dead with a body of flesh and bones, and sits today on the right hand of the Father as our judge and advocate."

SPENCER W. KIMBALL

"I know that Jesus Christ is the Son of the living God and that he was crucified for the sins of the world. He is my Friend, my Savior, my Lord, my God. With all my heart I pray that the Saints may keep his commandments, have his Spirit, and gain an eternal inheritance with him in celestial glory."

EZRA TAFT BENSON

"I testify that Jesus is the Christ and that He stands at the head of His Church today, even The Church of Jesus Christ of Latter-day Saints. I testify that He will come again in power and great glory and that He will leave nothing undone for our eternal welfare."

HOWARD W. HUNTER

"I give to you my solemn witness that Jesus Christ is in fact the Son of God. He is the Messiah. . . . It is by the power of the Holy Ghost that I bear my witness. . . . I know also that the Holy Spirit will confirm the truthfulness of my witness in the hearts of all those who listen with an ear of faith."

GORDON B. HINCKLEY

"I believe in the Lord Jesus Christ, the Son of the eternal, living God; . . . He is the Savior and the Redeemer of the world. I believe in Him. I declare His divinity without equivocation or compromise. I love Him. I speak His name in reverence and wonder. I worship Him as I worship His Father, in spirit and in truth. I thank Him and kneel before His wounded feet and hands and side, amazed at the love He offers me."

Brigham Young a few years after settling in Utah,
December 12, 1850 (Marsena Cannon, Church Archives)

Ezra Taft Benson blowing out the candles at his ninetieth birthday party,
August 4, 1989 (Church Archives)

Apostolic ordinations: The beginning of the call of one to be president of the Church actually begins when he is called, ordained, and set apart to become a member of the Quorum of the Twelve Apostles. . . . Each apostle so ordained under the hands of the president of the Church . . . has given to him the priesthood authority necessary to hold every position in the Church, even to a position of presidency over the Church. —HAROLD B. LEE

Ages of the presidents of the Church at the time of their calling: Some express concern that the president of the Church is likely always to be a rather elderly man, to which my response is, "What a blessing!" The work in this dispensation was first put in place through the instrumentality of the Prophet Joseph Smith. He was at the time young and vigorous, one whose mind was not set in the traditions of his day. His was a youthful mind which the Lord could mold as fresh, moist clay as he initiated the work. Joseph's successor was relatively young when he was faced with the terrible responsibility of leading an entire people

across the wilderness to pioneer a new land. But the basics of our doctrine are now well in place, and we are firmly established as a people, at least until the Lord should mandate another move. We do not need innovation. We need devotion in adherence to divinely spoken principles. We need loyalty to our leader, whom God has appointed. . . . To my mind there is something tremendously reassuring in knowing that for the foreseeable future we shall have a president who has been disciplined and schooled, tried and tested, whose fidelity to the work and whose integrity in the cause have been tempered in the forge of service, whose faith has matured, and whose nearness to God has been cultivated over a period of many years. —GORDON B. HINCKLEY

Tenure as president: Full provision has been made by our Lord for changes. . . . Since the death of his servants is in the power and control of the Lord, he permits to come to the first place only the one who is destined to take that leadership. Death and life become the controlling factors. —SPENCER W. KIMBALL

APOSTOLIC ORDINATIONS

Joseph Smith
Date ordained an apostle: May or June 1829
Age when called: 23 years 5 months
Date called as president: April 6, 1830
Age when called: 24 years 3 months
Tenure as president: 14 years 2 months

Brigham Young
Date ordained an apostle: February 14, 1835
Age when called: 33 years 8 months
Date called as president: December 27, 1847
Age when called: 46 years 7 months
Tenure as president: 29 years 8 months

John Taylor
Date ordained an apostle: December 19, 1838
Age when called: 30 years 2 months
Date called as president: October 10, 1880
Age when called: 71 years 11 months
Tenure as president: 6 years 9 months

Wilford Woodruff
Date ordained an apostle: April 26, 1839
Age when called: 32 years 2 months
Date called as president: April 7, 1889
Age when called: 82 years 1 month
Tenure as president: 9 years 4 months

Lorenzo Snow
Date ordained an apostle: February 12, 1849
Age when called: 34 years 10 months
Date called as president: September 13, 1898
Age when called: 84 years 5 months
Tenure as president: 3 years

Joseph F. Smith
Date ordained an apostle: July 1, 1866
Age when called: 27 years 7 months
Date called as president: October 17, 1901
Age when called: 62 years 11 months
Tenure as president: 17 years 1 month

Heber J. Grant
Date ordained an apostle: October 16, 1882
Age when called: 45 years 11 months
Dated called as president: November 23, 1918
Age when called: 62 years
Tenure as president: 26 years 5 months

George Albert Smith
Date ordained an apostle: October 8, 1903
Age when called: 33 years 6 months
Date called as president: May 21, 1945
Age when called: 75 years 2 months
Tenure as president: 5 years 10 months

David O. McKay
Date ordained an apostle: April 9, 1906
Age when called: 32 years 7 months
Date called as president: April 9, 1951
Age when called: 77 years 7 months
Tenure as president: 18 years 9 months

Joseph Fielding Smith
Date ordained an apostle: April 7, 1910
Age when called: 33 years 9 months
Date called as president: January 23, 1970
Age when called: 93 years 6 months
Tenure as president: 2 years 5 months

Harold B. Lee
Date ordained an apostle: April 10, 1941
Age when called: 42 years
Date called as president: July 7, 1972
Age when called: 73 years 3 months
Tenure as president: 1 year 5 months

Spencer W. Kimball
Date ordained an apostle: October 7, 1943
Age when called: 48 years 6 months
Dated called as president: December 30, 1973
Age when called: 78 years 9 months
Tenure as president: 11 years 10 months

Ezra Taft Benson
Date ordained an apostle: October 7, 1943
Age when called: 44 years 2 months
Date called as president: November 10, 1985
Age when called: 86 years 3 months
Tenure as president: 8 years 6 months

Howard W. Hunter
Date ordained an apostle: October 15, 1959
Age when called: 51 years 11 months
Date called as president: June 5, 1994
Age when called: 86 years 6 months
Tenure as president: 9 months

Gordon B. Hinckley
Date ordained an apostle: October 5, 1961
Age when called: 51 years 3 months
Date called as president: March 12, 1995
Age when called: 84 years 9 months
Current president

OLDEST TO YOUNGEST WHEN CALLED AS PRESIDENT

Joseph Fielding Smith 93 years 6 months	Gordon B. Hinckley 84 years 9 months	Spencer W. Kimball 78 years 9 months	Harold B. Lee 73 years 3 months	Heber J. Grant 62 years
Howard W. Hunter 86 years 6 months	Lorenzo Snow 84 years 5 months	David O. McKay 77 years 7 months	John Taylor 71 years 11 months	Brigham Young 46 years 7 months
Ezra Taft Benson 86 years 3 months	Wilford Woodruff 82 years 1 month	George Albert Smith 75 years 2 months	Joseph F. Smith 62 years 11 months	Joseph Smith 24 years 3 months

LONGEST TO SHORTEST TENURE AS PRESIDENT

Brigham Young 29 years 8 months	Joseph F. Smith 17 years 1 month	Wilford Woodruff 9 years 4 months	George Albert Smith 5 years 10 months	Harold B. Lee 1 year 5 months
Heber J. Grant 26 years 5 months	Joseph Smith 14 years 2 months	Ezra Taft Benson 8 years 6 months	Lorenzo Snow 3 years	Howard W. Hunter 9 months
David O. McKay 18 years 9 months	Spencer W. Kimball 11 years 10 months	John Taylor 6 years 9 months	Joseph Fielding Smith 2 years 5 months	Gordon B. Hinckley Currently Serving

Joseph Smith Jr

At midnight, May 14, 1844, two cousins docked at Nauvoo as part of a sight-seeing trip along the Mississippi River frontier. The men had not originally planned to stop at the center of Mormonism, but fellow travelers convinced them that a visit with the Mormon prophet was a must-do.

The gentlemen were Eastern elites with bloodlines reaching back to the founding of the United States. New Englander Josiah Quincy, born into wealth and prestige and son of the president of Harvard University, would be mayor of Boston within a year. Cousin Charles Francis Adams, son of former U.S. President John Quincy Adams, was a Massachusetts state senator and would later serve as Abraham Lincoln's minister to England.

The rough-hewn prophet they came to see was a man of the frontier—born and raised in poverty, wearing home-spun clothes, without proper pedigree, and, for the most part, self educated. Their two worlds could hardly be more different. In a May 16, 1844, letter to his wife, Mary Jane, Quincy sketched this quickly thought-out image: "We . . . arrived at the seat of this 'prophet, priest, king, Mayor, Lt. General and tavern keeper' for as each and all of these is he inspired to act. The door was surrounded by dirty loafers, from among which our quixotic guide selected a man, in a checked coat, dirty white pantaloons, a beard of some three days growth and introduced him as General Smith. He had the name but certainly but in few respects the look of a prophet. . . . We passed the whole day in his society, and had one of the most extraordinary conversations I ever participated in, he preached, prophesied for us, . . . and took us to his temple which he is now erecting on a most majestic site. Every inhabitant dedicates the labor of his tenth day."

A lifetime of experience allowed Quincy to reflect back on this meeting with greater depth of understanding and respect. In his 1883 *Figures of the Past*, he wrote, "It is by no means improbable that some future textbook, for the use of generations yet unborn, will contain a question something like this: What historical American of the nineteenth century has exerted the most powerful influence upon the destinies of his countrymen? And it is by no means impossible that the answer . . . may be thus written: *Joseph Smith, the Mormon prophet . . .*

(Left) Portrait by unknown artist, nineteenth century (MCHA)

(Above oval) Portrait by unknown artist, 1840s (Community of Christ)

BORN
DECEMBER 23, 1805
SHARON, VERMONT

PARENTS
JOSEPH SR. AND
LUCY MACK SMITH

BAPTIZED
MAY 15, 1829
(AGE 23)

STATURE
6' 0"
200–210 POUNDS

MARRIED
JANUARY 18, 1827
TO EMMA HALE (AGE 21)

APOSTLE
MAY OR JUNE
1829 (AGE 23)

PRESIDENT
APRIL 6, 1830
FIRST ELDER OF THE
CHURCH (AGE 24)

DIED
JUNE 27, 1844
CARTHAGE, ILLINOIS
(AGE 38)

THIS IS MY BELOVED SON. HEAR HIM!

Joseph Smith's vision in the spring of 1820 signaled the beginning of a new dispensation of the gospel (Lead stained glass, 1913, MCHA)

absurd as it doubtless seems to most men now living, may be an obvious commonplace to their descendants . . . the wonderful influence which this founder of religion exerted and still exerts throws him into relief before us, not as a rogue to be criminated, but as a phenomenon to be explained."

Instead of thinking of Joseph as a loafer in dirty pantaloons and rough beard, Quincy came to understand he had been with a hands-on frontiersman "clad in the costume of a journeyman carpenter when about his work. He was a hearty, athletic fellow . . . a fine-looking man. . . . A remarkable individual who had fashioned the mold which was to shape the feelings of so many thousands of his fellow mortals."

Joseph Smith's journey to Nauvoo began in eastern Vermont, where he was born on December 23, 1805. His parents, Joseph and Lucy Mack Smith, were continuously in the grip of poverty despite hard work and good habits. The Smith family worked a series of tenant farms where Joseph learned the arduous responsibilities of farming and family economics. From Vermont the Smiths moved in 1811 to Lebanon, New Hampshire. There Joseph had an operation that saved his leg but left him with a slight limp. Five years later the Smith family moved to Palmyra, New York, relocating two years after that to nearby Manchester.

Inspired by the great 1820 religious revivals in western New York and wanting to know his standing before God and which religious denomination to join, fourteen-

---

1805
Dec. 23 • Born in Sharon, Vermont
Lewis and Clark reach the Pacific Ocean

1811
Suffers from typhoid fever
U.S.-British War begins (1812)

1816
Winter • Family moves to New York
R.T.H. Laënnec invents stethoscope

1820
Spring • First Vision
U.S. population: 9,638,453

1823
Sept. 21–22 • Angel Moroni visits
Thomas Jefferson and John Adams die on same day, July 4 (1826)

1827
Jan. 18 • Marries Emma Hale
Sept. 22 • Obtains plates from Moroni
Construction begins on the first public railroad in the United States (1828)

1829
May 15 • Receives Aaronic Priesthood and is baptized
May or June • Receives Melchizedek Priesthood
June 11 • Secures copyright for Book of Mormon
Louis Braille invents reading system for the blind

1830
Mar. 26 • The first 5,000 copies of the Book of Mormon printed
Apr. 6 • Organizes the Church
U.S. population:12,866,020

1831
Jan. or Feb. • Leaves New York for Kirtland, Ohio
Aug. 3 • Dedicates first temple site, Independence, Missouri
Cyrus H. McCormick invents the first commercially successful grain reaper

1833
Jan. 23 • Organizes the School of the Prophets in Kirtland
Feb. 27 • Receives revelation on Word of Wisdom (D&C 89)
Mar. 18 • President of the High Priesthood (First Presidency)
Nov. 7 • Saints compelled to flee Jackson County
British abolish slavery throughout the Empire

1834
Feb. 17 • Organizes first stake, Kirtland, Ohio
May–July • Leads Zion's Camp to Missouri
Fur trappers establish Ft. Hall, Idaho

glory defy all description, standing above me in the air. One of them spake unto me, calling me by name and said—pointing to the other—'This is my beloved son, hear him.' Smith was commanded to join no sect, "for they were all wrong." This was the first in a series of divine visitations that not only changed his life but also changed the course of American religious history.

After the First Vision, the anticipated simple, uneventful life of a farmer would forever elude Joseph Smith. At seventeen year-old Joseph Smith retired to a secluded grove near his father's Palmyra farm, where he knelt to pray. He later described his experience: "I . . . began to offer up the desires of my heart to God. . . . I saw a pillar of light exactly over my head, above the brightness of the sun, which descended gradually until it fell upon me. . . . I saw two personages, whose brightness and

(Above) Rear view of the reconstructed Joseph and Lucy Mack Smith family log home, Manchester (Palmyra), New York (VRL)

(Right) View of Exchange Row in the business district of Palmyra, New York; E. B. Grandin's bookstore and printing establishment, where the Book of Mormon was printed and sold, was located in the section of building on the left identified by the L. W. Chase sign (Church Archives)

1835
Feb. 14 • Organizes Quorum of the Twelve Apostles
Feb. 28 • Organizes First Quorum of Seventy
Aug. 17 • Church accepts Doctrine and Covenants
Hans Christian Anderson publishes Tales, Told for Children

1836
Jan. 21 • Vision of the Celestial Kingdom (D&C 137)
Mar. 27 • Dedicates first temple, Kirtland, Ohio (D&C 109)
Apr. 3 • Visions in the Kirtland Temple (D&C 110)
Mexican forces defeat Texans at the Alamo

1837
June 13 • Sends first missionaries to Great Britain
Sept. 27 • Flees Kirtland for Missouri

1838
Apr. 26 • Receives revelation on the name of the Church (D&C 115)
Oct. 27 • Missouri Gov. Boggs issues extermination order
Dec. 1 • Imprisoned in Liberty Jail
Cherokees heading west on the Trail of Tears

1838–39
Winter • Saints flee Missouri seeking refuge in Illinois and Iowa

1839
Apr. 16 • Escapes Missouri imprisonment for Illinois
May 10 • Begins gathering to Commerce (Nauvoo)
Nov. 29 • Meets with U.S. president Martin Van Buren
Abner Doubleday creates rules for baseball

1840
June 6 • British converts begin immigration to Nauvoo.
Aug. 15 • Announces doctrine of baptism for the dead
U.S. population: 17,069,453

1841
Jan. 19 • Receives revelation on Nauvoo Temple (D&C 124)

1842
Mar. 17 • Organizes Navuoo Female Relief Society
May 4 • Administers endowment for the first time

1843
Apr.–May • Teaches about the Godhead and eternal marriage

1844
Mar. 11 • Delivers the "keys of the kingdom" to Brigham Young and the Twelve
June 27 • Martyred with Hyrum Smith in Carthage, Illinois
Morse sends first telegraph: "What hath God wrought?"

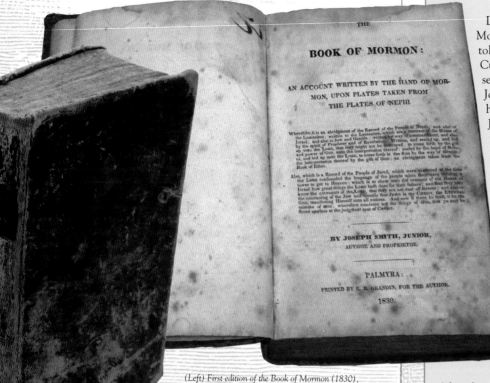

THE BOOK OF MORMON

During the night of September 21, 1823, the Angel Moroni visited seventeen-year-old Joseph Smith and told him about ancient gold plates buried in the Hill Cumorah near Palmyra. Moroni instructed Joseph to secure and translate this ancient record. The next day Joseph went to the Hill Cumorah, but Moroni told him he was not yet prepared to take on the task. Joseph returned yearly until September 27, 1827, at which time he was allowed to remove the plates from the hill. The plates had the appearance of gold but may have been a gold alloy. They measured about six inches by eight inches and six inches thick; some who lifted them said they weighed fifty to sixty pounds.

Joseph received a special instrument, called the Urim and Thummim, to help him translate the Book of Mormon. From December 1827 through June 1829, he was assisted at various times by his wife Emma, Martin Harris, Oliver Cowdery, and others who acted as scribes, writing as he dictated.

Martin Harris acted as Joseph's scribe from April 12 to June 14, 1828, during which time they produced 116 pages of translation. Unfortunately, these manuscript pages were lost when Martin took them to show his family. After this incident, Martin was no longer allowed to serve as scribe. Work on the Book of Mormon manuscript progressed slowly until April 7, 1829, when Oliver Cowdery began work as scribe. Laboring in earnest, Joseph and Oliver completed the translation by the last week of June 1829. The first edition of the Book of Mormon was printed in March 1830.

(Left) First edition of the Book of Mormon (1830), cover view (VRL)
(Above) First edition of the Book of Mormon (1830), title page view (MCHA)

REVELATIONS

From Adam to Moses and on to John the Revelator, God has revealed His word and will directly through chosen servants. In these latter days, Joseph Smith was chosen to reopen temporarily blocked communication from Heavenly Father to all His people.

To the elders assembled in Norton, Ohio, on April 21, 1834, the Prophet Joseph Smith rehearsed the coming forth of the Book of Mormon, the revelation of the Priesthood of Aaron, the 1830 organization of the Church, the importance of the gift of the Holy Ghost, and the revelation of the High Priesthood. He then emphasized a fundamental principle of this dispensation: "Take away the Book of Mormon and the revelations, and where is our religion?" He then asserted, "We have none."

Joseph Smith understood revelation to be so fundamentally necessary to understanding God that he wondered why it should be "thought a thing incredible that [God] should be pleased to speak again in these last days for their salvation." The Prophet felt that other churches condemned latter-day revelation because of a "consequence of tradition" that declared revelation merely "a thing of the past."

In 1842, as part of an answer to a newspaper editor's inquiry about Mormonism, the Prophet succinctly explained modern revelation: "We believe all that God has revealed, all that He does now reveal, and we believe that He will yet reveal many great and important things pertaining to the Kingdom of God" (9th Article of Faith).

(Above) Joseph Smith receiving a revelation (D&C 21) during the organizational meeting of the Church of Christ on April 6, 1830 (Painting by William Whitaker, about 1970, MCHA)

JOSEPH SMITH, FOUNDER OF MORMONISM.

Drawn by Henry Howe in 1846.
MORMON TEMPLE AT KIRTLAND.

JOSEPH SMITH JR.

years old, he was warned by the Angel Moroni that his "name should be had for good and evil among all nations, kindreds, and tongues, or that it should be both good and evil spoken of among all people." Indeed, Joseph was hated, loved, berated, and praised throughout his short life—with many people denouncing him as a blasphemous fraud. The barrage of verbal and physical harassment against the Prophet was constant and harsh.

Such was the case on the night of March 24, 1832. While Joseph and his wife, Emma, cared for their two adopted children, a mob burst open the door. Joseph later wrote: "I made a desperate struggle. . . . They then seized me by my throat and held on till I lost my breath. After I came to, as they passed along with me, I saw Elder Rigdon stretched out on the ground, whither they had dragged him by his heels. . . . They had concluded not to kill me, but to beat and scratch me well, tear off my shirt and drawers, and leave me naked. . . . They ran back and fetched the bucket of tar, . . . and one man fell on me and scratched my body with his nails like a mad cat, and then muttered out: 'G__ d____ ye, that's the way the Holy Ghost falls on folks!' They then left me, and I attempted to rise, but fell again; I pulled the tar away from my lips, so that I could breathe more freely. . . . My friends spent the night in

Joseph Smith profile, a photographic reproduction of an earlier Sutcliffe Maudsley view (Church Archives)

"LIEUTENANT-GENERAL" JOSEPH SMITH REVIEWING THE NAUVOO LEGION.

"Lieutenant General" Joseph Smith, about 1870, from J. H. Beadle's Life in Utah

scraping and removing the tar, and washing and cleansing my body."

The next morning, bruised, beaten to the bone, with flesh ripped from his body, Joseph insisted he be clothed and made ready for Sabbath morning meetings. He wrote that he joined the Saints "assembled for meeting at the usual hour of worship. . . . With my flesh all scarified and defaced, I preached to the congregation as usual, and in the afternoon of the same day baptized three individuals." In so many ways this incident and his response to it stand as a metaphor of his life. Rather than being brought down by adversity, he continually concentrated on the gospel and how wonderfully it blessed the lives of others.

Given his trials and tribulations, it would be easily understood, and even forgivable, if Joseph Smith had been austere and gloomy. Purposely avoiding the pompous, overblown sobriety of ministers, he was sociable, animated, approachable, and candid about his humanness. He taught that "happiness is the object and design of our existence." Simply put, Joseph Smith loved life and lived it exuberantly.

People who met him for the first time were usually surprised by his affable nature. When Jonathon Crosby met the Prophet for the first time, he noted that "he didn't appear exactly as I expected to see a Prophet of God. However, I was not stumbled at all. I found him to be a friendly, cheerful, pleasant, agreeable man." Illinois Governor Thomas Ford knew Joseph during the worst of times and maintained, "It must not be supposed that he was a dark and gloomy person, with a long beard, a grave and severe aspect, and a reserved and saintly carriage of his person; on the contrary, he was full of levity, even to boyish romping."

He was a playful, physical man who loved athletic games. Benjamin F. Johnson remembered the Prophet as "kind, generous, and mirth loving. For amusement, he would sometimes wrestle a with friend, or others; would test strength with others by sitting upon the floor with feet together and stick grasped between them. But he never met his match. Jokes, rebuses, matching couplets in rhymes, etc., were not uncommon. But to call for the singing of one or more of his favorite songs was more frequent. Of those, 'Wives, Children and Friends,' 'Battle of River Russen,' 'Soldier's Tear,' 'Soldier's Dream,' and 'Last Rose of Summer' were most common."

While looking over some horses in Nauvoo, the Prophet turned to his slight-built secretary, Howard Coray, and said, "Brother Coray I wish you were a little larger. I would like to have some fun with you"—which meant, "Let's wrestle." Coray responded, "Perhaps you can as it is," and later wrote, "The fact that Joseph was a man of over 200 pounds, while I was scarcely 130 pounds, made it not a l ittle ridiculous for me to think of engaging with him in anything like a scuffle." Joseph reached over, grappled him, and twisted him over and down—breaking his leg three inches above the ankle! Coray wrote, "He immediately carried me into the house, pulled off my boot, and found at once that my leg was decidedly broken, then got some splinters and bandaged it. A number of times that day he came in to see me, endeavoring to console me as much as possible." Later, a contrite Joseph checked on his friend, who suggested, "Brother Joseph, when Jacob wrestled with the angel and was lamed by him, the angel blessed him.

Portrait of Joseph Smith, 1840s (Unknown artist, Community of Christ)

Now I think I am also entitled to a blessing." Joseph, with his father the patriarch, gave the man a blessing. Coray recalled, "In nine days after my leg was broken I was able to get up and hobble about the house by the aid of a crutch, and in two weeks thereafter I was about recovered."

The Prophet's immense compassion for those around him often surfaced in spontaneous acts of simple but profound kindness. Mercy Thompson, a widow, remembered Joseph Smith's "tender sympathy and brotherly kindness he ever showed toward me and my fatherless child. When riding with him and his wife Emma in their carriage I have known him to alight and gather prairie flowers for my little girl."

(Above) "Joseph Smith and Friends," 1844
(Painting by William W. Major, about 1845, MCHA)

(Below) Nauvoo, Illinois, about 1845–46
(Attributed to Lucian Foster, Church Archives)

Margarette Burgess remembered she and her brother Wallace "were going to school, near . . . Joseph's store. It had been raining the previous day, causing the ground to be very muddy, especially along that street. My brother . . . and I both got fast in the mud and could not get out, and, childlike, we began to cry, for we thought we would have to stay there. But looking up, I beheld the loving friend of children, the Prophet Joseph, coming to us. He soon had us on higher and drier ground. Then he stooped down and cleaned the mud from our little, heavy-laden shoes, and took his handkerchief from his pocket and wiped our tear-stained faces. He spoke kind and cheering words to us, and sent us on our way to school rejoicing."

The Prophet was well aware of the possible effect his physical appearance had on strangers: "I was this morning [November 6, 1835] introduced to a man from

Lord and how to lead a happy life. . . . To these word also to add works, to our faith virtue, knowledge, temperence, Brotherly kindness, charity" (italics added).

After Joseph's and his brother Hyrum's murders on June 27, 1844, John Taylor, in Doctrine and Covenants 135, wrote that "Joseph Smith, the Prophet and Seer of the Lord, has done more, save Jesus only, for the salvation of men in this world, than any other man that ever lived in it. In the

the East. After hearing my name, he remarked that I was nothing but a man, indicating by this expression, that he had supposed that a person to whom the Lord should see fit to reveal His will, must be something more than a man." Joseph then reminds us of "the nature of prophets" as spoken from "the lips of St. James, that Elias was a man subject to like passions as we are, yet he had such power with God, that He, in answer to his prayers, shut the heavens that they gave no rain for the space of three years and six months; and again, in answer to his prayer, the heavens gave forth rain, and the earth gave forth fruit. Indeed, such is the darkness and ignorance of this generation, that they look upon it as incredible that a man should have any intercourse with his Maker."

As did the ancient prophets before him, Joseph Smith brought the word and the will of God to His people. The Prophet's ministry renewed a long-lost vision of life—the bright, the hopeful, and the possible now replaced a world blighted with darkness and negativity. Nauvoo resident George Laub clearly laid out what Joseph Smith's efforts meant to him: "The prophet . . . spake with great power and assurance. He expounded the Scripture that it could not be misunderstood for plainness. He also told us the will of the Lord concerning our present situation and state. *In this my soul found food, as a hungry man's body that sits to the luxuries of the Earth.* He told us how to walk before the

(*Top left*) *Joseph and Hyrum Smith, about 1842*
(*Reproduction based on an early David Rogers image, Church Archives*)

(*Above*) *Sutcliffe Maudsley's portrait of Lucy Mack Smith, about 1842 (MCHA)*

short space of twenty years, he has brought forth the Book of Mormon, which he translated by the gift and power of God, . . . has sent the fulness of the everlasting gospel, which it contained, to the four quarters of the earth; has brought forth the revelations and commandments which compose this book of Doctrine and Covenants, and many other wise documents and instructions for the benefit of the children of men."

However, Joseph was so much more than a list of great accomplishments. He was an instrument of God who profoundly touched and positively changed the lives "of so many thousands of his fellow-mortals." John Needham, in an 1843 letter to his parents, gave voice to the feelings of so many then and now: "Joseph Smith is a great man, a man of principle, a straight forward man; no saintish long-faced fellow, but quite the reverse. Indeed some stumble because he is such a straight forward, plain spoken, cheerful man, but that makes me love him the more; but if people will stumble, let them, for such miserable notions as many have got with regard to religion. . . . I have seen and been in the company of Joseph, and heard him speak. . . . I love him, and believe him to be a prophet of God."

Indeed, Josiah Quincy accurately gauged "the wonderful influence which this founder of religion exerted and still exerts."

(Above oval)
Emma Smith, about 1840s (Portrait by unknown artist, Community of Christ)

(Facing page)
"Monday, 24 June 1844, 4:15 a.m.: Beyond the Events"
(Portrait by Drago Pino, 1987, MCHA)

JOSEPH SMITH'S FAMILY

The Prophet's father, Joseph Smith Sr., and mother, Lucy Mack Smith, were married on January 24, 1796, in Tunbridge, Vermont. They were the parents of nine children who grew to adulthood—Alvin, Hyrum, Sophronia, Joseph, Samuel, William, Catherine, Don Carlos, and Lucy. The Prophet grew up in a religious, hard-working, close, and nurturing family.

Father Smith, as Joseph Sr. was known, asserted the veracity of his son's religious experiences from the time of the First Vision. He also was one of the Eight Witnesses to the Book of Mormon and was the Church's first patriarch.

Lucy Mack Smith's strong belief in God was central to her family life, and she tenaciously supported her son Joseph's teachings. She unfortunately lived to experience the trauma of the murder of her sons Hyrum and Joseph, as well as the untimely deaths of Samuel and Don Carlos.

Emma Hale Smith met Joseph Smith in October 1825 when he was boarding at her father's house while working for Josiah Stoal. They eloped on January 18, 1827, and eventually became the parents of eleven children, five of whom reached adulthood—Joseph III, Frederick Granger, Alexander Hale, David Hyrum, and adopted daughter Julia.

Joseph and Emma enjoyed a loving, close, and supportive relationship in which she helped with the Book of Mormon translation, selected hymns for the first hymnal, and helped found the Relief Society, of which she was the first president. Because Joseph was a man loved and hated, Emma was rarely free from anxiety and insecurity.

On July 12, 1843, Joseph Smith recorded the revelation on the "eternity of marriage" and the "plurality of wives" (D&C 132). In keeping with the Lord's direction, the Prophet was married and sealed to other wives.

Three and a half years after Joseph's martyrdom, Emma married Lewis Bidamon on December 23, 1847. They lived in Nauvoo, where she died April 30, 1879. She is buried with Joseph and Hyrum.

State of the Church at the time of Joseph Smith's death	
Year of death	1844
Church membership	26,146
Stakes	2
Temples	2
Missions	3
Missionaries set apart during administration	1,782
Book of Mormon translations completed during administration	1

JOSEPH SMITH JR.

TO BE A PROPHET

To be a prophet of the Lord, one does not need to "be everything to all men." He does not need to be youthful and athletic, an industrialist, a financier, nor an agriculturist; he does not need to be a musician, a poet, an entertainer, nor a banker, a physician, nor a college president, a military general, nor a scientist.

He does not need to be a linguist, to speak French and Japanese, German and Spanish, but he must understand the divine language and be able to receive messages from heaven.

He need not be an orator, for God can make his own. The Lord can present his divine messages through weak men made strong. He substituted a strong voice for the quiet, timid one of Moses, and gave to the young man Enoch power which made men tremble in his presence, for Enoch walked with God as Moses walked with God. . . .

What the world needs is a prophet-leader who gives example—clean, full of faith, godlike in his attitudes with an untarnished name, a beloved husband, a true father.

A prophet needs to be more than a priest or a minister or an elder. His voice becomes the voice of God to reveal new programs, new truths, new solutions. I make no claim of infallibility for him, but he does need to be recognized of God, an authoritative person. He is no pretender as numerous are who presumptuously assume position without appointment and authority that is not given. He must speak like his Lord, "as one having authority, and not as the scribes" (Matthew 7:29).

He must be bold enough to speak truth even against popular clamor for lessening restrictions. He must be certain of his divine appointment, of his celestial ordination, and of his authority to call to service, to ordain, to pass keys which fit eternal locks.

He must have commanding power like prophets of old, "to seal both on earth and in heaven, the unbelieving and rebellious . . . unto the day when the wrath of God shall be poured out upon the wicked without measure" (D&C 1:8–9), and rare powers, "that whatsoever you seal on earth shall be sealed in heaven; and whatsoever you bind on earth, in my name and by my word, saith the Lord, it shall be eternally bound in the heavens; and whosesoever sins you remit on earth shall be remitted eternally in the heavens; and whosesoever sins you retain on earth shall be retained in heaven" (D&C 132:46).

He needs not be an architect to construct houses and schools and high-rise buildings, but he will be one who builds structures to span time and eternity and to bridge the gap between man and his Maker.

—SPENCER W. KIMBALL

(Above) William Armitage's 1890 depiction of "Joseph Smith Preaching to the Indians" (MCHA)

Brigham Young

BORN
JUNE 1, 1801
WHITINGHAM, VERMONT

PARENTS
JOHN AND
ABIGAIL HOWE YOUNG

BAPTIZED
APRIL 14, 1832
(AGE 30)

STATURE
5' 10"
185–230 POUNDS

MARRIED
OCTOBER 5 OR 8, 1824
TO MIRIAM WORKS
(AGE 23)

APOSTLE
FEBRUARY 14, 1835
(AGE 33)

PRESIDENT
DECEMBER 27, 1847
(AGE 46)

DIED
AUGUST 29, 1877
SALT LAKE CITY, UTAH
(AGE 76)

Dark clouds of a summer storm were gathering in the distance on a hot day in August when Samuel Clemens accompanied his older brother and a group of Nevada territorial officials to a scheduled interview. It was a remarkable time: the Civil War had broken out only months before in South Carolina in April 1861. They were visiting an out-of-the-ordinary place: the city of the Saints in the valley of the Great Salt Lake. The much anticipated interview would be a rare treat and certainly engaging; they were scheduled to meet the Mormon prophet in his private office.

Clemens recalled that all the men "put on white shirts and went and paid a state visit to the king." The "king" was, of course, Brigham Young. He had served as Utah's first territorial governor but continued to play a dominant role in virtually every aspect of Utah society. He was a successful businessman, directing and participating in much of the economic activity in the region. He was a respected and influential member of the community, promoting art, drama, education, and music. And most important, he was the leader of a much-maligned but growing religious movement whose missionaries converted thousands each year. These converts became part of a large immigration wave augmenting an ever-increasing number of Mormon settlements throughout the Mountain West.

Clemens described President Young as a "quiet, kindly, easy-mannered, dignified, self-possessed old gentleman of fifty-five or sixty." He also noted that Brother Brigham "had a gentle craft in his eye that probably belonged there."

After a brief greeting, they began talking in earnest about the current topics of the day, "Utah, and the Indians, and Nevada, and general American matters and questions."

We will never know the exact details of the discussion, but Clemens did tell us that the Church leader "never paid any attention to me, notwithstanding I made several attempts to 'draw him out' on federal politics and his high-handed attitude toward Congress."

Blocked at every turn, Clemens finally subsided into an "indignant silence . . . hot and flushed" until the end of the interview. He said some intelligent and thoughtful things, he thought, but he reported, "[Brigham] merely looked around at me at distant intervals something as I have seen a benignant old cat look around to see which kitten was meddling with her tail."

(Left) Brigham Young portrait (Dan A. Weggeland, 1888, MCHA)

(Above oval) Brigham Young, 1855 (Attributed to Marsena Cannon, Church Archives)

No matter how hot and angry Clemens was inside, however, Brother Brigham "was calm—his conversation with those gentlemen flowed on as sweetly and as peacefully and musically as any summer brook."

Before they left the President's office, Brigham, having noticed the young man's frustration, gave the precocious Clemens one more thing to write about: "When the audience was ended and we were retiring from the presence, he put his hand on my head, beamed down on me in an admiring way, and said to my brother; 'Ah—your child, I presume? Boy or girl?'"

Later in the evening, the gathering clouds finally broke loose and showered down upon the Salt Lake Valley. Just as the light rain cooled the hot and thirsty ground, providing much-needed moisture, Brigham Young's quick wit had cooled down Clemens's hot temper and provided nourishment for

Brigham Young portrait, about 1850
(William W. Major, DUP)

1801
June 1 • Born in Whitingham, Vermont
Thomas Jefferson becomes U.S. president

1804
Family moves to New York
U.S. population: 7,239,881 (1810)

1824
Oct. 8 • Marries Miriam Works (dies Sept. 8, 1832)
Erie Canal opens (1825)

1830
Spring • Introduced to Book of Mormon
Jedediah Smith leads first covered wagons into Rocky Mountains

1832
Apr. 15 • Baptized in Mendon, New York

1834
Feb. 18 • Marries Mary Ann Angell
May–July • Member of Zion's Camp

1835
Feb. 14 • Ordained an apostle

1838
Fall • Organizes exodus from Missouri to Illinois
Louis Daguerre announces first type of photography, France (1839)

1840–41
Mission to England
Viscount Melbourne British prime minister (1840)

1842
May 4 • Endowed by Joseph Smith
900 people travel Oregon Trail for Oregon territory (1843)

1844
June 27 • Joseph and Hyrum martyred in Carthage, Illinois
Aug. 8 • Brigham Young and Quorum of the Twelve lead Church
James K. Polk wins U.S. presidency

1845–46
Dec.–Feb. • Labors in Nauvoo Temple giving endowments to the Saints

1846
Feb. 4 • Exodus begins from Nauvoo
July 20 • Mormon Battalion begins march to California
Sept. 23 • Establishes Winter Quarters as temporary Church headquarters
U.S. Congress creates Smithsonian Institution

1847
Jan. 14 • Receives "The Word and Will of the Lord" (D&C 136)
July 24 • Enters Salt Lake Valley
July 28 • Selects site for Salt Lake Temple
Dec. 27 • Sustained as president of the Church
Gold discovered near Sutter's Mill, California (1848)

his literary imagination years later when he wrote under a more famous pen-name, Mark Twain.

One observable characteristic that emerges from the personal writings of Brigham Young and the word-pictures left behind by those who met and knew him was his sharp wit. Sometimes Brigham's reaction to situations reflected a subtle humor, and at other times his reaction demonstrated an overt effort to produce a little laughter for himself and others.

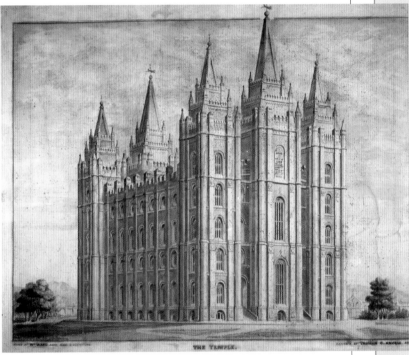

Rendering of the Salt Lake Temple that hung over Brigham Young's desk during his lifetime
(William W. Ward, 1853, MCHA)

BRIGHAM YOUNG AND THE TEMPLE

Brigham Young's life and ministry were tied to the temple and its ordinances. He helped build the Kirtland Temple, applying his training as a carpenter and glazier and also acting as superintendent for the painting on the upper and lower interior courts. Additionally, he was among those who received the washings and anointings performed therein. Later, in Nauvoo, he was among the first group to receive the holy endowment under the hands of Joseph Smith in May 1842.

Brother Brigham was intimately involved with all aspects of temple worship and construction until the death of Joseph Smith in 1844, after which he took over all responsibility for the completion of the Nauvoo Temple. He presided over the extraordinary effort to administer the endowment to more than six thousand Latter-day Saints during the emotional and spiritually powerful days of December and January 1845–1846.

Just a few days after Brigham Young identified the Salt Lake Valley as the new gathering place for the Saints, he walked to a spot between two creeks, waved his hand, and said, "Here is the [ten] acres for the temple." In April 1853, President Young recalled the visionary experience he had at the site: "I scarcely ever say much about revelations, or visions, but suffice it to say, five years ago last July [1847] I was here, and saw in the Spirit the Temple not ten feet from where we have laid the Chief Corner Stone. I have not inquired what kind of a Temple we should build. Why? Because it was represented before me. I have never looked upon that ground but the vision of it was there. I see it as plainly as if it was in reality before me. Wait until it is done. I will say, however, that it will have six towers."

Before his death in August 1877, Brigham Young oversaw the construction and dedication of the St. George Temple and identified sites for temples at Logan and Manti. He also foresaw the completion of other temples throughout the world.

1849
Oct. 6 • Establishes Perpetual Emigration Fund
Armand Fizeau measures speed of light

1850
Sept. 20 • Governor of Utah Territory
Australian Gold Rush begins (1851)

1853
Feb. 14 • Breaks ground for Salt Lake Temple
Florence Nightingale revolutionizes army medical care (1854)

1856
Fall • Coordinates rescue of handcart companies

1857
July 24 • Hears news of approaching U.S. Army
Sept. 11 • Mountain Meadows Massacre, Southern Utah
Elisha Otis installs first passenger elevator, New York City

1859
July 13 • Interviewed by Horace Greeley for *New York Herald*
U.S. Civil War begins (1861)

1862
July 8 • U.S. government initiates campaign against plural marriage
U.S. Civil War ends (1865)

1867
Oct. 6 • First conference held in Salt Lake Tabernacle
Dec. 2 • Reestablishes the School of the Prophets
Dec. 8 • Calls for the reestablishment of Relief Societies
British government declares the Commonwealth of Canada

1869
Nov. 28 • Young Ladies Cooperative Retrenchment Association founded
Transcontinental railroad joins in Utah

1875
June 10 • Young Men's Mutual Improvement Association founded
Oct. 16 • Founds Brigham Young Academy (University)
National League baseball plays first game (1876)

1876–77
Winter • Begins temple work in nearly completed St. George Temple

1877
Apr. 6 • Institutes massive reorganization of stakes
Apr. 25 • Dedicates Manti Temple site
May 17 • Dedicates Logan Temple site
Aug. 29 • Dies in Salt Lake City
Washington Post begins publication

(Above) Brigham Young and an unidentified wife, believed to have been taken in the early 1850s (Attributed to Marsena Cannon, Deseret News)

Such a sense of humor was necessary when we consider the situation in which the Saints found themselves following the death of Joseph Smith in 1844. During this time of turmoil and crisis, Brigham Young led the Church as the senior apostle through the stormy days of the Nauvoo exodus, the wet and muddy Iowa crossing, the cold and deadly season at Winter Quarters, and the eventual trek across the plains to the Great Basin. From the time he was sustained as the second president of the Church in December 1847, Brigham Young stood as the forceful-yet-fatherly, protective, prophetic leader. The dangers the Church faced during his presidency were real—death, destruction, and loss—both physical and spiritual hazards lurked just around the corner. The vicissitudes of pioneer life in Utah during his ministry were magnified by the political, economic, and religious storms that continued to cast a long, dark shadow from time to time across the Mormon landscape.

During a particularly difficult period in 1850, when the Saints were attempting to obtain "home rule" or self-government in their new promised land, news reached the Great Basin that U.S. President Zachary Taylor had passed away. Taylor had been elected twelfth president of the United States in November 1848 but died suddenly on July 9, 1850. And though he had been somewhat sympathetic to the Latter-day Saints at first, Taylor became an outspoken critic of the Church and its members, vowing never to let the Saints have a state or territory of their own. It was while the debate was raging in the halls of Congress what kind of government (state or territorial) would eventually be established in the region that Taylor's life was cut short by an attack of cholera.

President Young arose in a morning meeting on the Temple Block to announce the news and reportedly said, "We have just received word that Zachary Taylor is dead and has gone to hell." Some federally appointed officers present on the occasion objected and, during the break between meetings, asked Brigham to apologize. He said that he would oblige them. As the Saints gathered in the afternoon, Brigham again walked to the pulpit, where he said, "We announced this morning that Zachary Taylor was dead and gone to hell—I am sorry!"

Sometimes Brother Brigham's humor had a serious side—meant to cause his audience to pause and think. This was certainly the case when in 1851 Mormon convert

Colorized daguerreotype of Brigham Young and Margaret Pierce Young, about 1852–53 (Attributed to Marsena Cannon, courtesy Richard M. Young)

HARPER'S WEEKLY.
A JOURNAL OF CIVILIZATION.

VOL. III.—No. 140.]   NEW YORK, SATURDAY, SEPTEMB

Entered according to Act of Congress, in the Year 1859, by Harper & Brothers, in the Clerk's Office of the

BRIGHAM YOUNG'S RELIGION, WEALTH, WIVES, ETC.

THE accompanying illustration will convey to the beholder some idea of a very remarkable interview which took place a few days since between Brigham Young, the chief of the Mormons, and Horace Greeley, the Editor of the New York *Tribune*. Mr. Greeley, on his way across the continent by the overland route, stopped at Salt Lake City, and there fell in with an old acquaintance, Dr. Bernhisel, who was for some time Mormon delegate in Congress. The Doctor proposed to introduce Mr. Greeley to Governor Young, and the offer, as may be imagined, was gladly accepted. We give the rest in Mr. Greeley's own language, simply observing that Brigham Young's statements are the latest and most authentic expositions we have of the Mormon doctrine:

We were very cordially welcomed at the door by the President, who led us into the second-story parlor of the largest of his houses (he has three), where I was introduced to Heber C. Kimball, General Wells, General Ferguson, Albert Carrington, Elias Smith, and several other leading men in the Church, with two full-grown sons of the President. After some unimportant conversation on general topics, I stated that I had come in quest of fuller knowledge respecting the doctrines and polity of the Mormon Church; and would like to ask some questions bearing directly on these, if there were no objection. President Young avowed his willingness to respond to all pertinent inquiries. The conversation proceeded substantially as follows:

THE RELIGION OF MORMON.

GREELEY. "Am I to regard Mormonism (so-called) as a new religion, or as simply a new development of Christianity?"

BRIGHAM. "We hold that there can be no true Christian Church without a priesthood directly commissioned by, and in immediate communication with, the Son of God and Saviour of mankind. Such a Church is that of the Latter-Day Saints, called by their enemies Mormons. We know no other that even pretends to have present and direct revelations of God's will."

GREELEY. "Then I am to understand that you regard all other Churches professing to be Christian as the Church of Rome regards all Churches not in communion with itself—as schismatic, heretical, and out of the way of salvation?"

BRIGHAM. "Yes, substantially."

GREELEY. "Apart from this, in what respect do your doctrines differ essentially from those of our orthodox Protestant Churches—the Baptist or Methodist, for example?"

BRIGHAM. "We hold the doctrines of Christianity, as revealed in the Old and New Testaments; also in the Book of Mormon, which teaches the same cardinal truths, and those only."

GREELEY. "Do you believe in a personal devil—a distinct, conscious, spiritual being, whose nature and acts are essentially malignant and evil?"

BRIGHAM. "We do."

GREELEY. "Do you hold the doctrine of Eternal Punishment?"

BRIGHAM. "We do; though perhaps not exactly as other Churches do. We believe it as the Bible teaches it."

GREELEY. "I understand that you regard Baptism by Immersion as essential?"

BRIGHAM. "We do."

GREELEY. "Do you practice Infant Baptism?"

BRIGHAM. "No."

GREELEY. "Do you make removal to these valleys obligatory on your converts?"

BRIGHAM. "They would consider themselves greatly aggrieved if they were not invited thither. We hold to such a gathering together of God's people as the Bible foretells, and that this is th appointed for its consummatio

GREELEY. "The predictio usually, I think, been unde (or Judea) as the place of g

BRIGHAM. "Yes, for the g

HOW THE BISHOPS

GREELEY. "Let me now more especially to your C all the produces or earns fo

BRIGHAM. "That is a req is no compulsion as to the in the premises according to tates of his own conscience.

GREELEY. "What is don tithing?"

BRIGHAM. "Part of it is and other places of worship and needy converts on their largest portion to the sup Saints."

GREELEY. "Is none of it dignitaries of the Church?

BRIGHAM. "Not one pen deacon, or other Church offi tion for his official services. to put his hand in his own for the poor of his charge thing for his services."

GREELEY. "How, then, d first Apostles. Every bisho seen at work in the field or every minister of the Churc which he earns the bread o or will not do the Church's ed in her service; even our Ferguson and another presi yers of the Church) are pai

INTERVIEW BETWEEN BRIGHAM YOUNG AND HON. HORACE GREELEY AT SALT LAKE CITY.

INTERVIEW BETWEEN BRIGHAM YOUNG AND HON. HORACE GREELEY AT SALT LAKE CITY.

(Above)
"Brigham Young and Friends" about 1864 (Sarah Ann Burbage Long, MCHA)

(Left)
"Interview Between Brigham Young and Hon. Horace Greeley at Salt Lake City," illustration published in Harper's Weekly, September 3, 1859 (color added to original newspaper, a practice during the period to enhance illustrations) (Courtesy R. Q. and Susan Shupe)

Brigham Young portrait, about 1864–65 (Courtesy Truman F. Clawson)

PROPHETS OF THE LATTER DAYS

Brigham Young with top hat, about 1864
(Charles R. Savage, courtesy Neal A. and Colleen Hinckley Maxwell)

An unusual view of Brigham Young, about 1864
(Courtesy Brent F. Ashworth)

Elizabeth Green wrote to ask that he remove her name from the records of the Church because she had become a spiritualist. Brigham's reply in part was, "Madam: I have this day examined the records of the baptisms for the remission of sins in the Church of Jesus Christ of Latter Day Saints, and not being able to find the name of 'Elizabeth Green' recorded therein, I was saved the necessity of erasing your name there from. You may therefore consider that your sins have not been remitted you and you may consequently enjoy the benefits there from."

In another instance, Brigham Young's wit was a welcome respite for two Protestant ministers who had heard stories of Mormon vengeance, hatred, intolerance, and anger directed toward outsiders. William Van Orsdel came to Salt Lake City in 1875 to attend the Rocky Mountain Conference of the Methodist Church. He and a friend were admiring some of the houses near the president's home when "they saw the Mormon leader walking down the street."

Charles W. Carter tintype of Brigham Young, about 1868
(Courtesy Brent F. Ashworth)

(Above) Stereo view of Brigham Young, front view, about 1871
(Charles R. Savage, Church Archives)

(Right) Stereo view of Brigham Young, rear view, about 1871
(Charles R. Savage, Church Archives)

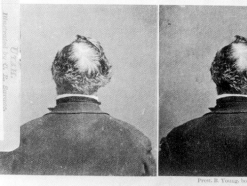

Brigham Young

Entered according to Act of Congress in the year 18__ by C. R. Savage,
in the Office of the Librarian of Congress at Washington.

DESCRIPTION OF MY FATHER

Perhaps my listeners would like a short word picture of my Father as I remember him on that occasion of our last meeting. He was large but not overly stout, having small hands and feet but an unusually large brain, his head measuring more than 23 inches in circumference; he was broad between the ears showing a large intelligent forehead. His nose was somewhat pointed, and of good size and what some might designate as Roman. His mouth was large but the lips were thin and firmly set, together with a long upper lip, giving him the appearance of great determination. In his later years he wore a chin beard which gave him rather a Patriarchal appearance. He had a head of beautiful golden hair and very expressive blue eyes that, when aroused, fairly blazed. He had a sweet melodious voice which was always used in the defense of truth.

—John W. Young

Brigham Young

*(Above) This image was taken during a brief time
when Brigham Young grew out his beard, about 1875
(Charles W. Carter, Courtesy R. Q. and Susan Shupe)*

*(Left) Brigham Young on his seventieth birthday, June 1, 1871
(Charles R. Savage, Church Archives)*

Brigham Young,

HEAD OF THE MORMON CHURCH, AND A PORTION OF HIS WIVES AND CHILDREN.

BRIGHAM YOUNG'S FAMILY

Born in Whitingham, Vermont, on June 1, 1801, Brigham Young was the ninth of eleven children born to John and Abigail (Nabby) Howe Young. As a young boy he moved with his parents to New York, where his mother died of tuberculosis in 1815, when he was fourteen. Brigham left home with only eleven days of formal schooling and became an apprentice carpenter, painter, and glazier. He married Miriam Works on October 5 or 8, 1824, and within a year Elizabeth, his first child, was born. In Mendon he experienced much joy and sorrow: His second child, Vilate, was born in 1830; he and his wife were baptized into the Church in 1832; and his wife died in September 1832. He gathered with the Saints in Kirtland, Ohio, where he married Mary Ann Angell in 1834. Later he reflected in a touching letter to Mary Ann, "I do think the Lord has blest me with one of the best families that any man ever had on the Earth." His sermons, conversations, and letters, compiled over a lifetime, reveal such feelings time and time again.

When William H. Seward, former governor of New York and secretary of state in the Lincoln cabinet, visited Brigham Young, he noted the special feelings Brigham had for his family as the Young children were introduced: "Brigham Young's manner toward his wives is respectful, and toward his children dignified and affectionate. In presenting them severally as they came in groups, with a kind smile for the particular mother, he spoke this way: 'This is our delicate little Lucy,' 'This is our musical daughter,' 'This is our son George, who has a mathematical genius,' and so on."

Fifty-six children, one hundred forty-six grandchildren, and twenty-two great-grandchildren were born during Brigham's lifetime. By the time of his death, Brigham had married numerous times, some for time and others for eternity. Sixteen women gave birth to Brigham's children. Emmeline Free had ten; six wives had only one child. The oldest child, Elizabeth Young Ellsworth, was fifty-two at Brigham's death, and the youngest, Fannie Young Clayton, was seven. Of the forty-six children he raised to maturity, seventeen were sons and twenty-nine were daughters. Eight wives, fourteen children, and twenty-three grandchildren preceded him in death.

(Top) "Brigham Young, Head of the Mormon Church, and a Portion of His Wives and Children," 1872 (J. S. Foy, courtesy Gary L. and Carol B. Bunker)

(Above) Brigham Young, about 1874–75 (Charles R. Savage, courtesy Kim N. Leavitt)

Brigham Young portrait, about 1882 (Attributed to John W. Clawson, MCHA)

PROPHETS OF THE LATTER DAYS

A spirit of curiosity and adventure gripped them both—prompting each of them to dare each other "to cross the street, speak to, and shake hands with the august leader of Mormonism." Both, emboldened by the challenge, "crossed the street and introduced themselves as Methodist preachers from the West and proffering eager hands." It was reported that Brother Brigham "looked at them with an amused twinkle in his eyes, and cordially shook hands, saying, 'I certainly am glad to shake hands with you. I was a Methodist once myself!'"

While such humor could be used to "break the ice" or put the pretentious in their place, Brigham also used his keen wit to open the minds and hearts of the Saints to their own shortcomings so they might feel the desire to improve. No doubt, too, the smiles he brought to their faces helped lighten burdens and make the people glad to find themselves in the world of Brigham Young.

(Right) Missionary certificate dated October 13, 1876, signed by the First Presidency (Courtesy Gregory P. and MarJane Christofferson)

(Below) The last-known photograph of Brigham Young taken during the year preceding his death, about 1877 (Charles R. Savage, courtesy Annetta Sharp Mower)

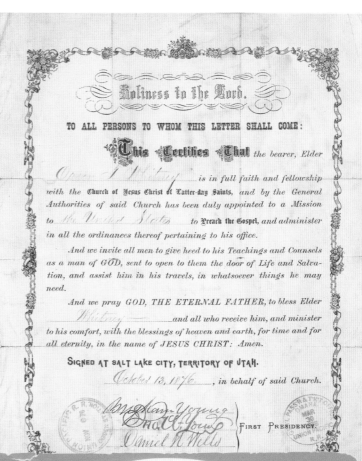

State of the Church at the time of Brigham Young's death	
Year of death	1877
Church membership	115,065
Stakes	20
Temples	1
Missions	8
Missionaries set apart during administration	2,826
Book of Mormon translations completed during administration	7

DEATH OF A PROPHET

The Lord told Jeremiah, "Before I formed thee in the belly I knew thee; and before thou camest forth out of the womb I sanctified thee, and I ordained thee a prophet unto the nations" (Jeremiah 1:5). Just as the Lord's eye is upon His prophets before their birth, so the Lord continues to watch over them throughout mortality until that moment when they pass on into eternity.

Harold B. Lee, who had just become the eleventh president of the Church, asked the Saints to follow the living prophet. To illustrate his point, President Lee recounted a meeting that he had attended at Carthage Jail while serving his mission. Here his mission president talked about Joseph Smith and then said, "When the Prophet Joseph Smith died, many died spiritually with him. So, he said, likewise with each of his successors as changes in administrations came, they died spiritually because they continued to pay their allegiance to their deceased leader rather than to look to his successor upon whom had descended the mantle of the special gift of prophecy, as the endowment of the Holy Ghost to the new leader."

During his address to the Saints, President Lee also quoted John Taylor's remarks following the death of Brigham Young: "'The keys of the kingdom are still here . . . with the Church. . . . The holy priesthood and apostleship which He restored to the earth, still remain to guide and govern, and to administer ordinances to the Church which He has established.' So I declare unto you faithful Saints that the Lord has not left you without a shepherd or shepherds. . . . He is revealing himself in ways that are clearly manifest and are understood by those of us who stand in responsible places in his church."

The death of the prophet is a special moment in eternity—a time of reflection as the Saints contemplate a faithful life that serves as a model of dedication, commitment, and service. It also makes way for the rare occasion when the Lord calls another whom He knew before birth and "ordained [him] a prophet unto the nations."

(Above) Gary Smith's moving depiction of Joseph and Hyrum Smith's martyrdom on June 27, 1844 (MCHA)

(Oval) Brigham Young's death mask, prepared by George M. Ottinger on September 1, 1877, shortly after the prophet's death (MCHA)

Funeral
of
Wilford Woodruff.

President of the Church of Jesus
Christ of Latter-day Saints.

September 8th, 1898,
Salt Lake City, Utah.

Program for the funeral services of
Wilford Woodruff, September 8, 1898
(Courtesy Gregory P. and
MarJane Christofferson)

The Church opened the historic Tabernacle for the first time since the beginning of
World War II to hold Heber J. Grant's funeral on May 18, 1945 (Church Archives)

(Below) Andrew E. Kimball Sr. and Camilla Kimball at the graveside service for
Spencer W. Kimball, November 9, 1985 (Courtesy Edward L. Kimball)

"Somber lobby of the Mormon Office Building";
the English-speaking world caught a brief glimpse of
the transition between presidencies when Life magazine
published photographs of George Albert Smith lying in
state in its April 23, 1951, issue (Life magazine)

Deseret News headlines announcing the
death of Harold B. Lee in December 1973
(Courtesy L. Brent Goates)

Ezra Taft Benson's headstone in Whitney, Idaho
(R. Clark Salisbury)

Pallbearers carrying Howard W. Hunter's casket at the
Salt Lake City Cemetery, March 8, 1995 (Ventura County Star)

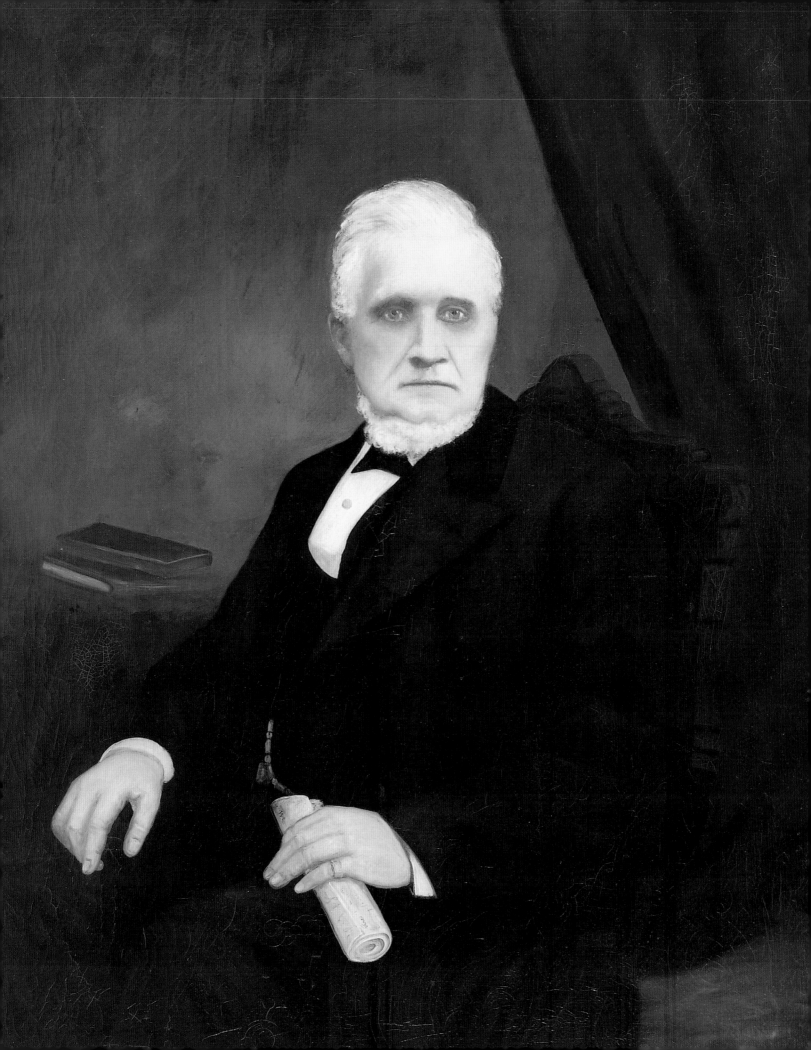

John Taylor

In April 1836, Apostle Parley P. Pratt arrived in Toronto, Canada, as a missionary for the Church of the Latter-day Saints (on April 26, 1838, the name was changed to The Church of Jesus Christ of Latter-day Saints). He had journeyed north from Kirtland, Ohio, with Heber C. Kimball's prophetic instruction to go "to the city of Toronto . . . there thou shalt find a people prepared for the gospel and they shall receive thee." Elder Pratt was soon invited to attend a Bible study group, where he found "a solemn, well dressed, and, apparently, serious and humble people, nearly filling the room. Each held a Bible, while Mr. Patrick presided in their midst, with a Bible in his hand. . . . In this manner, these people had assembled twice each week for about two years, for the professed purpose of seeking truth, independent of any sectarian organization to which any of them might nominally belong." In addition to their readings and research, the study group "prayed and fasted before God . . . that if He had a people upon the earth anywhere, and ministers who were authorized to preach the gospel, that he would send us one."

Among those in attendance was John Taylor, a well-spoken, politely affable, six-foot Englishman, who carried himself with gracious, dignified strength. In 1832 he had followed his parents, John and Agnes Taylor, to Canada, where he could continue his Methodist calling to preach the gospel of Christ. However, doubts concerning Methodist teachings crept through his contemplative mind. He shared his misgivings with his wife, Leonora, whom he had met and married in Canada. Referring to a revelation during his youth that he "go to America to preach the gospel," she inquired, "Are you not now preaching the gospel in America?" He responded, stating, "This is not the work; it is something of more importance."

At first Elder Pratt found John Taylor and his group courteously unreceptive. However, when the apostle was allowed to preach, the conviction and logic of his message squared with much of what the group had previously discovered in their studies. For three weeks, John Taylor determinedly studied the

(Left) John Taylor, 1882 (Painting by A. Westwood, MCHA)

(Above oval) John Taylor, about 1880 (Charles W. Carter, Church Archives)

BORN
NOVEMBER 1, 1808
MILNTHORPE, ENGLAND

PARENTS
JAMES AND AGNES TAYLOR

BAPTIZED
MAY 9, 1836
(AGE 27)

STATURE
5' 11"
180 POUNDS

MARRIED
JANUARY 28, 1833
TO LEONORA CANNON
(AGE 24)

APOSTLE
DECEMBER 19, 1838
(AGE 30)

PRESIDENT
OCTOBER 10, 1880
(AGE 71)

DIED
JULY 25, 1887
KAYSVILLE, UTAH
(AGE 78)

Book of Mormon and compared Elder Pratt's sermons to the Bible. Convinced of the truth of his teachings, John and Leonora Taylor were baptized on May 9, 1836.

Their lives were changed forever. John Taylor was now anchored in the truth he had been seeking since childhood when he envisioned a heavenly angel "holding a trumpet to his mouth, sounding a message to the nations." After his baptism, he devoted his life to the Church—continuously pursuing a deep understanding of the gospel in order to defend it and proclaim it through his powerful writing, preaching, and missionary work.

John Taylor first met the Prophet Joseph Smith in March 1837 at Kirtland, Ohio, during the bitter disaffection of many members toward the Prophet. Apostasy was rampant, and even John Taylor's mentor, Parley P. Pratt, voiced some doubts. During a meeting in which Joseph Smith's character was questioned, John Taylor spoke in his defense, courageously declaring, "How can we find out the mysteries of the kingdom? It was Joseph Smith, under

St. Peter's Church, the Parish Church of Heversham, was the site of John Taylor's christening on December 4, 1808. Like all the presidents of The Church of Jesus Christ of Latter-day Saints previous to Joseph F. Smith's presidency (1901–18), John Taylor was an adult convert to Mormonism. Born and reared in the Christian faith, John Taylor began a religious search that eventually led him to the fulness of the Gospel. (About 1993, Tod Fulwood, courtesy J. Lewis Taylor)

the Almighty, who developed the first principles, and to him we must look for further instructions. If the spirit which he manifests does not bring blessings, I am very much afraid that the one manifested by those who have spoken, will not be very likely to secure them."

It was an early example of John Taylor's loyalty to the Prophet and his teachings. On the terrible, fateful summer afternoon of June 27, 1844, this faithful man witnessed the murder of Joseph Smith and his brother Hyrum at Carthage Jail. True to his nature, John Taylor took up a large hickory stick to boldly fend off attackers who were shooting a barrage of gunfire into the humidly hot room. As the two brothers lay dead, John Taylor was wounded and bleeding. Miraculously, he survived four severe musket-ball wounds—one to the thigh, another just below the left knee, another just above his left wrist, and finally one to "the fleshy part" of his left hip. Section 135 of the Doctrine and Covenants, which was later canonized, is his graceful tribute to the two martyrs.

1808
Nov. 1 • Born in Milnthorpe, England
Duke of Portland British prime minister

1819
Summer • Family moves to Hale, England
King George III dies (1820)

1824
Joins Methodist Church
First passenger railway opens, England (1825)

1832
Follows family to Toronto, Canada

1833
Jan. 28 • Marries Leonora Cannon (dies Dec. 7, 1868)
Canadian Royal William becomes first steamship to cross Atlantic

1836
May 9 • Baptized in Toronto, Canada
Rebellions in Upper and Lower Canada fail (1837)

1838
Dec. 19 • Ordained an apostle

1839–41
Mission to Great Britain
British-Chinese Opium Wars begin (1839)

1842–46
Editor of *Times and Seasons*, Nauvoo, Illinois

1843–45
Editor of WASP and *Nauvoo Neighbor*
Charles Dickens publishes A Christmas Carol (1843)

1844
June 27 • Witnesses the martyrdom of Joseph and Hyrum Smith and is wounded

1846–47
Mission to Great Britain
Irish Potato blight causes famine and immigration to U.S. and Canada (1846)

1847
Sept. 29 • Arrives in Salt Lake Valley
Marx and Engels publish Communist Manifesto (1848)

1849–52
Mission to France and Germany

1852
Publishes first book, *Government of God*
Directs Book of Mormon translation into French and German
Native American/African American George Crum invents potato chip, New York (1853)

1854
Oct. 24 • Missionary work begins in New Zealand

1857
Speaker of Utah Territorial Legislature
Suez Canal opens (1869)

John Taylor's contribution to the gospel was considerable. He wrote, "I have traveled to preach these doctrines in most of the United States and in the Canadas; I have preached them in England, in Scotland, in Wales, in the Isles of Man and the Jerseys, in France, Germany, in the principal cities of America and Europe, and to many prominent men in the world." His strong defense of the Church through debate and extemporaneous speeches earned him a reputation as the "defender of the faith." Of his efforts, he stated, "I have not yet found a man that could controvert one principle of 'Mormonism' upon scriptural grounds. If there is a man, I have yet to find him."

President Taylor's gift for words was not confined to oratory alone. Brigham Young declared that John Taylor "has one of the strongest intellects that can be found. He is a powerful man, and we may say that he is a powerful editor. But I will use a term to suit myself and say that he is one of the strongest editors that ever wrote." He was the editor of the *Times and Seasons* and the

Sketch of John Taylor, 1853 (Frederick H. Piercy, based on daguerreotypes by Marsena Cannon taken about 1852 in Salt Lake City, Church Archives)

Nauvoo Neighbor; directed the translation and publication of French and German translations of the Book of Mormon; and published *The Mormon* in New York City. In 1852 he authored *The Government of God,* in which he tackled a favorite subject of his—comparing God's government to man's government. His long-term study of this topic moved him to conclude, "in God's government there is perfect order, harmony, beauty, magnificence, and grandeur; in the government of man, confusion, disorder, instability, misery, discord, and death."

Amid the consuming responsibilities as Church president, President Taylor compiled, wrote, and issued in 1882 *The Mediation and Atonement of Our Lord and Savior Jesus Christ*—a compilation of scriptural passages and his commentary concerning Christ's atonement. He was the first president of the Church to write and publish a book.

During his years of Church service, John Taylor braved the tragic persecutions of Missouri, the rise and collapse of Nauvoo, the murder of the Prophet Joseph Smith, the

---

1875
Apr. 10 • Seniority adjusted in Quorum, making John Taylor senior apostle
Alexander Graham Bell invents the telephone

1877
Aug. 29 • Brigham Young dies
Sept. 4 • John Taylor and Quorum of the Twelve lead Church

1878
Aug. 25 • Primary founded

1879
Jan. 6 • Anti-plural marriage legislation upheld by U.S. Supreme Court
Mar. 1 • First telephone call made in Utah
E. W. von Siemans demonstrates first electric locomotive

1880
Apr. 6 • Declares "Year of Jubilee" and cancels many debts owed the Church
Oct. 10 • Sustained as president of the Church
Dec. 18 • Places first telephone call to Wilford Woodruff, Salt Lake City
Clara Barton establishes the American Red Cross (1881)

1882
Jan. 8 • Assembly Hall dedicated
Publishes *The Mediation and Atonement,* first book written by a Church president as president
Celebration of first Labor Day, New York City

1882–87
U.S. government crusade against plural marriage intensified

1883
Apr. 14 • Receives revelation on the Seventy
Mormon crews work on Canadian Pacific Railway
Brooklyn Bridge opens

1884
May 17 • Dedicates Logan Temple
May • Receives revelation concerning Logan Temple
Grover Cleveland wins U.S. presidency

1885
Jan. 8 • Church representatives arrive in Chihuahua, Mexico, to rent or buy land for new colony
Feb. 1 • Delivers last public address before going into exile to avoid arrest

1885
Apr. 5 • General Epistle from First Presidency read at conference in their absence

1886
Summer • Sends Charles O. Card to find a place for settlement in Canada
Native American Apache Chief Geronimo surrenders

1887
Apr. 26 • First Mormon settlement established in Canada, Cardston, Alberta
July 25 • Dies in Kaysville, Utah
Queen Victoria celebrates Golden Jubilee

Portrait of John Taylor, about 1852 (Lorus Pratt, MCHA)

John Taylor, about 1852 (Marsena Cannon, Church Archives)

arduous trek west, the settlement of Utah, cultural harassment, and federal prosecution. He never knew a time when the Church was not persecuted and seen as going against the grain of American society. Yet, through it all, he remained fiercely proud to be an American—he became a citizen in 1849. He often spoke on the U.S. Constitution, noting that "our fathers were inspired to write the Constitution . . . and that it is an instrument, full, lucid, and comprehensive . . . the great bulwark of American liberty." Over the years, in addition to his Church service, writing, and farming, he served as an associate judge, a member of the territorial legislature (speaker of the house for five sessions), probate judge, and superintendent of schools.

IT IS BETTER TO REPRESENT OURSELVES, THAN TO BE REPRESENTED BY OTHERS.

VOL. II.—NO. 18.   NEW-YORK, SATURDAY, JUNE 21, 1856.   PRICE FIVE CENTS.

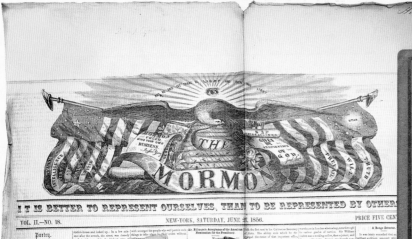

The Mormon *masthead* (MCHA)

THE MORMON MASTHEAD

The Church established four major newspapers (John Taylor's *The Mormon* in New York City, Erastus Snow's *The St. Louis Luminary* in St. Louis, George Q. Cannon's *The Western Standard* in San Francisco, and Orson Pratt's *The Seer* in Washington, D.C.) with the firm belief that it was "better to represent ourselves, than to be represented by others." Between February 1855 and September 1857, *The Mormon* was published weekly on the same street as the famous *New York Tribune* and *New York Herald*. The masthead created by Elder Taylor for this publication depicted certain Latter-day Saint sayings and ideas, such as the Mormon Creed ("Mind your own business") and "Truth will prevail." These are interlaced with symbols of America, the U.S. flag, a bald eagle, and the Constitution. The masthead occupied almost half of the entire front page.

John Taylor about the time of Brigham Young's death in 1877
(Savage and Ottinger, Church Archives)

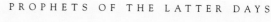

AN EXAMINATION INTO AND AN ELUCIDATION OF THE
GREAT PRINCIPLE OF THE

MEDIATION AND ATONEMENT

OF

OUR LORD AND SAVIOR JESUS CHRIST.

BY PRESIDENT JOHN TAYLOR.

"Wherefore the fruit of thy loins shall write, and the fruit of the loins of Judah shall write; and that which shall be written by the fruit of thy loins, and also that which shall be written by the fruit of the loins of Judah, shall grow together unto the confounding of false doctrines, and laying down of contentions."—Gen., 1, 31, Inspired Translation.

"For I command all men, both in the east and in the west, and in the north and in the south, and in the islands of the sea, that they shall write the words which I speak unto them: for out of the books which shall be written, I will judge the world, every man according to their works, according that which is written. For behold, I shall speak unto the Jews, and they shall write it; and I shall also speak unto the Nephites, and they shall write it; and I shall also speak unto the other tribes of the house of Israel, which I have led away, and they shall write it; and I shall also speak unto all nations of the earth, and they shall write it. And it shall come to pass that the Jews shall have the words of the Nephites, and the Nephites shall have the words of the Jews; and the Nephites and the Jews shall have the words of the lost tribes of Israel; and the lost tribes of Israel shall have the words of the Nephites and the Jews. And it shall come to pass that my people which are of the house of Israel, shall be gathered home unto the lands of their possessions; and my word also shall be gathered in one."—2 Nephi, xxix, 11—14.

SALT LAKE CITY, UTAH.

DESERET NEWS COMPANY, PRINTERS AND PUBLISHERS,

1882.

(Above) First Presidency (George Q. Cannon, John Taylor, Joseph F. Smith) in 1880 at the time of the Jubilee (50th anniversary) Celebration of the Church's organization (Church Archives)

(Left) Title page from The Mediation and Atonement (1882), the first book written and published by a president of the Church. President Taylor provides a brief synopsis of the focus of this 205-page work: "An examination into and an elucidation of the great principle of the mediation and atonement of Our Lord and Savior Jesus Christ."

(Below) "A Revelation given through President John Taylor, at Salt Lake City, Utah Territory, on Saturday, April 14th, 1883," from a pamphlet, To the Seventies. President Taylor had earlier published "A Revelation through John Taylor, at Salt Lake City, Utah Territory, October 13, 1883, to fill vacancies in the Twelve." John Taylor received several revelations, including these two published for the members of the Church during his ministry. (Courtesy R. Q. and Susan Shupe)

A Revelation given through President John Taylor, at Salt Lake City, Utah Territory, on Saturday, April 14th, 1883, in answer to the question: "Show unto us Thy will, O Lord, concerning the organization of the Seventies."

What ye have written is my will, and is acceptable unto me: and furthermore,

Thus saith the Lord unto the First Presidency, unto the Twelve, unto the Seventies and unto all my holy Priesthood, let not your hearts be troubled, neither be ye concerned about the management and organization of my Church and Priesthood and the accomplishment of my work. Fear me and observe my laws and I will reveal unto you, from time to time, through the channels that I have appointed, everything that shall be necessary for the future development and perfection of my Church, for the adjustment and rolling forth of my kingdom, and for the building up and the establishment of my Zion. For ye are my Priesthood and I am your God. Even so. Amen.

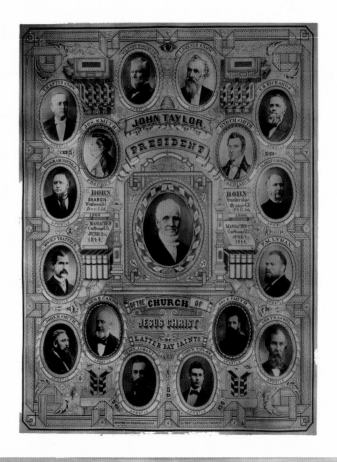

(Top left) "John Taylor President of the Church of
Jesus Christ of Latter Day Saints," about 1884 (USHS)

(Top right) John Taylor, about 1884 (Charles R. Savage, Church Archives)

(Above) Painting of Logan, Utah, 1892 (Christian Eisele, MCHA)

(Right) Logan Temple Dedication pass dated
May 17, 1884, and signed by John Taylor
(Courtesy Gregory P. and MarJane Christofferson)

No. 1.

Admit the Bearer to the Dedication Services of the Logan
Temple, May 17th, 1884.

John Taylor.

(Top left) Popular business-card-sized
photograph of John Taylor,
about 1884 (Church Archives)

(Top middle) John Taylor seated, about 1884
(Charles W. Carter, Church Archives)

(Top right) John Taylor's profile,
about 1884 (Church Archives)

(Right) Full view of John Taylor standing
by chair, about 1885 (Church Archives)

His knowledge and championing of truth allowed President Taylor to successfully guide the Saints through troubled times. He held the Church together during the increasingly horrific antipolygamy, anti-Mormon campaigns of the 1880s. During his time he created four new missions; forgave half the debts owed to the Perpetual Emigration Fund, and saw to the distribution of 1,500 head of livestock to the poor as part of the Church's jubilee celebration; established LDS settlements in Canada and Mexico; canonized the Pearl of Great Price; oversaw the Church-wide establishment of the Primary and Young Ladies Mutual

Improvement Association; dedicated the Logan Temple; began weekly bishopric meetings and quarterly stake conferences; and further defined the role of the bishop, Aaronic Priesthood, and Melchizedek Priesthood.

To avoid the constant harassment and possible arrest by federal marshals, John Taylor and other Church leaders "went underground" (into hiding) in 1885, directing the Church through letters, messengers, and personal meetings. He died at the Thomas Roueche home in Kaysville, Utah, on July 25, 1887—a "double martyr" for his near-fatal wounds at Carthage, Illinois, and his dying in exile.

James and Agnes Taylor, about 1868 (Church Archives)

JOHN TAYLOR'S FAMILY

John Taylor was born in Milnthorpe, England, on November 1, 1808—the second of ten children born to Agnes and James Taylor. The Taylors' close-knit family was religiously oriented, and infant John was baptized into the Church of England. As a youth he gained a strong foundation in prayer, music, and the scriptures as well as a strong desire for spiritual understanding. His parents created a home life that encouraged the boy to become a cultured, learned, fastidious man who also enjoyed a keen sense of humor. When his formal education ended at age fourteen, the young Taylor apprenticed first as a cooper and then as a lathe turner.

After imigrating to Canada in 1832, John Taylor met Leonora Cannon, and they were married January 28, 1833. Following their baptisms, they experienced the blessings and the hardships of their new religion until Leonora's death in 1868. Following the personal counsel of the Prophet Joseph Smith, John Taylor entered into the practice of plural marriage when he and Elizabeth Haigham were wed on December 12, 1843. President Taylor was the father of thirty-five children by seven wives—Leonora Cannon, Elizabeth Haigham, Jane Ballantyne, Mary Ann Oakley, Sophia Whitaker, Harriet Whitaker, and Margaret Young. Featured below is a glimpse into the home life of President John Taylor written by his daughter Ida Oakley Taylor Whitaker (1860–1946), whose mother was Mary Ann Oakley Taylor.

"My father, John Taylor, stood for so many fine principles of living that I have time only to mention a few. Father loved his family and treated his wives so graciously. With all his many responsibilities he took the time to get his family together and teach them how to live the Gospel. He wanted them to be well educated, so the first school was held over the granary where the older children taught the younger ones. He also had neighbor children in the school.

"In the home he wanted things clean and orderly, and at mealtimes to have family prayer, pleasant times, and did not bring up unpleasant subjects at the table. He was so hospitable and loved to have folks come into his home and entertain them.

"An honorable character meant so much to him. The incident of the chickens, for instance, showed how he tried to impress upon them the principles of honesty. A neighbor by the name of Angus Cannon had some chickens that happened to run on the east lot. Angus Cannon said that if Brig and Ebb could catch the chickens, they could have them. Well, the chickens were caught and sold. When Father heard of it he held court with the family around, and took out the family Bible and read where it said to pay four-fold. And the boys had to pay four-fold. Brig had some money saved up for a shirt—that went into the payment of it also.

"Each year on his anniversary he had all his wives and children present. It was his Home Night. Games, talks, and other interesting matters were given, refreshments served, all of which bound the family together. Since father's death 53 years ago, his family's families have met together to honor him and renew old friendships. I am certainly proud to be the daughter of such a loving, illustrious father."

"Salt Lake City, Utah—Morning," about 1887 (Frederick Ferdinand Schafer, MCHA)

Ever studying, seeking, and praying to gain greater understanding of the truth, President Taylor gave perspective to Mormonism, declaring, "Our religion . . . embraces every principle of truth and intelligence pertaining to us as moral, intellectual, mortal and immortal beings, pertaining to this world and the world that is to come. We are open to truth of every kind, no matter whence it comes, where it originates or who believes in it. . . . A man in search of the truth has no peculiar system to sustain, no peculiar dogma to defend or theory to uphold."

State of the Church at the time of John Taylor's death	
Year of death	1887
Church membership	173,029
Stakes	31
Temples	12
Missions	12
Missionaries set apart during administration	2,165
Book of Mormon translations completed during administration	1

SALT LAKE CITY, UTAH—MORNING

German-born landscape artist Frederick Schafer captured Salt Lake City sometime around the death of President John Taylor in 1887. His breathtaking painting, highlighting not only the city but also the rugged landscape, hides the dark cloud of persecution covering every Latter-day Saint community at this time, including Salt Lake City.

Deputy Marshals increased their harassment of members of the Church in the 1880s as the full power of the federal government came to bear upon the political, economic, social, and religious life of the members of the Church during what has been aptly called the "Federal Raid." No other religious body in the United States suffered as poorly as the Saints at the hand of the government, yet they remained loyal to the Lord, the Church, and the Prophet.

President Taylor went "underground" in early 1885 to avoid arrest, moving periodically until November 1886, when he found refuge in the Thomas and Margaret Rouche home in Kaysville, Utah. He remained there until his death in July 1887. President Taylor's body was sent to Salt Lake City, where a public funeral was held in his honor in the Tabernacle under the shadow of the uncompleted Salt Lake Temple.

SUCCESSION IN THE PRESIDENCY

(Left) Six weeks after Joseph and Hyrum Smith's death, the Saints met in conference in Nauvoo. Brigham Young, president of the Quorum of the Twelve Apostles, spoke twice during the course of the day. Several Latter-day Saints in attendance testified that the mantle of the prophet fell upon Brother Brigham—he sounded and appeared like Joseph Smith. For others, the Spirit witnessed that Brigham was to lead the Church. (July 1845, Seal Van Sickle, DUP)

(Below) The First Presidency and Quorum of the Twelve, October 9, 1868. This may be the first photograph ever taken of the entire First Presidency and Quorum of the Twelve Apostles together. Thirty-two years had elapsed since all the First Presidency and Quorum of the Twelve were together in one place in Kirtland in 1836, three years before the invention of photography. (Charles R. Savage, USHS)

(Below) Epistle of the Twelve Apostles, 1877. John Taylor and his associates in the Quorum of the Twelve sent this four-page epistle to the Saints, providing details of President Young's death and an overview of his productive ministry. Finally, they solemnly proclaimed, "Once more the necessity for the Twelve Apostles to step forward and take the Presidency of the Church of Jesus Christ of Latter-day Saints has arisen." The process of succession was underway. (Courtesy R. Q. and Susan Shupe)

(Right) President Howard W. Hunter and the First Presidency, June 6, 1994. Today, through modern technological advances, members of the Church hear almost instantly about a change in presidency and often watch the events unfold as was the case when President Howard W. Hunter met in a press conference at the Church Administration Building to introduce the new presidency. At this time he pledged his life and the full measure of his soul to his new calling, and he invited members to live with "ever more attention to the life and example of the Lord Jesus Christ." (Church Archives)

Today, the transition following the death of the president of the Church is simple and orderly. However, this process was established through the Lord "line upon line" during the early period of Church history. In the beginning, several succession options were in operation until March 1844, when the Prophet gave the keys of the kingdom to the Twelve Apostles, laying the foundation for our current procedure. While some segments of the Church membership may have wondered who should succeed Joseph Smith following his death

President Gordon B. Hinckley holds his first press conference as president of the Church in the lobby of the Joseph Smith Memorial Building on March 13, 1995. (Mark J. Scott, Church Archives)

in June 1844, the Twelve knew they held the keys of the kingdom. Brigham Young, as president of that quorum, was de facto president of the Church as the senior apostle in the quorum. For many Latter-day Saints, the August 8, 1844, meeting held in Nauvoo confirmed that the prophet's mantle had fallen on Brother Brigham. An important revelation, dated January 14, 1847, indicated that the "people of the Church of Jesus Christ of Latter-day Saints" were to organize themselves under the "direction of the Twelve Apostles" (D&C 136:1–3). In December 1847, Brigham Young was sustained as the second president of the Church in Kanesville, Iowa, during a conference of Saints. As the principles of succession unfolded, questions arose and Church leaders sought inspiration during this pivotal period. Issues of how seniority in the Quorum were eventually settled. By the time of Joseph F. Smith's presidency (1901–18), the smooth process based on inspired clarifications was firmly established—the senior apostle with the longest continuous service as a member of the Twelve (or as a member in the First Presidency following a call to the Twelve) will become the new president of the Church.

Another important procedure was adopted following Wilford Woodruff's death in 1898—the First Presidency was organized within a few days of the death of the president rather than waiting for a longer period as had been the case before.

Nothing better illustrates our current smooth succession than what happened in a small hospital waiting room at the time of Harold B. Lee's death in 1973. When President Lee was hospitalized on December 26, Spencer W. Kimball, president of the Quorum of the Twelve and senior apostle after Harold B. Lee, greeted President Marion G. Romney, counselor in the First Presidency. Spencer W. Kimball asked President Romney what he could do to help. Later, when they were told President Lee had died, Marion G. Romney turned and asked what he could do to help, as Spencer W. Kimball was now the senior apostle on earth. President Kimball immediately assumed the mantle of leadership of the Church when President Lee's heartbeat stopped. A few days later, on December 30, 1973, Spencer W. Kimball was ordained the twelfth president of The Church of Jesus Christ of Latter-day Saints.

Matthias F. Cowley provides a vivid picture of young Wilford Woodruff's personality and character when he said that he "was a boy of great vitality and given to the sports incident to the community and the times in which he lived. . . . The sports of fishing and hunting which he practiced in early boyhood were enjoyed by him throughout his entire life. . . . Wilford was an industrious boy. His mind was filled with lofty thoughts, and his education as time went on, took on a religious character. He was by nature a devoted son and observed carefully the divine command which enjoined obedience to his parents."

Born in 1804, Wilford grew up around family and friends in Farmington, Connecticut. His love of life and inherent curiosity found an instinctive outlet in fishing, playing, and the exploration of the natural world and man-made wonders around him. Yet, there was danger lurking at nearly every turn. When he was three years old, he fell into a cauldron of scalding water. He was rescued immediately, but Wilford was badly burned. For the next nine months, no one could be sure if the young boy would survive this life-threatening accident.

Of course, in the early nineteenth century, children and adults commonly experienced accidents that caused severe bodily injury and even death. Indeed, the very nature of life was fraught with danger—open cooking-fires and hard physical labor around animals and dangerous machinery. However, Wilford's diary records an exceptionally high number of accidents during his childhood and young adult years, including being hit by a large beam, falling down a stair-well, falling off a porch, being chased by an angry bull, being caught in sawmill gears, being kicked by an ox, being involved with a runaway wagon that turned over, falling out of a tree, nearly drowning in a river, being caught in a blizzard and nearly freezing to death, being hit with an ax, being bitten by a mad dog, falling off an out-of-control horse, being nearly crushed to death at a flour mill, barely escaping being kicked in the head by a horse, just being missed when a gun accidentally went off and blew his hat from his head, and narrowly escaping death when a gun misfired as it was pointed at his chest. He later reflected on his accident-prone life: "Evidently I have been numbered with those who are apparently the marked victims of misfortunes. It has seemed to me at times as

(Left) Wilford Woodruff (Lewis A. Ramsey, 1912, MCHA)

(Above oval) Wilford Woodruff, about 1887 (Charles R. Savage, Church Archives)

BORN
MARCH 1, 1807
FARMINGTON, CONNECTICUT

PARENTS
APHEK AND BEULAH
THOMPSON WOODRUFF

BAPTIZED
DECEMBER 31, 1833
(AGE 26)

STATURE
5' 8"
135–70 POUNDS

MARRIED
APRIL 13, 1837
TO PHOEBE CARTER
(AGE 30)

APOSTLE
APRIL 26, 1839
(AGE 32)

PRESIDENT
APRIL 7, 1889
(AGE 82)

DIED
SEPTEMBER 2, 1898
SAN FRANCISCO, CALIFORNIA
(AGE 91)

Phoebe Carter Woodruff and son Joseph, 1845 or 1846 (Thomas Ward, MCHA)

though some invisible power were watching my footsteps in search of an opportunity to destroy my life. I, therefore, ascribe my preservation on earth to the watch care of a merciful Providence, whose hand has been stretched out to rescue me from death when I was in the presence of the most threatening dangers."

Wilford was a guileless man of deep faith who would have remained a good neighbor, friend, and family man even if he had never heard of the restored gospel of Jesus Christ. But the Lord had other plans for this Connecticut Yankee. At twenty-six years of age, Wilford took his first step in a long and arduous religious journey when he traveled to hear Zera Pulsipher preach the gospel in Richland, New York: "I felt the spirit of God to bear witness that he was the servant of God. He then commenced preaching and that too as with authority, and when he had finished his discourse I truly felt that it was the first gospel sermon that I had ever heard. I thought it was what I had long

WILFORD WOODRUFF'S FAMILY

Wilford Woodruff's love of his family is reflected in his remarkable journals and numerous letters that highlight the concern of a dedicated son, brother, husband, son-in-law, father, uncle, grandfather, and great-grandfather. Following his own conversion in 1833, Wilford diligently sought to bring his relatives into the Church of Jesus Christ. Later, when he married Phoebe Carter in 1837, he continued to exert his efforts to preach the gospel to a larger family circle. Wilford and Phoebe accepted the Abrahamic test when called upon to accept and practice plural marriage. This unexpected revelation tested their discipleship, but they faithfully picked up their crosses and followed the Lord. Wilford eventually married three women in 1846, four others during the 1850s, and in 1870 was sealed to a ninth. Five of these wives bore him thirty-three children. As in a monogamous relationship, Wilford experienced the joys and setbacks of building a relationship that is tested by time and circumstances. Additionally, he experienced the pain of death and divorce—all of which shaped his character and gave him experience. The portrait of Phoebe and her son Joseph was a special treasure, as it was painted before young Joseph died. Wilford and Phoebe were sealed in the Nauvoo Temple, and therefore Joseph was born in the covenant with special promises. Though both parents mourned their son's death, they held firm to the belief that family ties can survive death—they believed that through the atonement of Jesus Christ and the ordinances of the priesthood, Phoebe, Wilford, and Joseph would be united again.

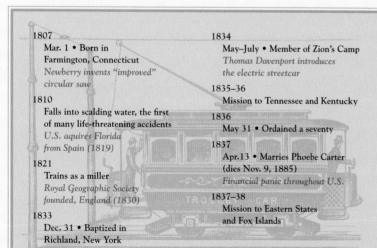

1807
Mar. 1 • Born in Farmington, Connecticut
Newberry invents "improved" circular saw

1810
Falls into scalding water, the first of many life-threatening accidents
U.S. aquires Florida from Spain (1819)

1821
Trains as a miller
Royal Geographic Society founded, England (1830)

1833
Dec. 31 • Baptized in Richland, New York

1834
May–July • Member of Zion's Camp
Thomas Davenport introduces the electric streetcar

1835–36
Mission to Tennessee and Kentucky

1836
May 31 • Ordained a seventy

1837
Apr.13 • Marries Phoebe Carter (dies Nov. 9, 1885)
Financial panic throughout U.S.

1837–38
Mission to Eastern States and Fox Islands

1838
July 1 • Baptizes parents and sister
U.S. abolitionists organize "Underground Railroad"

1839
Apr. 26 • Ordained an apostle

1839–41
Mission to Great Britain

1844
June 27 • Joseph and Hyrum Smith martyred in Carthage, Illinois

1844–46
President of British mission
Sir Robert Peel British prime minister (1841–46)

1847
July 24 • Enters Salt Lake Valley

1848–50
President of Eastern States and Canada mission
U.S. population: 23,191,876 (1850)

1856
Apr. 7 • Assistant Church historian
Edwin Drake strikes first oil well in U.S., Pennsylvania (1859)

1862
Mar. 18–26 • Compiles information for H.H. Bancroft's *History of Utah*
U.S. acquires Alaska from Russia (1867)

1875
Apr. 10 • Seniority adjusted in Quorum, placing Wilford Woodruff ahead of Orson Hyde and Orson Pratt
Rutherford B. Hayes loses popular vote but becomes U.S. president (1876)

*"I then lay down
and dreamed of ketching fish."*
—Wilford Woodruff
September 21, 1840

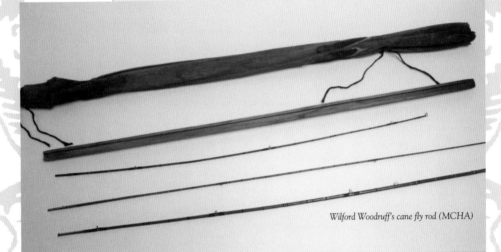

Wilford Woodruff's cane fly rod (MCHA)

Wilford Woodruff was an avid fisherman throughout his life. He wrote, "I was born on March 1, 1807, at Avon, Harford County, Conn., on the banks of a trout brook which had turned the wheels of a flour mill and a saw mill, owned by my grandfather and father, for many years. As soon as I was old enough to carry a fish-rod I commenced catching trout, which I have continued to do, from time to time, for nearly 80 years."

While his love for fishing never abated, his life was redirected in 1833 when he himself was captured in the gospel net. From age twenty-six Wilford Woodruff labored as a missionary, apostle, and prophet of the Lord until he died in 1898. His missions in the United States and Great Britain are now legendary, and though he continued to enjoy fishing when he had a chance, he beheld something symbolic in it all: "Behold, I will send for many fishers, saith the Lord, and they shall fish them" (Jeremiah 16:16). Wilford was one of those fishers—a "mighty fisher" of men and women.

1877
Jan. 1 • President of St. George Temple
Aug. 21 • Baptized in behalf of notable men, including the U.S. Founding Fathers
Aug. 29 • Brigham Young dies
Thomas Edison invents sound recording

1881
Spring • Salt Lake City Light, Heat, and Power Co. starts supplying electricity in Utah

1882
Aug. 10 • Attends concert in Tabernacle which is electrically lighted

1883
Oct. 7 • Church historian
William LeBaron Jenny completes the first "skyscraper," Chicago (1885)

1887
July 25 • John Taylor dies
Wilford Woodruff and Quorum of Twelve lead Church

1888
May 17 • Dedicates Manti Temple
George Eastman manufactures "Kodak" camera

1889
Apr. 7 • Ordained president of the Church

1890
Sept. 24 • Issues Manifesto (Official Declaration 1)

1891
May 9 • Meets U.S. President William H. Harrison, Salt Lake City
Canadian James Naismith creates basketball rules

1893
Apr. 6 • Dedicates Salt Lake Temple
World's Fair opens, Chicago

1894
Apr. 5 • Receives revelation concerning temple and family history work
Nov. 13 • Establishes the Genealogical Society of Utah
Milton Hershey develops "milk chocolate bar"

1895
June–July • Excursion to Oregon, Washington, Alaska

1896
Jan. 4 • Utah becomes 45th state
Sir Wilfrid Laurier becomes Canadian prime minister

1897
Mar. 19 • Records testimony into a "talking machine"
Nov. • *Improvement Era* begins publication (until 1970)
Church membership exceeds 250,000

1898
Apr. 1 • First single sister missionaries called
Sept. 2 • Dies in San Francisco, California
Spanish-American War breaks out

been looking for." Two days later, on December 31, 1833, Wilford and his brother Azmon entered the icy waters of baptism to begin a new life in Christ.

Few, including Wilford himself, could have known that this young convert would play such a significant role in the establishment of The Church of Jesus Christ of Latter-day Saints. Later, Wilford acknowledged that while his fellow Saints may not have known, the Lord and the devil certainly knew what role he would eventually play in the kingdom of God, and as a result there had been a real battle for his life.

Wilford is well known for his diligent, detailed, daily journal-keeping from the time of his 1833 conversion until just days before his death in 1898. Likewise, his missionary efforts are legendary. Others knew of his intense loyalty to Joseph Smith and to those who followed as president of The Church of Jesus Christ of Latter-day Saints—Brigham Young and John Taylor. However, when John Taylor died in July 1887, Wilford was an eighty-six-year-old with major health problems, and the Church was going through its most difficult period. Some thought that a younger, healthier, and more sophisticated man should step forward at this difficult moment to take the leadership reins of the Church. However, the mantle fell upon this simple, devout disciple of Jesus Christ. During the next twelve years, Wilford led the Church through troubled waters and, in the end, witnessed a new dawn of Church growth and peace preceding the twentieth century, when the Church came out of obscurity.

Wilford Woodruff, February 18, 1850. Wilford noted, "I called upon Br. Cannon, 123 Washington Street [Boston, Massachusetts]. He took my daguerreotype likeness and put it in a bosom pin for Mrs. Woodruff." In addition, a strand of Wilford's hair was also placed in the broach behind the photograph as a keepsake for his wife Phoebe Carter Woodruff. (Marsena Cannon, MCHA)

The Church's physical move from New York to Ohio and Missouri, from Nauvoo to Winter Quarters and eventually the Great Basin, was coupled with a spiritual move from one plane to another as the practices and doctrines of the Church unfolded during this critical period. It was a time of profound joy and sorrow, birth and death, and renewal and challenge. Nothing challenged the Saints and their neighbors more than plural marriage. At John Taylor's death, the Church was under unprecedented attack for the faithful acceptance of plural marriage. Defending their right to live the "principle," as they called it, the Saints' belief was based on the Lord's commandments and the inspired U.S. Constitution's guarantee of freedom to obey the revelations of God. During this intense time of prosecution and persecution, Church members held fast as they faced the storm of criticism, censure, and, for many, life on the run to avoid arrest and imprisonment as the federal government tried to destroy the Church. Many Saints were arrested, sentenced, and incarcerated in the Utah Territorial Prison—bishops and patriarchs imprisoned with murderers and cattle thieves—a unique situation, to say the least. Other faithful Saints sat in lonesome and dirty prisons in Arizona, Idaho, North Dakota, and Michigan. The very life of the Church was under attack, much as Wilford's own life had been from the life-threatening accidents that nearly destroyed him.

Wilford Woodruff was not only the Church president but also the prophet, seer, and revelator of the kingdom of God, and in this capacity the Lord worked through him to bring about His eternal purposes. Wilford had been prepared, as well as protected, to stand at this time at the head of the Church under the direction of Jesus Christ.

It seems clear that Wilford's greatest contribution to the kingdom was his ability to see more clearly than anyone else that prioritization was an essential responsibility of the Lord's anointed servant. In the storms of life, it takes a unique person to discern which of all the things that can be done should be done first. However, this process began much earlier in Wilford's life. His involvement as a missionary and in the restoration of temple worship in the new dispensation began with the blessings poured out at the Kirtland Temple, proceeded with the additional temple blessings restored in Nauvoo, and then continued when he accompanied Brigham Young to identify the site of the Salt Lake Temple in 1847. Later, he served as the president of the St. George Temple when it was completed in 1877, the first temple finished by the Saints in Utah. He privately dedicated the Manti Temple in 1888.

In the political pressure of the late 1880s, Wilford Woodruff's sincere humility and deep spiritual nature allowed the Lord to reveal two important and far-reaching changes in Church practice—prioritizing the things that mattered most and salvation for the living and the dead through temple worship. As God's prophet, he stressed that the Church's primary missions were preaching the gospel to living and the continual performance of saving ordinances for both the living and the dead.

It was Wilford's intuitive nature to contemplate what was most important to the Lord's eternal program. Should

Wilford Woodruff, 1866 (Enoch Wood Perry Jr., MCHA)

the Saints continue the practice of plural marriage, which involved a relatively small number of people, or should their energies be turned to establishing missionary and temple work in significant ways, reaching beyond the present capacity to an ever-increasing number of people on earth and in the spirit world?

The 1890 Manifesto is the Lord's confirmation of Wilford's thoughtful and prayerful decision to begin the process that would end the practice of plural marriage, a practice that substantially served its scriptural purpose to raise up a second and third generation of members committed to Jesus Christ (see Jacob 2:30) and that sharpened the discipleship of the first generation of Latter-day Saints—an "Abrahamic test" (see D&C 132:50). In turn, the change of policy now allowed Saints to continue missionary labors to the nations of the earth (many of whom had threatened to close their doors to the Church), providing those who listened the opportunity to receive the first ordinances of the gospel that allow men and women to become the sons and daughters of Christ. Moreover, this change allowed those who embraced the restored gospel to enter temples to receive ordinances necessary to preserve the family beyond death. Finally, this change also provided an opportunity to complete the work for the dead.

In 1894, a second revelation completed the process President Woodruff identified as a "revolution" when he announced to the First Presidency, "The Lord has told me that it is right for children to be sealed to their parents, and they to their parents just as far back as we can possibly

Wilford Woodruff, about 1867 (Edward Martin, Church Archives)

Wilford Woodruff, about 1870 (Courtesy Gregory P. and MarJane Christofferson)

obtain the records." This new revelation greatly expanded the Saints' understanding and lifted a fairly limited practice of work for the dead. The revelation was presented to the Church in general conference on April 8, a few days later. Soon the Genealogical Society of Utah was founded (predecessor to the Church's Family History Department), and Church members expanded their family history efforts. Temple work enabled them to "proclaim liberty to the captives, and the opening of the prison to them that are found" (Isaiah 61:1).

In August 1898, as Wilford Woodruff traveled west to San Francisco, he did not know that he would never return to his beloved Salt Lake City. The fourth president of the Church died on September 2, away from his dedicated fellow Saints. His body was transported to Utah, and on Thursday, September 8, thousands of grateful Church members arose as his casket entered the famed Tabernacle

on the Temple Block. Following the service, Wilford Woodruff was laid to rest—symbolic of the status of the Church as he left it in 1898. The Church and the Latter-day Saints had finally begun to find rest; the U.S. prison doors were opened so members could return home (1890); Church leaders were granted amnesty by the president of the United States, allowing them to minister to the Saints (1891); the Salt Lake Temple was completed after forty years of labor (1893); Church leaders and the Mormon Tabernacle Choir were warmly greeted by the leaders of nations at the Chicago World's Fair (1893); Utah was granted home rule when it became the forty-fifth state in the union (1896); and the missionary efforts increased as did temple work for the living and the dead, resulting from the newfound freedom provided by the Lord.

Elder Franklin D. Richards "spoke of the first time he met Wilford Woodruff, and stated that he was impressed

WILFORD WOODRUFF'S JOURNAL

Wilford Woodruff's remarkable journals provide detailed information about his life and labors. In 1889 he took a red and black pen to express to a later generation his feelings on this important day. Within the heart is a key, symbolic of the sealing power of the priesthood in turning the hearts of the children to the fathers and the fathers to the children. Inside the heart he wrote, "Wilford Woodruff was appointed president of the Church of Jesus Christ of Latter Days Saints April 7, 1889." The entry for the day continues, "This 7 day of April 1889 was one of the most important days of my life, for upon this Sabbath day I was appointed the president of the Church of Jesus Christ of Latter[-day] Saints by the unanimous vote of ten thousand Latter Day Saints. The vote was first taken by quorums, then by the whole assembly of the Saints of God. Then my two councilors, George Q. Cannon and Joseph F. Smith, were voted in the same manner. This is the highest office ever conferred upon man in the flesh and what a responsibility it places upon me or any other man in the same position. This office is placed upon me in my 83 year of my life. I pray God to protect me during my remaining days and give me power to magnify my calling to the end of my days. The Lord has watched over me from my birth until the present day."

(Right) Wilford Woodruff, possibly December 10, 1887. Wilford noted, "I came to Savages Gallery and set for a likeness." This image may be the one alluded to in his journal. Charles Savage copyrighted the image in 1888 and published it later on card stock with the caption "Wilford Woodruff, Fourth President of the Church of Jesus Christ of Latter-day Saints, Born March 1, 1807," sometime after Wilford Woodruff was ordained as president in 1889. (Charles R. Savage, Church Archives)

(Below) Wilford Woodruff Journal, April 7, 1889 (Church Archives)

(Left) Wilford Woodruff sitting for a photograph, about 1890 (MCHA)

Wilford Woodruff, about 1891 (Charles R. Savage, Church Archives)

President Woodruff's
MANIFESTO.

PROCEEDINGS AT THE SEMI-ANNUAL GENERAL CONFERENCE OF THE CHURCH OF JESUS CHRIST OF LATTER-DAY SAINTS.

MONDAY FORENOON, OCTOBER 6, 1890.

President Woodruff

Said: I will say, as the question is often asked, "What do the Latter-day Saints believe in?" we feel disposed to read the Articles of Faith of the Church of Jesus Christ of Latter-day Saints, and should there be any strangers present, they may understand our faith in this respect. The question is often asked, "Do the Mormon people believe in the Bible?" so the principles that are read will show our faith and belief appertaining to the Gospel of Christ.

The articles were then read by Bishop Orson F. Whitney. They are here introduced:

ARTICLES OF FAITH

Of the Church of Jesus Christ of Latter day Saints.

1. We believe in God, the Eternal Father, and in His Son, Jesus Christ, and in the Holy Ghost.
2. We believe that men will be punished for their own sins, and not for Adam's transgression.
3. We believe that through the atonement of Christ all mankind may be saved, by obedience to the laws and ordinances of the Gospel.
4. We believe that these ordinances are: First faith in the Lord Jesus Christ; second repentance; third, baptism by immersion for the remission of sins; fourth, laying on of hands for the gift of the Holy Ghost.
5. We believe that a man must be called of God by "prophecy, and by the laying on of hands," by those who are in authority, to preach the Gospel and administer in the ordinances thereof.
6. We believe in the same organization that existed in the primitive church, viz.: apostles, prophets, pastors, teachers, evangelists, etc.
7. We believe in the gift of tongues, prophecy, revelation, visions, healing, interpretation of tongues, etc.
8. We believe the Bible to be the word of God, as far as it is translated correctly; we also believe the Book of Mormon to be the word of God.
9. We believe all that God has revealed, all that he does now reveal, and we believe that He will yet reveal many great and important things pertaining to the Kingdom of God.
10. We believe in the literal gathering of Israel and in the restoration of the Ten Tribes. That Zion will be built upon this continent. That Christ will reign personally upon the earth, and that the earth will be renewed and receive its paradisic glory.

THE MANIFESTO

President Woodruff's journal entry for September 25, 1890, provides personal insight into an important event: "I have arrived at a point in the history of my life as the President of the Church of Jesus Christ of Latter Day Saints where I am under the necessity of acting for the temporal salvation of the Church. The United States Government has taken a stand and passed laws to destroy the Latter day Saints upon the subject of polygamy or patriarchal order of marriage. And after praying to the Lord and feeling inspired by his spirit I have issued the following proclamation which is sustained by my councilors and the 12 Apostles."

The "Official Declaration," known as the Manifesto, is now titled "Official Declaration 2" as published in the Doctrine and Covenants. Eleven days later Wilford continued, "Oct. 6 Conference met at 10 o'clock. . . . The Authorities of the Church presented and sustained. The Articles of Faith were read and accepted by all of the people. Then W. Woodruff manifesto was read and accepted by a vote of the whole conference which act created a sensation throughout the whole United States."

Wilford Woodruff, about the time the Salt Lake Temple capstone was set amid great celebration in Salt Lake City on April 6, 1892 (Charles Johnson, courtesy Gregory P. and MarJane Christofferson)

Wilford Woodruff profile, sometime before the dedication of the Salt Lake Temple, about 1892 (Sainsbury and Johnson, Church Archives)

(Left) Woodruff Manifesto pamphlet, 1890 (BYU)

very strongly with the directness and simplicity of his character, and his perfect guilelessness. He had been a great exemplar of the work in which he had been engaged, by his implicit obedience to the dictates of the spirit. . . . President Woodruff's enemies had been led to become his friends. He had assisted in the building and dedication of the temples, had established an honorable family on the earth and had performed great missionary labors in different parts of the world. He had been a mighty fisher of men bringing into the Church almost two thousand persons."

Another honor was paid by Elder Matthias F. Cowley: "President Woodruff was an unassuming man, very unaffected and childlike in his demeanor. He did no man an injury, nor was he too proud, even in his Apostolic calling, to toil as other men toiled. His traits and characteristics were ennobling, and so energetic was he that nothing

was too burdensome for him even in his advanced years. . . . He was of a sweet disposition and possessed a character so lovely as to draw unto him friends in every walk of life. . . . He was free, sociable, and amiable in every respect. No jealousy lurked in his bosom. He looked upon all mankind as his equals and was one who cherished the most profound respect for all with whom he associated. . . . In spite of his high and holy calling, he . . . was unpretentious, unassuming, and his character and life were as transparent as glass. He hid nothing from his brethren, but was candid, outspoken, and free to all."

Certainly, Church presidents who followed had their own challenges to face, but Wilford Woodruff led the Church through an important transition, providing for it the central focus of its mission to bring souls, both living and dead, to Jesus Christ.

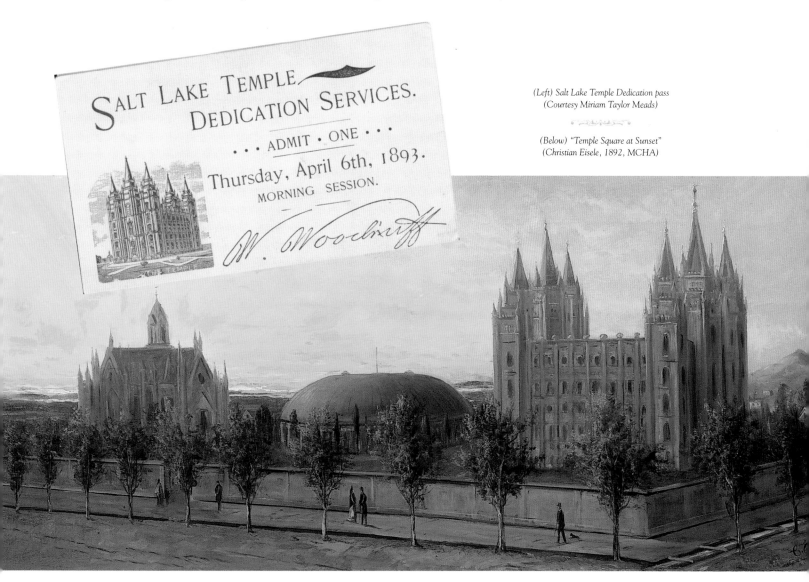

(Left) Salt Lake Temple Dedication pass
(Courtesy Miriam Taylor Meads)

(Below) "Temple Square at Sunset"
(Christian Eisele, 1892, MCHA)

(Above) Wilford Woodruff, about 1894
(Fox and Symons, Church Archives)

Wilford Woodruff, April 6, 1893. Wilford Woodruff saw the dedication of the Salt Lake Temple as one of the most important events of his life. Sainsbury and Johnson captured the First Presidency in three different poses on the first day of dedication services. This final image, showing President Woodruff alone, is reprinted from the original glass-plate negative, now housed in L. Tom Perry Special Collections at the Harold B. Lee Library at Brigham Young University. When printed at the time, the image would have been cropped not to include the entire area of the negative. (BYU)

(Left) Wilford Woodruff party at the Hotel Del Coronado, California, August 29, 1896. President Woodruff noted, "We went out on the pier. Got a fish pole and line. Caught a small stinger fish. The location of this hotel is excellent, and as a winter resort has few equals in the land. The summers are mild the weather cool and bracing, but the heat now is greater than had been felt. It was said by old residents, for 25 years." (S. P. Tresslar, Church Archives)

(Bottom left) Wilford Woodruff four-generation photo, August 16, 1897. (Charles Johnson, Church Archives)

(Below) Wilford and his wife Emma, about a year before Wilford's death in 1898. (Fox and Symons, Church Archives)

FOUR GENERATIONS
OF THE FAMILY OF
PRESIDENT WILFORD WOODRUFF.
Copyright 1899, by The Johnson Co., Salt Lake, Utah.

State of the Church at the time of Wilford Woodruff's death	
Year of death	1898
Church membership	267,251
Stakes	40
Temples	4
Missions	20
Missionaries set apart during administration	5,780
Book of Mormon translations completed during administration	2

The President's Office

(Below) Reconstructed Red Brick Store, Nauvoo, Illinois (Courtesy John Telford)

Reconstructed Whitmer Cabin, Fayette, New York (VRL)

President's Office sign from the Red Brick Store, Nauvoo, Illinois (MCHA)

Joseph Smith lived at the Whitmer farm in Fayette, New York, when the Church of Christ was organized on April 6, 1830—making the Whitmer cabin the headquarters of the Church during this period. Later, the Prophet moved to Ohio and lived in various locations, including the Johnson home (Hiram, Ohio); the Morley farm; the Whitney store; and his own home (Kirtland, Ohio). Each in its turn served as the president's office. Later, there are references to an office apart from his residence that may have stood near the temple, then under construction. When completed, however, the new Kirtland Temple had an office for the president in the attic story. In the wake of persecution, the Saints left their temple, homes, farms, and businesses for Missouri in 1838. During his brief stay in Missouri, Joseph Smith may have had a separate office in Far West, as one source from this period suggests. Again a

Brigham Young home and office complex, Salt Lake City, about 1855 (Louis Rice Chaffin, Church Archives)

storm of persecution forced the Saints to find refuge in another location, this time Illinois.

Eventually, following his escape from Missouri imprisonment, the Prophet joined the Saints in Illinois. On a bend of the Mississippi River, he identified Nauvoo as the new Mormon gathering place and Church headquarters. In 1842, Joseph Smith built a store, known as the Red Brick Store. In the upper floor of this building he had an office, which served as the president's office until his death in June 1844.

Administratively, the headquarters of the Church moved from the Red Brick Store to Brigham Young's home following the martyrdom in 1844. Brigham added a wing to his two-story brick home. This wing served as a meeting place for Church leaders until the Nauvoo Temple was nearly completed in 1845. Again, the leadership of the Church used rooms in the attic of the temple as offices.

Following the exodus in February 1846, the Church headquarters moved with Brigham Young and was located in wagons and tents along the trail to the Great Basin. When he was sustained as the second president of the Church of Jesus Christ in December 1847, the president's office was in Winter Quarters until Brigham Young made his way back to Utah in 1848. Upon his return to Salt Lake City in September, the president's office was located in various places in the growing community, including Brigham Young's homes (early residences before the completion of the Beehive House in late 1854). In 1852, a separate and distinct president's office was built on a lot east of the temple. Eventually, Brigham Young constructed the Beehive House (his new residence) and Lion House (residence for several members of his family) on either side of an office complex, now consisting of two attached buildings (known as the east and west offices). This complex served as the president's office for Brigham Young, Wilford Woodruff, Lorenzo Snow, and Joseph F. Smith.

Near the end of his ministry, Joseph F. Smith authorized the construction of a new Church office building. Completed in 1917, the Church Administration Building housed the offices of the First Presidency and the Quorum of the Twelve. It was the first time that these general officers of the Church were located in one building. Today, this beautiful granite building continues to house the president's office.

"Brigham Young in his office," from Harper's Weekly, November 25, 1871 (Courtesy Gary L. and Carol B. Bunker)

Heber J. Grant working in his office, about 1925; from left: Anthony W. Ivins, Heber J. Grant, Charles W. Nibley (USHS)

Church Administration Building, Salt Lake City. Built in 1917, this granite building remains the site of the office of the president of the Church (to the left can be seen the Joseph Smith Memorial Building, formerly the Hotel Utah, built in 1911; looming in the background is the Church Office Building, dedicated in 1975). (VRL)

Spencer W. Kimball in his office, about 1980 (Church Archives)

Gordon B. Hinckley and grandchildren in his office, December 1996 (Richard M. Romney, courtesy Hinckley Family)

Lorenzo Snow

On the afternoon of May 15, 1899, President Lorenzo Snow and party departed from Salt Lake City aboard a private Pullman railway car headed to Modena, the southern Utah terminus of the Utah and Pacific "Salt Lake Route." From Modena, they traveled in horse-drawn carriages and wagons over the seventy miles of rough dirt road leading to St. George, Utah.

After twenty-six hours of travel, the tired and sore party pulled into St. George on the night of May 16, 1899. An exhausted Lorenzo Snow visited with his hosts and then retired to his room, where he rested but a few minutes before anxiously pacing back and forth. He was sure of one thing—the Lord had directed him to go to St. George. But he did not know why the Lord wanted him in Utah's Dixie. Aloud he wondered, "O why have I come to St. George and why have I brought so many of the Church authorities when we are so much needed at home to look after the important affairs of the Church? Haven't I made a mistake? Why have I come here?"

When Lorenzo Snow became president on September 13, 1898, the Church was close to financial ruin, with an outstanding debt in excess of more than 1.25 million dollars. This terrible situation was brought on by the federal government's confiscation of Church property, a drop in tithing receipts, and borrowing of money, often at an interest rate of 10 percent. Deeply concerned and seeking a solution, President Snow studied and prayed for guidance. In answer, the Lord directed him to travel to and address a special conference at St. George. As he was wont to do, Lorenzo faithfully obeyed.

A long, varied life journey prepared Lorenzo Snow for this moment and the unique problems facing the Saints at the end of the nineteenth century. In fact, his life resonated with trust and dependency upon the spiritual. As a student at Oberlin College in 1835, the ambitious young man was "full of worldly aspirations, with bright prospects and means to gratify my ambition in acquiring a liberal, collegiate education. Besides I had many wealthy, proud, aristocratical friends and relatives who watched eagerly for me to achieve high honors in life." Lorenzo, whose mother and two older sisters were already members of the Church, was familiar with the Prophet Joseph's teachings. Indeed, contrary to

(Left) Lorenzo Snow (Lewis A. Ramsey, 1911, MCHA)

(Above oval) Lorenzo Snow, about 1893 (Church Archives)

BORN
APRIL 3, 1814
MANTUA, OHIO

PARENTS
OLIVER AND ROSETTA
LEONORA PETTIBONE SNOW

BAPTIZED
JUNE 19, 1836
(AGE 22)

STATURE
5' 6"
140 POUNDS

MARRIED
APRIL 21, 1845
TO SARAH ANN PRICHARD
(AGE 30)

APOSTLE
FEBRUARY 12, 1849
(AGE 34)

PRESIDENT
SEPTEMBER 13, 1898
(AGE 84)

DIED
OCTOBER 10, 1901
SALT LAKE CITY, UTAH
(AGE 87)

many of his peers, Lorenzo liked Joseph Smith, believing him to be "honest and sincere." In determining his course in life, Lorenzo fought what he called "the fiercest struggle of heart and soul I ever experienced." He continued, "However, through the help of the Lord—for I feel certain He must have helped me—I laid my pride, worldly ambition and aspirations upon the altar, and, humble as a child, went to the waters of baptism, and received the ordinances of the gospel."

For two weeks after his baptism, Lorenzo daily retired to a grove near his Kirtland lodgings and prayed for the reception of the Holy Ghost. One evening, although in a "gloomy and disconsolate" mood, he again knelt in prayer. What happened next forever refocused his life and established a life true to the promptings of the Lord. As he began to pray, Lorenzo heard, above his head, a sound "like the rustling of silken robes." He wrote, "Immediately the Spirit of God descended upon me, completely enveloping my whole person, filling me from the crown of my head to the soles of my feet, and O, the joy and happiness I felt! No language can describe the

Sketch of Lorenzo Snow, 1853 (Frederick H. Piercy, based on a daguerreotype taken by Marsena Cannon about 1852 in Salt Lake City, Church Archives)

instantaneous transition from a dense cloud of mental and spiritual darkness into a refulgence of light and knowledge. . . . I then received a perfect knowledge that God lives, that Jesus Christ is the Son of God, and of the restoration of the Holy Priesthood, and the fulness of the gospel."

Lorenzo Snow no longer sought to further his formal education; instead, he committed and devoted his life to the Lord and the gospel. As a missionary he served in his home state of Ohio, then in Illinois and Kentucky, and then in England and Italy, where he directed the translation of the Book of Mormon into Italian. He also served short missions to Hawaii and to the Indians of the Pacific Northwest. As a pioneer he led a company of Saints across the plains to the Salt Lake Valley.

As a colonizer, he was called in the autumn of 1853 to organize some fifty families to establish a community in northern Utah's Box Elder County. Naming the settlement Brigham City, Lorenzo Snow, over the next twenty years, energetically guided its growth from "a receptacle for bed bugs" into a progressive and thriving town, complete with city

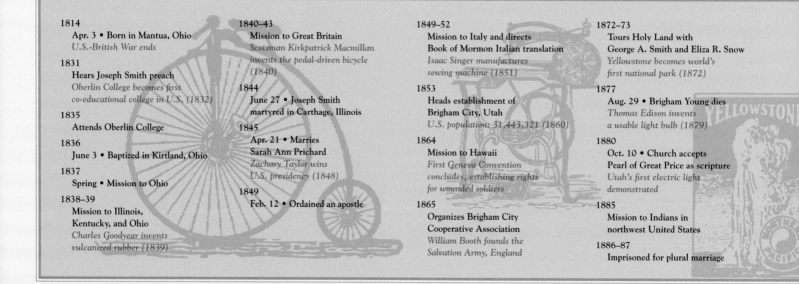

1814
Apr. 3 • Born in Mantua, Ohio
U.S.-British War ends

1831
Hears Joseph Smith preach
Oberlin College becomes first co-educational college in U.S. (1832)

1835
Attends Oberlin College

1836
June 3 • Baptized in Kirtland, Ohio

1837
Spring • Mission to Ohio

1838–39
Mission to Illinois, Kentucky, and Ohio
Charles Goodyear invents vulcanized rubber (1839)

1840–43
Mission to Great Britain
Scotsman Kirkpatrick Macmillan invents the pedal-driven bicycle (1840)

1844
June 27 • Joseph Smith martyred in Carthage, Illinois

1845
Apr. 21 • Marries Sarah Ann Prichard
Zachary Taylor wins U.S. presidency (1848)

1849
Feb. 12 • Ordained an apostle

1849–52
Mission to Italy and directs Book of Mormon Italian translation
Isaac Singer manufactures sewing machine (1851)

1853
Heads establishment of Brigham City, Utah
U.S. population: 31,443,321 (1860)

1864
Mission to Hawaii
First Geneva Convention concludes, establishing rights for wounded soldiers

1865
Organizes Brigham City Cooperative Association
William Booth founds the Salvation Army, England

1872–73
Tours Holy Land with George A. Smith and Eliza R. Snow
Yellowstone becomes world's first national park (1872)

1877
Aug. 29 • Brigham Young dies
Thomas Edison invents a usable light bulb (1879)

1880
Oct. 10 • Church accepts Pearl of Great Price as scripture
Utah's first electric light demonstrated

1885
Mission to Indians in northwest United States

1886–87
Imprisoned for plural marriage

planning, public schools, drama society, and the prosperous, communally owned Brigham City Mercantile and Manufacturing Association.

In 1872–73, with his sister Eliza R. Snow, George A Smith, and others, Elder Snow journeyed to the Holy Land to dedicate the land for the return of the children of Abraham. On their way, they extensively toured Europe to "observe closely what openings now exist . . . for the introduction of the Gospel." Their visits included Liverpool, London, Amsterdam, Paris, Lyon, Venice, the Vatican, Cairo, and the Mount of Olives.

Upon learning of President Wilford Woodruff's death on September 2, 1898, Lorenzo Snow humbly secured himself in the sanctity of the inner rooms of the Salt Lake Temple, where he poured out his heart to the Lord, pleading, "I have not sought this responsibility, but if it be Thy will, I now present myself before Thee for Thy guidance and instruction. I ask that Thou show me what Thou wouldst have me do." Intelligent, gracious, cultured, and humble, Lorenzo Snow had served the Lord for forty-nine years as an apostle. Now, taking his place as prophet, seer, and revelator, he adamantly let his brethren know, "I do not want this administration to be known as Lorenzo Snow's administration, but as God's in and through Lorenzo Snow."

On May 17, 1899, with a lifetime of experience behind him, President Snow stood before expectant Saints crowding the St. George Tabernacle. In the midst of a severe drought, they looked forward to their prophet's

The Only Way to Be Saved, published in 1851 by Lorenzo Snow (Courtesy R. Q. and Susan Shupe)

1887

Feb. 7 • Freed following U.S. Supreme Court's decision reversing earlier conviction

Thomas Edison patents motion picture camera (1891)

1892

Apr. 6 • Leads 40,000 Saints in Hosanna Shout at Salt Lake Temple capstone ceremony

1893

May 30 • Begins service as the first Salt Lake Temple president

Karl Benz constructs four-wheel car

1898

Sept. 2 • Wilford Woodruff dies

Sept. • Vision of Jesus Christ in Salt Lake Temple

Sept. 13 • Ordained president of the Church

Conference Reports begins regular biannual publication

Count Zeppelin patents airship

1899

May 8 • Reemphasizes tithing

July 2 • Church leaders accept tithing as the "word and will of the Lord"

Latter-day Saint William Aldridge drills first oil well in Alberta, Canada

Henry Ford starts Detroit Automobile Company

1900

Jan. 1 • Speaks at special meeting in Tabernacle welcoming the new century

Jan. 10 • Issues "Greeting to the World"

Jan. 8 • Purchases Lion House and President's Office from Young Family

July 24 • Brigham Young Monument unveiling

Dec. 5 • Clarifies apostolic seniority

Dec. 31 • Church membership: 283,765

U.S. establishes gold standard

1901

Feb. 7 • LDS Business College building dedicated

Feb. 14 • Announces expansion of missionary work to Japan

May 4 • Tabernacle organ reconstructed by Kimball Organ Company

May 12 • Instructs the Twelve to preach tithing until all are converted

Oct. 10 • Dies in Salt Lake City

Queen Victoria of England dies

Oil portrait of Lorenzo Snow, about 1866 (Enoch Wood Perry, MCHA)

Lorenzo Snow at Charles R. Savage's gallery in the late 1860s
(Charles R. Savage, Church Archives)

A rare photograph by Edward Martin, about 1867,
from a photo album (Church Archives)

comforting counsel. As he spoke, he touched on gospel principles, but suddenly, as his son LeRoi Snow reported: "Father paused in his discourse, complete stillness filled the room. When he commenced to speak again his voice strengthened and the inspiration of God seemed suddenly to come over him, as well as over the entire assembly. Then he revealed to the Latter-day Saints the vision that was before him. God manifested to him there and then the purpose of the call to visit the Saints in the south. He told them that he could see, as he had never realized before, how the law of tithing had been neglected by the people, also that the Saints, themselves, were heavily in debt, as well as the Church, and now through strict obedience to this law—the paying of a full and honest tithing—not only would the Church be relieved of its great indebtedness, but through the blessings of the Lord this would also be the means of freeing the Latter-day Saints from their individual obligations and they would become a prosperous people."

President Snow's seemingly peculiar combination of heightened spiritual sensitivity and financial pragmatism enabled Church members to spiritually unite and begin the road back to financial solvency. By August 1899 rains returned to southern Utah, promising improved prosperity to the farmers and ranchers. To end Church debt, the First Presidency cut expenditures, consolidated debts, offered two $500,000 bonds, sold nonessential property, and quit borrowing money for investments—and the Saints

C-62

Image from a Charles W. Carter glass-plate negative, about 1870 (Church Archives)

(Below) United Order Shop, Brigham City, about 1885. Lorenzo Snow is standing at the far right (Church Archives)

SAYINGS OF PRESIDENT SNOW

The reward for righteousness is exaltation.

Godliness cannot be conferred, but must be acquired.

We approach godliness as fast as we approach perfection.

Before I die I hope to see the Church cleared of debt and in a commanding position financially.

If we are faithful, we shall at some time do our own work, but now we are doing the work of our Father.

The Lord has shown me most clearly and completely that Joseph Smith was a prophet of God.

Greater work was never done by man since the days of Adam than is being done here in the temple.

We have all the possibilities of God himself, and we should so act that every faculty shall be developed to the utmost.

A mother who has brought up a family of faithful children ought to be saved, if she never does another good thing.

The glorious opportunity of becoming truly great belongs to every faithful elder in Israel; it is his by right divine.

Before the lion and the lamb shall lie down together in peace, man must desist from hunting, killing, and eating the flesh of animals.

I would like to live to see the time when the old bitterness between "Mormons" and non-"Mormons" shall have disappeared.

(Above) Image from a Charles W. Carter glass-plate negative, about 1886 (Church Archives)

(Left) A popular business-card-sized photograph of Lorenzo Snow, about 1880 (Church Archives)

increased their contributions. President Snow's financial undertakings allowed the Church to be debt-free by 1907.

Lorenzo Snow died of pneumonia on October 10, 1901. His journey through life positively affected many men and women, including the Reverend Dr. Prentice, a writer and lecturer from South Carolina. Dr. Prentice believed that "upon the countenance of the aged saint or sinner, every line, every shade, every tracing speaks unerringly of a history of glorious triumph or disastrous defeat. Before the story is told and the character completed, regularity of feature lines, of texture, and delicacy of coloring may cover up from careless eyes the deadly work of spiritual destruction going on beneath the specious appearances but when . . . the hoar frost of winter whitens the head and furrows the smooth skin, the

history of the life can no longer be hid, and men may read it as in an open book."

When he first met and visited with President Snow in 1898, the reverend "expected to find intellect, intellectuality, benevolence, dignity, composure and strength depicted upon the face of the president of the Church of Jesus Christ of Latter-day Saints." However, Dr. Prentice beheld "the holiest face, but one, that I had ever been privileged to look upon. His face was a poem of peace; his presence a benediction of peace. In the tranquil depths of his eyes were the 'home of silent prayer' and the abode of spiritual strength. . . . The picture of that slight, venerable form haloed with the aura of an ineffable peace will haunt my heart like the vision of a celestial picture."

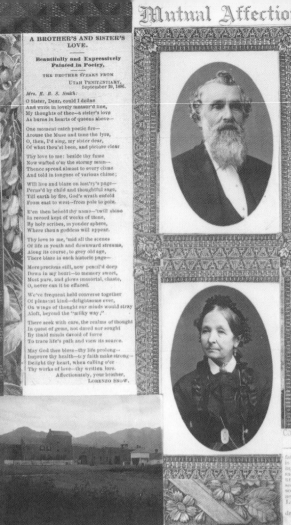

(Left) "Mutual Affection" (Charles W. Carter, Church Archives)

MUTUAL AFFECTION

Church leaders and members faced significant challenges during the 1880s, when the U.S. government passed laws against plural marriage. Since the public announcement of the practice in 1852, Church leaders and members attempted to convince the world that it was their religious and moral duty to obey the Lord's command to restore biblical plural marriage.

In the face of increased persecution and prosecution, many Saints went "underground" to avoid confrontation with government officers. Hundreds, however, were arrested, convicted, and incarcerated during the "Federal Raid" period. One of the unintended consequences of this stressful period was an explosion of literary activities among those underground and in prison, including the production of numerous letters, diaries, autograph albums, and poems.

While in the Utah territorial prison, Lorenzo Snow wrote to his sister, Eliza R. Snow. Extracts of his letters were later used by Charles W. Carter to create "Mutual Affection." The seventy-two-year-old Church leader was among the more than eight hundred Saints imprisoned in Utah for plural marriage.

He retained his sense of humor during his incarceration, as indicated by a few lines from one of his many letters to family members: "In a general sense, we are here as the invited guests of the nation, boarded and lodged all at Government expense, a remarkable instance illustrating in a striking manner that spirit of philanthropy pervading the bosom of our mighty republic."

Utah Territorial Penitentiary, 1886 (Francis M. Treseder, Springville Museum of Art)

LORENZO SNOW'S FAMILY

Born on April 3, 1814, in Mantua, Ohio, Lorenzo Snow was the fifth child and first son of seven children born to Oliver and Rosetta Lenora Snow. Hardworking and relatively well-to-do, the Snows were active Baptists who hosted religious discussions in their home. His family encouraged Lorenzo's love of reading and intellectual curiosity, which was balanced with helping to maintain the family farm.

Lorenzo Snow was husband to nine wives and father to forty-two children. His wives were Mary Adaline Goddard, Caroline Horton, Eleanor Houtz, Mary Elizabeth Houtz, Sarah Minnie Jensen, Sarah Ann Prichard, Charlotte Squires, Harriet Amelia Squires, and Phoebe Amelia Woodruff.

In 1920, Rosetta Adaline Snow Loveland, daughter of Lorenzo Snow and Mary Adaline Goddard, wrote down "incidents of her life" as she remembered them. Mrs. Loveland included her memories of her father's family life in the early days of Utah:

"When I was three years of age, Father was called on a mission to Italy [1849–1852]. . . . After performing a three-and-a-half year mission he returned and as soon as possible built us a house on Brigham Street [Salt Lake City]. Here I attended school for the first time, in the basement, with Aunt Harriot Snow as instructor.

"We experienced many hardships at this time, going sometimes six weeks at a time without bread. But not withstanding this we had many good times. There was a big hall upstairs in this house where dances were given. Father was very anxious that his children should have good wholesome amusements. One very noticeable thing was the love and harmony that existed between the wives and children. Quarreling was not allowed in Father's household and we had great respect for our Father and Mother and were taught to obey from our infancy. Music was a favorite pastime. First, Father bought an accordion, then a melodian, then an organ, and finally a piano. Every evening we seven older children would sing for the others. Then Father would relate stories with some good moral, and I am sure this had an effect for good. If there were any grievances, they were brought up and settled at these little family gatherings, and the Spirit of the Lord was there. The mothers enjoyed this very much, as they were usually tired, and an hour's rest before retiring was much appreciated. Each morning and evening the bell would ring, which was a signal for us all to assemble in the spacious dining room for prayer."

Eliza R. Snow in Cairo, Egypt, 1873, while on a tour of the Holy Land with her brother Lorenzo Snow (Delie & E. Bechard Photography, Church Archives)

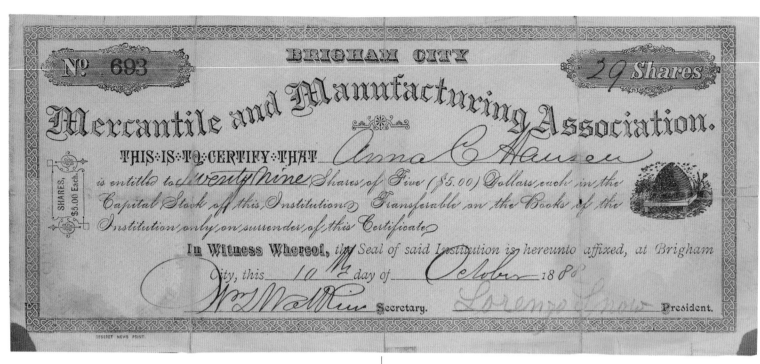

(Above) Brigham City Mercantile and Manufacturing Association
share certificate dated October 10, 1888, signed by Lorenzo Snow
(Courtesy Gregory P. and MarJane Christofferson)

(Lower left) Lorenzo Snow, about 1888 (Church Archives)

(Lower right) Profile of Lorenzo Snow, about 1892 (Charles R. Savage, Church Archives)

(Above) The First Presidency and Quorum of the Twelve,
October 10, 1898 (Fox and Symons, Church Archives)

(Below) Lorenzo Snow about the time of his appointment as the first Salt Lake
Temple president, about 1893 (Charles R. Savage, Church Archives)

Lorenzo Snow in the Salt Lake Temple shortly before his death, about 1901 (USHS)

State of the Church at the time of Lorenzo Snow's death	
Year of death	1901
Church membership	292,931
Stakes	50
Temples	4
Missions	21
Total Missionaries set apart during administration	1,642
Book of Mormon translations completed during administration	0

COME LISTEN TO A PROPHET'S VOICE

Color sketch of Joseph Smith at general conference, April 1844 (George Lloyd, Church Archives)

From the earliest days of the Restoration, people were eager to see and hear the young prophet, Joseph Smith. By 1839 the practice of holding regular general conferences was well established, giving the faithful an opportunity to receive counsel and be spiritually uplifted by the words of the living prophet. However, the challenge to accommodate all who wanted to see and hear the Lord's anointed was already formidable. During this "premeeting-house" period, Joseph Smith addressed the Saints in one of several groves in Nauvoo. Speaking in the open air provided difficult challenges as the Prophet tried to be heard: "My lungs are failing with continual preaching in the open air to large assemblies," he once noted.

Within the first decade of the founding of Salt Lake City, the Saints built several structures on the Temple Block to accommodate those who wanted to listen to a prophet's voice. In October 1867, Church members gathered in a historic meeting held in the new Tabernacle where the acoustics were better, allowing those attending to hear. Nevertheless, there was not enough room in this building to accommodate all those wishing to "see and hear" the prophet. In 1889, the Church offered concurrent sessions of conference in both the Tabernacle and the Assembly Hall, dedicated in 1882 just south of the Tabernacle.

(Above left) Stereo card, old and new Tabernacles, about 1867 (Courtesy R. Q. and Susan Shupe)
(Above middle) Stereo card, interior view of new Tabernacle, about 1867 (Courtesy R. Q. and Susan Shupe)
(Above right) Latter-day Saints gather at the Temple Block on April 2, 1892 (Church Archives)

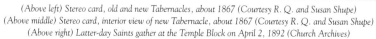

Technological progress in the twentieth century expanded the opportunity for many more people to receive counsel from the prophet at general conference. In April 1923, the Church used amplifiers for the first time, allowing those gathered in the Assembly Hall to join those seated in the Tabernacle. Only eighteen months later, the radio expanded the audience to a million in the local area. Another significant advance occurred in October 1949 when conference was broadcast by television, allowing people not only to hear a prophet's voice but to see him as well. Short-wave radio transmission brought the conference to those beyond the confines of Utah and the West beginning in 1962.

Feeling a need to fulfill the desire of an increasing number of Saints who wanted to see and hear the prophet in person, the Church began holding area conferences in 1972. In 1975, satellites started carrying conference proceedings around the world. Still, to "see and hear" the prophet in person was denied many who wanted such an opportunity, and so it was with special feeling that President Gordon B. Hinckley welcomed twenty thousand Saints gathered at the recently completed Conference Center in April 2000. He spoke of the pulpit "in this great hall where the voices of prophets will go out to all the world in testimony of the Redeemer of mankind."

President Heber J. Grant delivering his first message to the world in a radio station May 6, 1922 (Church Archives)

President David O. McKay speaking at general conference, about 1968 (VRL)

Joseph Fielding Smith addressing the first area conference, Manchester, England, August 27, 1971 (Deseret News)

Interior of the new Conference Center, April 2003 (Courtesy Corey Perrine)

Joseph F. Smith

A group of angry men entered a cabin in Far West, Missouri, and began ransacking the tiny home of Hyrum and Mary Fielding Smith. They were looking for guns, documents, and other valuables from the homes of Church leaders who were now under their guard. Mary had delivered her first child just days before and was therefore in no position to stop the men from doing what they pleased. Lying helpless on her bed, Mary watched the melee unfold as her newborn son slept nearby. Joseph F. Smith later said of the situation, "When the mob entered the room where I was, the bed on the floor was thrown on to the other completely smothering me up, and here I was permitted to remain until after the excitement subsided. When thought of, and discovered, my existence was supposed to have come to an end; but subsequent events have proven their suppositions erroneous, however well founded!"

Joseph F. Smith was born into a cauldron of intense persecution on November 13, 1838, at Far West, Missouri. Named after his uncle (Joseph Smith the Prophet) and after his mother (Mary Fielding Smith), Joseph Fielding Smith was known as Joseph F. Smith during his lifetime. When the Angel Moroni visited Joseph Smith in 1823, he told the young man that his "name should be had for good and evil among all nations, kindreds, and tongues, or that it should be both good and evil spoken of among all people" (Joseph Smith—History 1:33). Later events proved the prophecy to be true.

Joseph F. Smith inherited not only his uncle's name but also his legacy of having his name known "for good and evil." The name Joseph, which brought both comfort and joy along with ridicule and hatred, was not selected without some thought. His mother and father chose the name as a way to honor each of their families—and the infant as well.

Of all the presidents of the Church, only Joseph Smith, Brigham Young, and Joseph F. Smith experienced intense and continuous personal attacks during most of their ministry, having their names known "for good and evil." John Taylor, Wilford Woodruff, and Lorenzo Snow were rarely exposed to the personal abuse Joseph Smith and Brigham Young experienced during their lives. John Taylor, along with the other Latter-day Saints, was persecuted during his presidency, yet he avoided personal vilification. Those who followed Joseph F. Smith, beginning

(Left) Portrait of Joseph F. Smith (John W. Clawson, 1916, MCHA)

(Above oval) Portrait of Joseph F. Smith (Grant Romney Clawson, MCHA)

BORN
NOVEMBER 13, 1838
FAR WEST, MISSOURI

PARENTS
HYRUM AND
MARY FIELDING SMITH

BAPTIZED
MAY 21, 1852
(AGE 13)

STATURE
5' 11"
180–85 POUNDS

MARRIED
MAY 5, 1866
TO JULINA LAMBSON
(AGE 27)

APOSTLE
JULY 1, 1866
(AGE 27)

PRESIDENT
OCTOBER 17, 1901
(AGE 62)

DIED
NOVEMBER 19, 1918
SALT LAKE CITY, UTAH
(AGE 80)

with Heber J. Grant and George Albert Smith, were not exposed to the defamation of character that Joseph Smith, Brigham Young, and Joseph F. Smith were subjected to during their lives. In most cases, the Church leaders since the mid-twentieth century have generally been honored in the press (George Albert Smith appeared on the cover of *Time* in 1947 with a generally complimentary article about the Church).

Not since the days of Brigham Young did newspapers, magazines, and book authors and publishers direct vicious attention on the president of the Church as they did during Joseph F. Smith's presidency. He was, however, prepared by the Lord to face these challenges.

Loyalty was one of the main characteristics for which Joseph F. was known during his lifetime. Even his enemies acknowledged this pronounced characteristic. Joseph F. Smith declared during a general conference address, "We should set an example; we should be true to the faith, as Brother Stephens sings to us; true to the faith! We should

Joseph F. Smith shortly after his return from his mission in Hawaii, about 1857 (Church Archives)

be true to our covenants, true to our God, and true to one another, and to the interests of Zion, no matter what the consequences may be, no matter what may result. I can tell you that the man who is not true to Zion and to the interests of the people will be the man who will be found, by and by, left out and in a pitiable spiritual condition. The man who stays with the kingdom of God, the man who is true to this people, the man who keeps himself pure and unspotted from the world, is the man that God will accept, that God will uphold, that he will sustain, and that will prosper in the land, whether he be in the enjoyment of his liberty or be confined in prison cells, it makes no difference where he is, he will come out all right."

Loyalty was important to Joseph F. Smith—loyalty to the Prophet Joseph Smith, the restored gospel, and his family was a constant throughout his life. One former missionary companion recalled a story that demonstrated his allegiance to his name and family. Shortly after boarding a ship for his first Hawaiian mission, his traveling companion

1838
Nov. 13 • Born in Far West, Missouri
Christian F. Schoenbein discovers ozone

1844
June 27 • Father and uncle murdered in Carthage Jail

1848
Drives ox team to Salt Lake Valley
United States acquires present-day Utah and other western areas

1852
May 21 • Baptized in Salt Lake City
Henry David Thoreau publishes Walden (1854)

1854–57
Mission to Hawaii
John L. Mason receives a patent for "Mason jars" (1858)

1860–63
Mission to Great Britain
First underground railway system begins service, London (1860)

1864
Second mission to Hawaii

1866
May 5 • Marries Julina Lambson
July 1 • Ordained an apostle
William Gladstone becomes British prime minister (1868)

1874–75
President of British and European missions
Battle of the Little Big Horn (1876)

1877
President of British and European missions
Aug. 29 • Brigham Young dies

1878
Mission to eastern U.S.

1880
Oct. 10 • Second counselor in First Presidency to John Taylor
U.S. population: 50,155,783

1884–91
Forced into exile to avoid anti–plural marriage persecution
Canadian Pacific Railway completed (1886)

1887
July 25 • John Taylor dies

1889
Second counselor in First Presidency to Wilford Woodruff
U.S. population: 62,947,714 (1890)

1898
Sept. 2 • Wilford Woodruff dies
Second counselor in First Presidency to Lorenzo Snow
United States annexes Hawaii

1901
Oct. 10 • Lorenzo Snow dies
Oct. 17 • Ordained president of the Church
British government declares the Commonwealth of Australia

1902
Jan. • *Children's Friend* begins publication (until 1970)
Aug. 4 • Bureau of Information established on Temple Square

(Above) Joseph F. Smith, about 1860 (Church Archives)

(Right) Joseph F. Smith while serving on his first British mission,
about 1861 (Church Archives)

1903
Nov. 5 • Purchases Church's
first historical site, Carthage Jail
*Wright brothers make their first
flight, North Carolina*

1904
Mar. 2–9 • Testifies before U.S.
Senate Committee on Church
history, doctrine, and practice

1905
Dec. 23 • Dedicates Joseph Smith
Monument, Sharon, Vermont

1906
Summer • Visits members and
missionaries in Europe, the
first president to do so
*Alois Alzheimer identifies a disorder
known today as Alzheimer's disease*

1907
Jan. 10 • Retires Church debt
*Sir Joseph Ward becomes New
Zealand's first prime minister*

1908
Apr. 8 • Creates General
Priesthood Committee
*Henry Ford introduces
Model T*

1909
Nov. • Issues statement
on the origin of man

1910
Jan. 27 • Dedicates Bishop Building
*William Boyce founds the
Boy Scouts of America*

1912
May 12 • Approves construction
of first seminary, Granite High
School, Salt Lake City

1913
May 21 • Church adopts
Boy Scout program
Apr. • Maori Agricultural
College dedicated, New Zealand
World War I begins (1914)

1915
Jan. • *Relief Society Magazine*
begins publication (until 1970)
James E. Talmage publishes
Jesus the Christ

1916
June 30 • Issues *The Father and
the Son: A Doctrinal Exposition*

1917
Oct. 2 • Church Administration
Building completed
U.S. enters World War I

1918
Oct. 3 • Receives revelation on
the redemption of dead (D&C 138)
Nov. 19 • Dies in Salt Lake City
World War I ends

THIS CERTIFIES THAT

The RITE of

Holy Matrimony

WAS CELEBRATED BETWEEN

Joseph F. Smith of *Salt Lake City*
and *Julina Lambson* of " " "
on *Satur. May 5. 1866* at *The E. H., S. L. City, Utah.*
by *Elder Heber Chase Kimball, of the 1st Pres.y*
of the *Church of Jesus Christ of Latterday Saints.*
Witness *Geo. A. Smith* Witness *John Lyon*.

(Above) Joseph F. Smith and Julina
Lambson were married on Saturday,
May 5, 1866, by Elder Heber C.
Kimball of the First Presidency. This
marriage certificate indicates that
George Albert Smith and John Lyon
acted as witnesses. (Courtesy Mary
Louise Richardson Walker)

(Left) Joseph F. and Julina Lambson
Smith about the time of their marriage
in 1866 (Courtesy Miriam Taylor
Meads)

recalled: "After working two months in the harvest field to earn his passage money, Joseph with the other elders, sailed steerage passage, on the bark Yankee, for the islands. As soon as the ship was clear from the wharf, the passengers were lined up on the deck and their names read off to see if there were any stowaways. When the purser called, 'Joseph Smith' the captain asked, 'Any relation to old Joe Smith?' 'No, sir,' was the prompt answer, 'I never had a relative by that name; but if you had reference to the Prophet Joseph Smith, I am proud to say, he was my uncle.' 'Oh, I see,' said the captain, and he did see a man who had the nerve and manhood to demand that proper respect be shown to the name of the Prophet, whom he loved and honored." This loyalty to the name Joseph explains, in part, the honor and the animosity Joseph F. Smith experienced in his life.

Shortly following President Lorenzo Snow's funeral in October 1901, and before Joseph F. Smith was sustained as his successor in November 1901, Juab Utah Stake president James W. Paxman reported a recent dream he had had that foretold, in part, the struggles and eventual victory that lay ahead of the next president of the Church: "He had beheld a mighty struggle between [Joseph F. Smith], the [Salt Lake] Tribune & Herald which wore ugly masks, worn by men. President Smith conquered and crushed the life out of both of them."

From the beginning of his presidency through 1912, President Smith was in a mighty struggle with the press, especially the *Salt Lake Tribune*, the leading anti-Mormon newspaper in America at the time. In the *Salt Lake Tribune* alone there were some eight hundred cartoons dealing with the Church from 1890 through 1914. More than six hundred of these appeared from 1905 to 1909.

Although different aspects of the Church and, in some cases, individuals were targeted, more than three hundred of the cartoons appearing at this time depicted President

(Above) Family Bible photograph section showing Joseph F. Smith and three of his wives, Julina Lambson, Sarah Richards, and Edna Lambson (Courtesy Mary Louise Richardson Walker)

(Below) Joseph F. Smith in Liverpool, England, September 25, 1874 (Richard Brown and A. Vandyke, Church Archives)

Joseph F. Smith. What was true in Utah was also true in the United States during this period of yellow journalism. The most personal attacks came between 1910 and 1911 in such popular magazines as *Cosmopolitan, Everybody's Magazine, McClure's,* and *Pearsons.*

Although the *Salt Lake Tribune* was among President Smith's most vocal critics, attacking him almost daily during some periods of his ministry, the tone and tenor slowly changed. In 1912, the *Salt Lake Tribune* printed fewer and fewer of its vindictive cartoons and dropped most of its personal attacks. The climate changed so drastically that the *Tribune* honored Joseph F. Smith at his passing in 1918 with this tribute: "It seems but a little while since President Joseph F. Smith was a familiar figure on the streets of Salt Lake City. With his alert glance, his erect figure, his brisk walk, his benign countenance, his dignified bearing and his cordial greeting, he was a striking personality wherever he went. . . . Joseph F. Smith was sincere and intense in whatever he believed; he was loyal and courageous under whatever banner he marched, whether as a churchman, as a partisan, as an advocate of war or of peace, as a business associate or as a personal friend. In later years he made many friends in every walk of life, in every circle of society, in every cult or congregation with which he came in contact. He was a preacher of the gospel as he understood it, and an orator of exceptional power and eloquence. He was a leader upon whom his people leaned because of the simplicity of his character and the frankness of his disposition. . . . He will be mourned throughout the west and missed by all classes of our citizens, because, after all is said and done, he was very much a man, with the courage of his convictions and a sincere affection for his followers; he exhorted them to obey the laws, to honor the flag, to aid and defend the government in the war just ended, and he goes now to his final rest covered with all

FISHING ON THE WEBER

Joseph F. Smith wrote his son Calvin on August 10, 1907, highlighting his activities, including a reference to a fishing trip on the Weber River. The trip was preserved in a wonderful photograph (see facing page). He wrote: "Your letter of July 24th reached me July 27th. I have been too busy to answer sooner. However for the last week I have attended the Summit Stake conference and spent two or three days with Pres. Frank Y. Taylor, the head of the Weber Canyon. I suppose Mamma [Mary Taylor Schwartz Smith] has kept you posted on home affairs. Little Royal, and little Margery, have both got whopping cough. You know that Grandma Schwartz had gone to Idaho for a short time. We got nice letters from Wesley, who is at Hilo, on the Island of Hawaii. Alvin, Millie, and Chase expect to sail from Liverpool for home on the 14th inst. They will probably land in Boston Aug. 22nd and may reach home about Aug. 31st. Coulsen and Lileth expect to go to Boston to meet them there. Aunts Julina and Sarah [Joseph F.'s wives] and little girls went to the Canyon this morning. I send your return ticket, extended until Aug. 31. It will be no good after that day. All well."

(Upper left) Joseph F. Smith about 1885, when he moved to Hawaii to avoid arrest by federal authorities in Utah for his practice of plural marriage (Charles R. Savage, courtesy Ann Alice Smith Nebeker)

(Lower left) Missionary certificate signed by Joseph F. Smith and his counselors, calling Elder Mischa Markow on a mission to Turkey in 1903 (Church Archives)

(Below) Joseph F. Smith, about 1889 (Charles R. Savage, Church Archives)

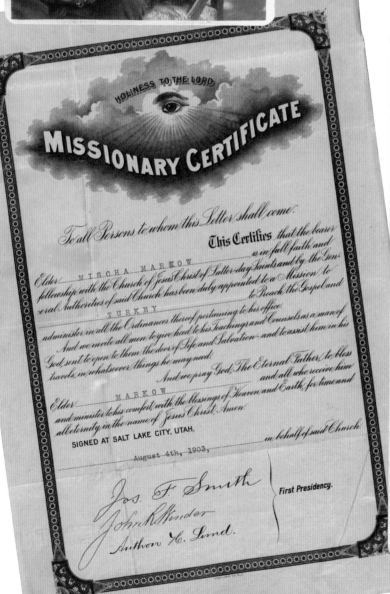

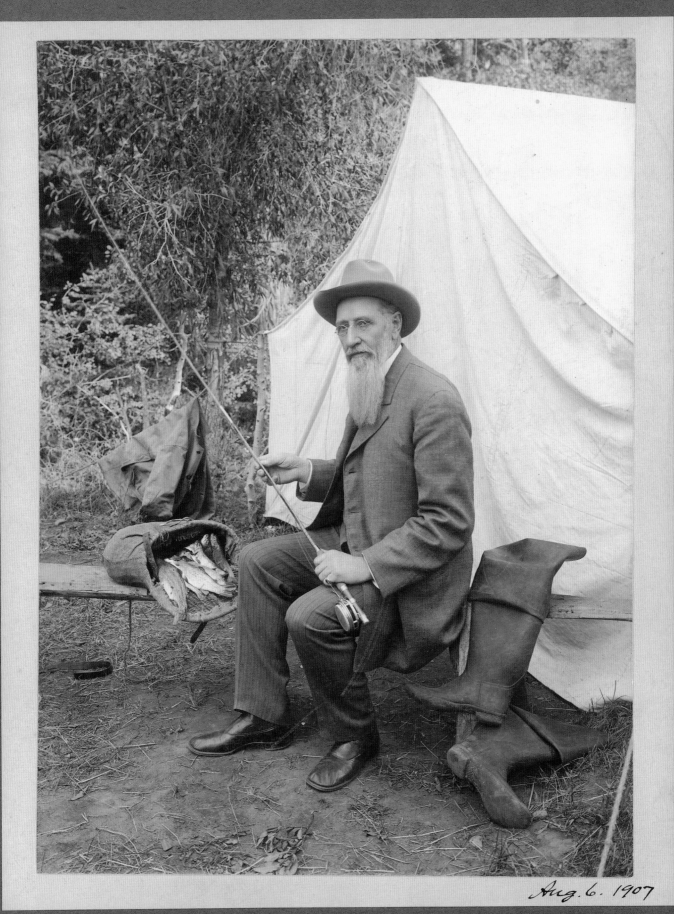

Aug. 6. 1907

Joseph F. Smith and Hyrum M. Smith attended a stake conference in Coalsville, Utah, August 6, 1907. While there President Smith went fishing with local stake president, Frank Taylor, on the Weber River. Charles R. Savage captured President Smith with a creel full of fish. (Courtesy Rita C. Smith)

the earthly glory he ever sought or that his people could bestow. Even those who differed radically from him in the past have doubtless forgotten it in the presence of death, if it had not already passed from their memories in close acquaintance through mutual interests and activities of later years."

President Harold B. Lee noted, "He presided during the stormy days when an antagonistic press maligned the Church, but his was the steady arm by the Lord's appointment to carry off the Church triumphantly."

Given a common name at birth, Joseph F. Smith proved to be more than a common person. Preserved and prepared by the Lord in significant and miraculous ways, he led the Latter-day Saints from 1901 until his death in 1918. During his lifetime, he remained loyal to his name, his uncle (the Prophet Joseph Smith), his family, and the gospel of Jesus Christ. And, like the Prophet, his name was literally known for "good and evil." Before he died in November 1918, those who once hated and abused him in print had, for the

(Above) Joseph F. Smith family celebrating Joseph F. and Julina's fiftieth wedding anniversary on May 5, 1916 (Courtesy Ann Alice Smith Nebeker)

(Left) Portrait of Joseph F. Smith, about 1915 (Albert Salzbrenner, MCHA)

most part, silenced their voices. Of them, many, in fact, joined in honoring him as one of the greatest leaders of the twentieth century. Of course, during this same period, hundreds of thousands honored him as a mighty apostle, prophet, seer, and revelator. Their testimonies, letters, diaries, and reminiscences speak of his name with reverence, fulfilling the prophecy that his name would be known for good also among many people and nations. By the time he passed from this life, Joseph F. Smith had become a tender father figure for a whole generation of Saints—a genuinely humble, warm, faithful, and fearless disciple of the Lord Jesus Christ.

JOSEPH F. SMITH ON FILM

Joseph F. Smith was the first Church president to be captured in motion pictures. And while these movie clips are in black and white and without sound, they capture his movement instead of the still, formal portraits we generally see of him. Produced by Shirley Y. and Chester Clawson (brothers who did commercial and Church work), these motion-picture clips show President Smith, beginning in 1911, walking with the General Authorities from the Salt Lake Temple, getting into an automobile, greeting Church leaders, visiting with his family on the lawn of his home in Southern California, talking in close-up images (no sound in the film), taking his hat off, and removing his glasses—all giving us several profiles.

Several frames from a film showing Joseph F. Smith taking off his hat and glasses.
(Courtesy Joseph Fielding and Brenda McConkie)

FIRST PRESIDENCY DOCTRINAL STATEMENTS AND TEACHINGS OF JOSEPH F. SMITH

During Joseph F. Smith's presidency, several important documents signed by the First Presidency were issued that still serve as touchstones of Latter-day Saint belief. One such document, "The Origin of Man," was issued in 1909 during a time when evolution was gaining attention in the academic world. Another important doctrinal statement issued during Joseph F. Smith's presidency, released in 1916, was titled "The Father and The Son: A Doctrinal Exposition by The First Presidency and The Twelve." It appeared in the *Improvement Era* in August 1916 and as a separate pamphlet at about the same time. These official statements provided the Latter-day Saints with responses to important questions and remain, to this day, the basis of Church doctrine on the subjects. In addition to official statements by the First Presidency, Joseph F. Smith left a legacy of important talks and essays. The most comprehensive, single-volume collection of Joseph F. Smith's teachings is the book *Gospel Doctrine: Selections from the Sermons and Writings of Joseph F. Smith*, originally published in 1919. Reprinted numerous times, this book is found in many homes and libraries throughout the Church. Shortly after being called as the new president of the Church in 1972, President Harold B. Lee said, "When I want to seek for a more clear definition of doctrinal subjects, I have usually turned to the writings and sermons of President Joseph F. Smith." It has been so for many before and since President Lee.

Joseph F. Smith writings, from left: "Vision of the Redemption of the Dead," published in the Improvement Era *22 (December 1918); "The Father and The Son: A Doctrinal Exposition by the First Presidency and the Twelve," published in June 1916; Gospel Doctrine, published in 1919; and Joseph F. Smith to John McCarthy letter dated February 25, 1896 (MCHA)*

The Redemption of the Dead

Joseph F. Smith's greatest doctrinal legacy is the vision he had shortly before his death. With decades of spiritual preparation, he was given a vision in Salt Lake City on October 3, 1918. As he spoke to the Saints in what would be his last general conference in October 1918, President Smith provided those gathered in the historic Tabernacle some insights about the events of the previous few months: "I will not, I dare not, attempt to enter upon many things that are resting upon my mind this morning, and I shall postpone until some future time, the Lord being willing, my attempt to tell you some of the things that are in my mind, and that dwell in my heart. I have not lived alone these five months. I have dwelt in the spirit of prayer, of supplication, of faith and of determination; and I have had my communication with the Spirit of the Lord continuously." Only later did the Saints discover that he had received an important vision just the day before. The vision, now contained in Doctrine and Covenants 138, is actually a series of visions and has become known as "The Vision of the Redemption of the Dead." It was accepted unanimously by the First Presidency

and the Quorum of the Twelve when it was presented to them in late October of 1918.

Elder James E. Talmage highlighted the momentous occasion in a diary entry at the time of the meeting in the Salt Lake Temple: "Attended meeting of the First Presidency and the Twelve. Today President Smith, who is still confined to his home by illness, sent to the Brethren the account of a vision through which, as he states, were revealed to him important facts relating to the work of the disembodied Savior in the realm of departed spirits, and of the missionary work in progress on the other side of the veil. By united action the Council of the Twelve, with the Counselors in the First Presidency, and the Presiding patriarch accepted and endorsed the revelation as the Word of the Lord. President Smith's signed statement will be published in the next issue (December) of the Improvement Era."

In 1976 the revelation was presented to the body of the Church, accepted as canonized scripture, and published with the scriptures.

Joseph F. Smith's Bible; according to family tradition, this King James Version of the Bible was in Joseph F. Smith's possession and was probably the one he was reading during the period when the vision of the Redemption of the Dead was received (Courtesy Scott T. Jackson)

"Mary Fielding Smith and Joseph F. Smith Crossing the Plains"
(Glen S. Hopkinson, VRL)

JOSEPH F. SMITH'S FAMILY

The Smith family was a tight-knit group—faithful to each other through thick and thin. Joseph F. Smith's father and mother profoundly influenced him, even though they both died while Joseph F. was still young. Following his father's murder in 1844, when the boy was only five years old, Joseph F.'s mother became the single most important influence in his life. Her courage and devotion to the restored gospel was the link between young Joseph F. and his father, Hyrum, and his uncle, the Prophet Joseph Smith. Even following her death in 1852, when Joseph F. was only thirteen years old, his mother's life and testimony continued to guide and influence the young man as he served as a missionary, apostle, and eventually president of the Church. Theirs had been a unique relationship—love between a boy and his mother rarely equaled. Other Smith family members, including his younger sister Martha Ann and his uncle George A. Smith, each played a part of his maturing into a great prophet. Later, his own personal family, five wives, Alice Ann Kimball, Edna Lambson, Julina Lambson, Sarah Ellen Richards, Mary Taylor Schwartz, and forty-eight children, also became a focus of his life's concerns and happiness. Tender moments, encouraging letters, and family activities among them during sixty years of family life helped mold this prophet of the Lord.

State of the Church at the time of Joseph F. Smith's death

Year of death	1918	Missions	22
Church membership	495,962	Total Missionaries set apart during administration	12,751
Stakes	75	Book of Mormon translations completed	
Temples	4	during administration	4

PROPHETS AND TEMPLES

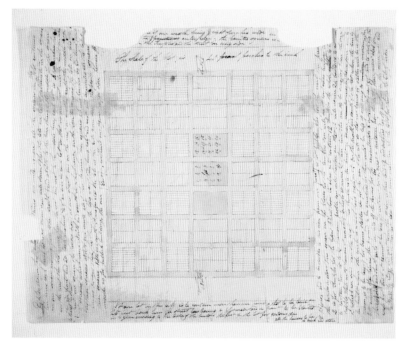

Joseph Smith plan for Zion, showing the place for the temple in Jackson County, Missouri (Church Archives)

Nauvoo Temple, 1845–1846 (Louis R. Chaffin, DUP)

In an early revelation, the Lord commanded Joseph Smith to "establish a house, even a house of prayer, a house of fasting, a house of faith, a house of learning, a house of glory, a house of order, a house of God" (D&C 88:119). The Lord promised faithful Saints an endowment of power from on high in the special houses of God, or temples, that they built. Temple sites were designated in Ohio, Missouri, and Illinois during the first two decades of the Church's existence (1830–1846). Notable spiritual experiences followed years of sacrifice when the first two temples were completed in Kirtland and Nauvoo. The Kirtland "Pentecostal" period began several weeks preceding the actual dedication of the Kirtland Temple in January of 1836 and lasted until May. The Saints were again rewarded for their efforts in constructing the Nauvoo Temple on the banks of the Mississippi River. During the Spirit-filled winter of 1845–1846, more than six thousand Saints received their sacred blessings in the temple as they prepared for their exodus and eventual removal to the Great Basin.

Within a few days of his arrival in the new promised land, Brigham Young designated the temple site where the Salt Lake Temple stands today. Temple construction in and around Utah continued, and soon the prophets directed that these sacred buildings arise beyond the confines of the United States. Always interested in providing faithful Saints the opportunity to secure the blessings reserved in temples, Church presidents were building them in increasing numbers throughout the world by the end of the twentieth century. Building temples, however, was not their only concern. When President Howard W. Hunter began his ministry, he invited members of the Church to live with "ever more attention to the life and example of Jesus Christ, especially the love and hope and compassion he displayed," and "to establish the temple of the Lord as the great symbol of membership and the supernal setting for your most sacred covenants." Additionally, he added, "It would be the deepest desire of my heart to have every member of the Church to be temple worthy."

Part of a latter-day prophet's mission is not only to establish these houses of worship but also to challenge the Saints to live worthily so they can secure the blessings available in the House of the Lord.

No. 1.
Admit the Bearer
to the
Dedication Service of the
Manti Temple, May 21, 1888.
Wilford Woodruff

The Church of Jesus Christ of Latter-day Saints
CORDIALLY INVITES YOU TO ATTEND THE PRE-VIEWING OF THE

Oakland Temple
4780 Lincoln Ave., Oakland, Calif.

Please Type or Print

Name

Address
Number   Street

City   State

ADMIT ONE

Please visit the Temple During
The Week Beginning
October 5, 1964
OPEN 9:00 A.M. TO 8:00 P.M.
MONDAY THRU SATURDAY
IF MEMBER, PLEASE DESIGNATE

WARD

STAKE

PLEASE SEE
REVERSE SIDE

(Top left) Manti Temple dedication pass
dated May 31, 1888 (Courtesy Gregory P.
and MarJane Christofferson)

(Above) C.C.A. Christensen's painting
of the Manti Temple, 1889 (MCHA)

(Left) Palmyra Temple dedication pass dated
April 6, 2000 (Courtesy Bailey York Holzapfel)

(Right) Gordon B. Hinckley placing mortar on
the cornerstone of the Perth Australia Temple,
May 20, 2001 (Intellectual Reserve Inc.)

(Below) Palmyra Temple, 2000 (VRL)

(Top right) Oakland Temple dedication pass dated October 5, 1964
(Courtesy Gregory P. and MarJane Christofferson)
(Above) Al Rounds painting of the Oakland Temple (Courtesy Al Rounds)

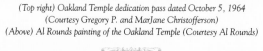

THURSDAY, 6 APRIL 2000
MORNING SESSION, ____ A.M.
OR
EVENING SESSION, 7:00 P.M.

PALMYRA NEW YORK
TEMPLE DEDICATION

BAILEY Y. HOLZAPFEL
RECOMMEND HOLDER'S NAME

BISHOP'S SIGNATURE

BORN
NOVEMBER 22, 1856
SALT LAKE CITY, UTAH

PARENTS
JEDEDIAH MORGAN
AND RACHEL RIDGEWAY
IVINS GRANT

BAPTIZED
JUNE 2, 1864
(AGE 7)

STATURE
6' 1"
175–80 POUNDS

MARRIED
NOVEMBER 1, 1877
TO LUCY STRINGHAM
(AGE 20)

APOSTLE
OCTOBER 16, 1882
(AGE 25)

PRESIDENT
NOVEMBER 23, 1918
(AGE 62)

DIED
MAY 14, 1945
SALT LAKE CITY, UTAH
(AGE 88)

It was a winter's day in 1863 when six-year-old Heber decided to catch a free ride home on a passing sleigh. "I ran out and took hold of the back of the sleigh, intending to ride a block" he later recalled. To his surprise, however, the horses drawing the sleigh increased their speed, forcing Heber to hold on for dear life. "I dared not let go," he remembered. The sleigh continued flying beyond the city into the countryside before finally slowing down enough so that Heber could make an undetected escape. As he did, he heard the sleigh's owner yell, "Stop, Brother Isaac, stop!" Instead of being angry upon finding a stowaway, the man said to his driver, "The little boy is nearly frozen. Put him under the buffalo robe and get him warm." Heber sat right next to the kind gentleman and was just settling in when the man asked, "What's your name?" He replied "Heber Jeddy Grant." The old man was delighted and began to tell the young boy stories about his parents. Heber began to feel a warm glow inside, specifically as the conversation turned to Heber's father, Jedediah M. Grant—a father he had never known, as Jedediah died just days after Heber's birth in 1856.

When Heber was finally delivered safely to his home in Salt Lake City, the owner asked him to inform his mother that she should send young Heber to his office for a visit in the near future. At the appropriate time, he did as requested and went to the man's office on South Temple. When he arrived, he informed the clerk in the office that he had been requested to visit. Heber fondly recalled some fifty-four years later, "From that time . . . until the day of his death I was intimately acquainted with President Young." Thus began Heber J. Grant's walk among prophets and apostles that eventually led him to be ordained the seventh president of The Church of Jesus Christ of Latter-day Saints.

The invitation to visit Brother Brigham and the close association that followed thereafter was not a surprise turn of events for Rachel Ridgeway Ivins Grant, Heber's mother. She knew for some time that the Lord was watching and preparing her son for service in the kingdom of God, as the Lord had revealed that he would "become a great man in the Church of Jesus Christ of Latter-day Saints and one of the Apostles of the Lord Jesus Christ" on several occasions while he was an infant and a toddler.

(Left) Lee Greene Richards portrait of Heber J. Grant, 1945 (MCHA)

(Above oval) C. J. Fox portrait of Heber J. Grant (MCHA)

The widow Grant poured love and affection upon her only child, and she never missed an opportunity to remind Heber that he had been promised great blessings if he lived worthy of them. Frustrated by her constant insistence on the role he would someday play in the Church, he finally told her, "Mother get it out of your head. I do not want to be an Apostle; I do not want to be a bishop; I do not want to be anything but a businessman. Just get it out of your head."

Despite his own wishes, the Lord had other plans for Heber J. Grant. One month before his twenty-sixth birthday, he was called to a meeting in Salt Lake City where he heard the secretary of the First Presidency, George Reynolds, read aloud a revelation given to John Taylor a few days earlier: "Thus saith the Lord to the Twelve and to the Priesthood and people of my church: Let my servants George Teasdale and Heber J. Grant be appointed to fill the vacancies in the Twelve." On that day, Elder Heber J. Grant began a ministry that lasted sixty-three years as an apostle, during which time, as the senior apostle on earth, he was called to preside over the Church.

Heber's determination to excel is renowned. *Persistent*

Rachel and son Heber J. Grant, about 1868 (Church Archives)

and *determined* may be the best words to describe his personality. By sheer willpower and constant effort, he learned to throw a baseball, perfected his penmanship, and achieved at least a degree of musical ability when singing. As an adult, the same personality made him an exceptional businessman. He liked to work. He liked to make money. He liked to get things done.

Heber's work ethic and personality did not change following his call to serve as a General Authority. He plunged into the work despite initial concerns about his own worthiness. Once he knew that it was the Lord's will for him to serve in the Quorum of the Twelve, he redoubled his efforts to fulfill his responsibilities by keeping a busy and hectic schedule traveling, speaking, writing letters, and serving the interest of the Church in a variety of ways. During this long service as a member of the Twelve, the Lord continued to prepare him for even greater responsibilities. Additionally, as was common practice of the day, Heber continued with his business interests as he faithfully fulfilled his ecclesiastical responsibilities.

While Heber always recognized the value of recreation—he played tennis, worked out at the gym, and

1856
Nov. 22 • Born in Salt Lake City
James Buchanan wins
U.S. presidency

1864
June 2 • Baptized in Salt Lake City
U.S. President Abraham
Lincoln assassinated (1865)

1871
Employed as a bank clerk
Great fire destroys Chicago

1877
Aug. 29 • Brigham Young dies
Nov. 1 • Marries Lucy Stringham
(dies Jan. 3, 1893)

1880
Oct. 30 • President of Tooele Stake

1882
Oct. 16 • Ordained an apostle
Sir Francis Galton proves the
individuality of fingerprints (1885)

1887
July 25 • John Taylor dies
Klondike Gold Rush begins,
Canada (1897)

1898
Sept. 2 • Wilford Woodruff dies

1901
Aug. 12 • Dedicates
Japan for missionary work
Oct. 10 • Lorenzo Snow dies
Sir Edmund Burton becomes
Australia's first prime minister

1904–1906
President of British and European
missions
William Hoover markets first portable
electric vacuum cleaner (1908)

1918
Nov. 19 • Joseph F. Smith dies
Nov. 23 • Ordained president
of the Church
Worldwide flu pandemic
kills 25 million people (1918–19)

1919
Nov. 27 • Dedicates Hawaiian
Temple
Church membership exceeds 500,000
Prohibition begins in the U.S.

1920
Constructing chapel, classrooms,
and cultural hall as connected
complexes begins
KDKA begins first radio
broadcast, Pittsburg

1922
May 6 • Speaks on new radio station
KZN (KSL)

1923
Aug. 26 • Dedicates
Cardston Alberta Temple, first
temple outside United States
Australian C. K. Smith flies from
California to Australia (1928)

1924
Oct. 3 • KSL radio begins
broadcasting general conference

(Left) Manuscript of John Taylor's 1882
revelation calling Heber J. Grant to be an apostle (BYU)

(Above) Lacquerware photograph album and
porcelain jar with cover—Grant family mementos from Japan (MCHA)

Missionary calling card of Heber J. Grant, 1901–1903 (MCHA)

First Church missionary tract in Japanese,
written by Heber J. Grant and published in 1908 (MCHA)

1925
Jan. 23 • Mission Home opens,
Salt Lake City

1927
Oct. 23 • Dedicates Arizona Temple

1928
Sept. 25 • First institute class
commences (University of Idaho),
Moscow, Idaho

1929
July 15 • Tabernacle Choir starts
weekly national radio broadcast
U.S. stock market crash (1929)

1930
Apr. 6 • Celebrates Church
centennial
*Prohibition repealed in the U.S.
(1933)*

1935
Jun. 30 • First stake outside
North America organized, Hawaii
Oct. 14 • Latter-day Saint
John Blackmore wins seat
in Canadian Parliament
*U.S. Congress passes the
Social Security Act*

1936
Apr. 7 • Introduces Church
welfare program
Church membership exceeds 750,000
*Volkswagen introduces
the Beetle*

1938
Aug. 14 • First Deseret Industries
store opens, Salt Lake City
Nov. • Microfilming
genealogical records begins
World War II begins (1939)

1940
Mar. 15 • Portuguese Book of
Mormon printed, Sao Paulo, Brazil
Aug. 23 • 20th Century Fox hosts
world premier of movie *Brigham
Young*, Salt Lake City
*Winston Churchill becomes
British prime minister*

1941
Apr. 6 • Calls first
assistants to the Twelve
Aug. 18 • Last 1847 pioneer,
Mary Ann Park Broadbank, dies
*United States enters
World War II*

1942
Apr. 5 • Salt Lake Tabernacle
closed for World War II
Aug. 17 • USS Brigham Young,
a Liberty class ship, commissioned
Oct. • Establishes LDS
Servicemen's Committee

1943
May 22 • USS Joseph Smith, a
Liberty class ship, commissioned
*Allied forces land in France,
D-Day*

1945
May 14 • Dies in Salt Lake City
World War II ends

attended the theater—there was apparently one more important lesson to be learned before assuming the role of Church president. His mentor, Joseph F. Smith, was the one prepared to teach him about the value of the game of golf. Heber recalled the lesson many years later: "Pres. Joseph F. Smith played golf, far more than I thought he should," he said. Heber, as the president of the Twelve, often had important papers that needed the signature of the Church president. On several occasions when he went to Joseph F. Smith's office, he learned that President Smith was golfing. On such an occasion, Heber felt that the business at hand could not wait until Joseph F. Smith returned to the

Four generations of Grants: Rachel Ivins Grant, Lucy Taylor, Susan Rachel Grant Taylor, and Heber J. Grant, about 1902 (Courtesy Bertram C. and Christine Willis)

Church headquarters, so he decided to track the president down at the golf course. When Heber arrived, President Smith sensed that he was upset. "Heber, you are tense and overworked," he said. "You should learn to play this game." He was stunned by the suggestion—there was simply too much work and already not enough time to complete it. President Smith continued, "Many times I, myself, get overworked, weary and so tense I can accomplish but little. So I drop everything and come and play golf." He tried to reassure Heber that in the end he was more productive: "There is something about this game that relaxes me and causes me to forget my anxieties. When I get back

Heber J. Grant with a men's group at the Deseret Gym in 1913; included in the photograph are Stephen L Richards (5); William E. Day, the instructor, (11); Bryant S. Hinckley (10); and Joseph Fielding Smith (17) (Church Archives)

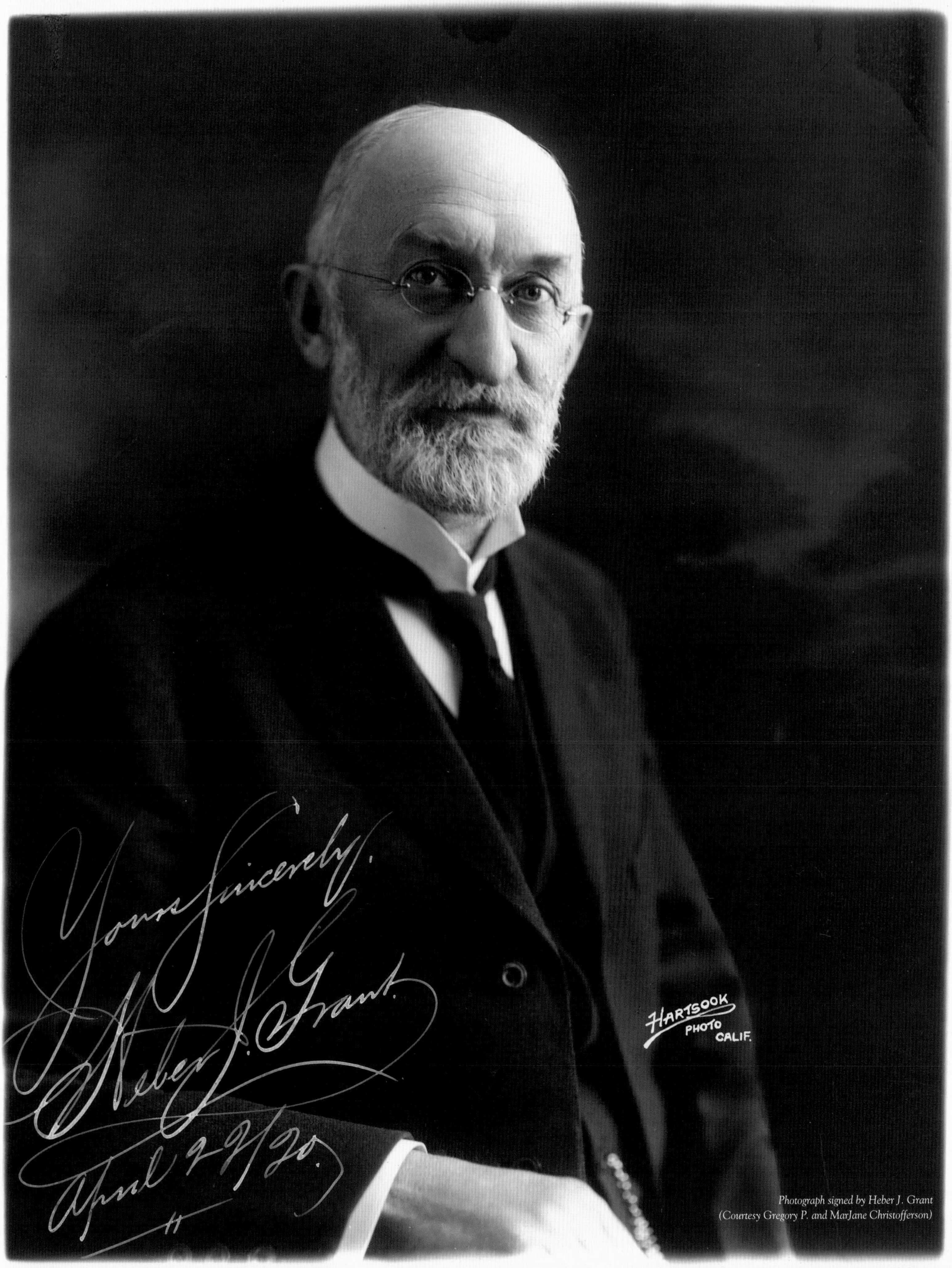

Yours Sincerely.
Heber J. Grant.
April 29/20.
HARTSOOK
PHOTO
CALIF.

Photograph signed by Heber J. Grant
(Courtesy Gregory P. and MarJane Christofferson)

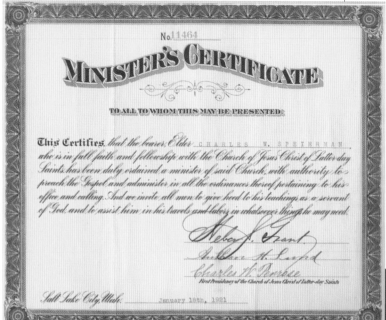

(Left) Elder Charles W. Speierman's Minister's Certificate signed by Heber J. Grant (Courtesy Susannah Speierman Langenheim)

(Below left) Arizona Temple Dedication pass signed by Heber J. Grant, October 23, 1927 (Courtesy Gregory P. and MarJane Chistofferson)

(Below) The Arizona Temple (VRL)

to the office I can accomplish more in a few hours then I could in days when I am so tense."

Heber stood firm, unwilling to consider that it was possible to get more done by taking a break from his busy schedule. "You will never catch me wasting my time playing that silly game," he said. "Now sign these papers and let me get back to work." Joseph F. Smith decided it was now time to teach Heber this important lesson. "No, Heber," he said. "I will not sign a thing until you take my partner's club and finish out this round with me."

Heber refused the offer: "Not on your life—I've got too much to do to fool away my time here." In order to get Heber to try the medicine he was prescribing, Joseph F. Smith spoke with presidential authority: "Heber, I command you to take that club and play out this round with me."

"Well," Heber replied, "if you are going to use your Priesthood on me I guess I'll have to." After a brief lesson, Heber stood poised to take his first swing. "I swung at it—I was very mad. I swung and knocked the ball a quarter of a mile down the fairway. Never since, in all my golf playing have I knocked a ball so far, and I have tried so hard and so many times to do it."

GORDON B. HINCKLEY
REMEMBERS PRESIDENT GRANT

I recall sitting in this Tabernacle when I was fourteen or fifteen—up in the balcony right behind the clock—and hearing President Heber J. Grant tell of his experience in reading the Book of Mormon when he was a boy. He spoke of Nephi and of the great influence he had upon his life. And then, with a voice ringing with a conviction that I shall never forget, he quoted those great words of Nephi: "I will go and do the things which the Lord hath commanded, for I know that the Lord giveth no commandments unto the children of men, save he shall prepare a way for them that they may accomplish the thing which he commandeth them" (1 Nephi 3:7). There came into my young heart on that occasion a resolution to try to do what the Lord has commanded.

(Above) Heber J. Grant, George Albert Smith, Andrew Jenson, and Oscar Kirkham at the dedication of a marker at Independence Rock, Wyoming, on July 4, 1930 (Church Archives)

(Right) Plate signed by Heber J. Grant in 1923 (Courtesy Jeni Broberg Holzapfel)

BOOKS! BOOKS!

Heber J. Grant loved to give books to family, friends, and visitors. This was especially true during the holiday season. There was always a message placed inside—each one personally signed by President Grant. It is estimated that he gave away more than a hundred thousand books. His journal often reveals the efforts involved, as was the case on Christmas Eve 1926: "Day spent with books. Books! Books! . . . I am sending books to all the members of the [Church auxiliary] boards, and to the directors of [some thirteen businesses], to say nothing about personal friends. . . . I am giving over one hundred copies of the Lecture on Martin Luther to the employees in the Church office. . . . It was a little after nine o'clock p.m. when I left the office."

Heber J. Grant standing with David O. McKay,
George Albert Smith, Melvin J. Ballard, and others
at the dedication of the Hill Cumorah monument
on July 21, 1935 (Church Archives)

Heber J. Grant in Basil, Switzerland, while on a tour of
Europe during the Centennial Celebration of the
European Mission, July 4, 1937 (Church Archives)

First Presidency (J. Reuben Clark, Heber J. Grant, David O. McKay),
about 1934 (Courtesy Edward L. Kimball)

HEBER J. GRANT'S MOTTO TO LIVE BY

"That which we persist in doing becomes easier for us to do;
not that the nature of the thing itself is changed, but that our
power to do is increased." —Ralph Waldo Emerson

PROPHETS OF THE LATTER DAYS

Lee Greene Richards portrait of Heber J. Grant, said to be his favorite, 1934
(Courtesy Warren Vincent and Lou Jean Willis Huber)

He then related: "I took to playing golf and learned that President Smith was right. Nothing I can do relaxes me half as much as two hours on the golf course. I can return to the office and unravel problems that seemed unsolvable when I was tired and tense."

Obviously Joseph F. Smith had achieved a sense of balance in his own ministry, allowing him to be more productive as he fulfilled his duties as the Lord's prophet. Such a life-changing lesson was one way in which Heber was being prepared for the future responsibilities when the tremendous weight of the Church would rest squarely upon his shoulders.

From 1918 until his death in 1945, Heber J. Grant served the Lord faithfully as prophet, seer, and revelator. During his ministry he implemented important policies and practices that continue to influence the Church today. Three of these seem especially significant. First, he more than any other person made the Word of Wisdom the standard of orthodoxy we know today. Second, he instituted the Church Welfare system that continues to bless the lives of the Saints. Finally, he called to Church leadership J. Reuben Clark Jr., Harold B. Lee, Spencer W. Kimball, and Ezra Taft Benson, all of whom have had a profound impact on Church history.

HEBER J. GRANT'S FAMILY

Rachel Ridgeway Ivins Grant welcomed her only child into the world on November 22, 1856. Shortly thereafter, during the first week of December 1856, she buried her forty-year-old husband, Jedediah Morgan Grant, leaving mother and child alone. In this situation Heber developed a special bond with his mother, who lived long enough to watch her son become an apostle and president of the Quorum of the Twelve. In 1877, Heber began his own family when he married Lucy Stringham (they had six children). Later he married Hulda Augusta Winters (they had one child) and Emily J. Harris Wells (they had five). When Heber passed from this world to the next in the late afternoon of May 14, 1945, he was reunited with his loved ones who preceded him and then waited for those left behind to join him in a glorious reunion. To him, the "wonderful joy and satisfaction and happiness" enjoyed by the righteous in the spirit world "robs the grave of its sting."

(Above) Heber J. and Hulda Augusta Winters Grant surrounded by their grandchildren at a family gathering, November 22, 1938 (Church Archives)

(Right) Heber J. and Lucy Stringham Grant family on the Grants' tenth wedding anniversary in 1887 (with children Susan Rachel, Lucy, Florence, Edith, and Anna) (Charles R. Savage, Church Archives)

(Below) Heber J. Grant and Leah Jeanne Swenson, April 18, 1937 (Courtesy Leah Jeanne Swenson Christofferson)

LEAH JEANNE SWENSON:
A VISIT WITH HEBER J. GRANT

April 18, 1937

President Grant came to our ward to dedicate a new addition to the chapel in Manila (located in Utah County) on April 18, 1937. Before the dedicatory service, President Grant came to my parents' home for dinner (my Father, Helge V. Swenson, was a counselor in the bishopric at the time). After dinner we all had the opportunity to have our pictures taken with President Grant on the front lawn of our home in Pleasant Grove. I was 12 years old and you can see by the smile on my face that I was thrilled to have my picture taken with the Prophet. He was such a friendly, sweet man. I vividly remember him hugging me and telling me that he loved me and that the Lord loved me.

My mother sent copies of the pictures to my brother Calvin, then serving a mission in Norway. Later, during a tour of the Norwegian mission, President Grant met my brother. Calvin showed President Grant the photographs taken at our home. He remembered the occasion well and autographed the pictures for my brother. These photographs and our memories of the Prophet's visit remain a special family treasure.

State of the Church at the time of Heber J. Grant's death	
Year of death	*1945*
Church membership	*954,004*
Stakes	*149*
Temples	*7*
Missions	*38*
Total Missionaries set apart during administration	*24,288*
Book of Mormon translations completed during administration	*4*

DIARIES AND LETTERS

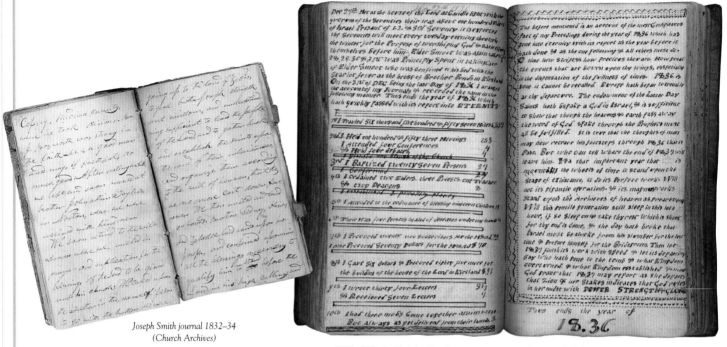

Joseph Smith journal 1832–34
(Church Archives)

Wilford Woodruff left the Church many important records, particularly his personal journals covering
the period shortly after his conversion in 1833 until his death in 1898. Without this treasure, the
Saints would have lost important information about the past. Especially prized are the teachings
of Joseph Smith and Brigham Young that Wilford felt compelled to record (Church Archives)

WILFORD WOODRUFF ON KEEPING A JOURNAL

I seldom ever heard Brother Joseph or the Twelve preach or teach any principle but what I felt as uneasy as a fish out of water until I had written it. Then I felt right. I could write a sermon of Joseph's a week after it was delivered almost word for word and after it was written it was taken from me or from my mind. This was a gift from God unto me. . . . I have never spent any of my time more profitably for the benefit of mankind than in my Journal writing for . . . some of the most glorious Gospel sermons, truths and revelations that were given from God to this people through the mouth of the Prophets Joseph, Brigham, Heber and the Twelve could not be found upon the Earth on record only in my Journals.

On the day the Church was established in 1830, the Lord said, "Behold, there shall be a record kept among you" (D&C 21:1). Since that day, Church leaders and members have strived to fulfill this commandment. As a result, Latter-day Saints have become known as "a record keeping people," a boon to historians and a blessing to the faithful who treasure the counsel and teachings of the prophets contained in their diaries and letters.

Visual images (paintings, photographs, and motion-picture film) provide a wonderful way to see the mighty prophets of the latter days. Another way to "see" these anointed servants of the Lord is through the word-pictures they have left for us through their own writings (journals, letters, books, and talks). Many of the presidents of the Church have produced sizable collections of papers, primarily housed in the Church Archives in Salt Lake City. Each letter or diary is, in its own way, an expression of the writer's most intimate thoughts, feelings, reflections, and desires. In a few cases, as in ancient times, these letters have even become scripture (see D&C 121–23, 127–28). Our historic and gospel understanding is greatly enhanced because these prophets took the time to pen the events of their lives or to provide counsel and direction in letters to family members, friends, or Church leaders.

Joseph F. Smith letter to Martha Ann Smith Harris dated December 23, 1915 (Courtesy Carol Call King)

Joseph F. Smith at his desk (Church Archives)

David O. McKay at his desk preparing a letter following a trip to Europe in 1952 (Church Archives)

(Left) Howard W. Hunter's first journal, 1918 (Courtesy Richard and Nan Hunter)

(Below) Entry from Howard W. Hunter's first journal, August 5, 1918 (Courtesy Richard and Nan Hunter)

(Below) Spencer W. Kimball's journal, 1973 (Courtesy Edward L. Kimball)

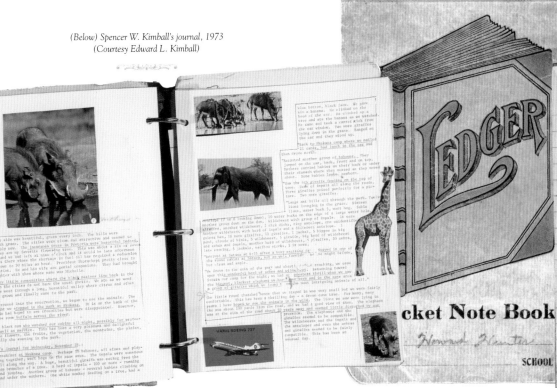

DIARIES AND LETTERS

George Albert Smith (signature)

BORN
APRIL 4, 1870
SALT LAKE CITY, UTAH

PARENTS
JOHN HENRY
AND SARAH FARR SMITH

BAPTIZED
JUNE 6, 1878
(AGE 8)

STATURE
6' 0"
160 POUNDS

MARRIED
MAY 25, 1892
TO LUCY EMILY WOODRUFF
(AGE 22)

APOSTLE
OCTOBER 8, 1903
(AGE 33)

PRESIDENT
MAY 21, 1945
(AGE 75)

DIED
APRIL 4, 1951
SALT LAKE CITY, UTAH
(AGE 81)

As twelve-year-old Doug Scalley embarked on a summer vacation of hiking, climbing, and exploring in the greater Yellowstone Snake River area, he met another boy who shared his sense of adventure. Soon they were planning and preparing for a day-long quest. The night before "the big day," Doug's friend unloaded worrisome news—his seventy-six-year-old grandfather wanted to join the quest.

Although anxious that an old man would slow them down, Doug figured the "grandfather will only last a few miles." On the appointed day the two boys began their trek in the company of a tall, thin gentleman wearing a "wide-brimmed Scout hat, a heavy Scouting jacket, a neckerchief around his collar, knee-length pants, and laced-up hiking boots."

The three headed up the trail together, but soon the boys excitedly hurried along "the narrow path" until the friend's grandfather called for them to come back. Assuming he was going to announce his return to the cabin, the boys were surprised when the grandfather pointed down at two sets of animal prints in the dirt. As the three knelt for a closer look, he explained: "This one is the mother deer. The imprint isn't very deep, and the strides are short. That's how you can tell it's not a buck; it's a doe. She has a little one with her."

Far from tiring, the grandfather walked on, pointing out different wildflowers, trees, bushes, and edible plants. Over the next few hours, he taught the young boys different ways to track animals—broken branches, rubbed tree-moss, over-turned rocks, and rarely noticed, narrow woodland pathways. After practicing their tracking skills, the three returned to their cabins as the sun began to go down. The boys were exuberantly exhausted.

The next morning Doug appreciatively delivered his mother's freshly baked rolls to his friend's grandfather. Doug and his family were not Latter-day Saints, but his mother mentioned that the man "was someone important in The Church of Jesus Christ of Latter-day Saints—'Maybe you should ask for his autograph.'"

After thanking him for a wonderful day, Doug asked the gentleman to sign the paper and the piece of kindling wood he brought with him. After leaving the cabin, Doug looked at the wood on which was written "George Albert Smith—Scouter." On the paper was written, "The pathway of righteousness is the high-way of happiness. Don't lose your way." They were messages Doug Scalley never forgot, especially later when he prepared to be baptized.

(Left) Portrait by Lee Greene Richards, 1928 (MCHA)

(Above oval) George Albert Smith, about 1945 (Church Archives)

Four-year-old George Albert Smith, about 1874 (Church Archives)

John Howard and George Albert Smith, about 1886
(George Edward Anderson, Church Archives)

1870
Apr. 4 • Born in Salt Lake City
U.S. population: 39,818,449

1877
Aug. 29 • Brigham Young dies

1878
June 6 • Baptized in
Salt Lake City

1878
Begins work at ZCMI
clothing factory
Canada's Sir Sandford Fleming
proposes worldwide time zones (1883)

1884
Jan. 16 • Receives Patriarchal
Blessing, indicating he would
be an apostle

1887
July 25 • John Taylor dies
Eiffel Tower built for
Paris Exhibition (1889)

1891
Sept.–Nov. • YMMIA
mission to southern Utah

1892
May 25 • Marries Lucy Emily
Woodruff (dies Nov. 5, 1937)

1892–1894
Mission to southern states
Greece hosts the first
modern Olympics (1896)

1898
Sept. 2 • Wilford Woodruff dies
Hague Peace Conference sets down
rules for conduct of war (1899)

1901
Sept. • Travels to Pan American
Exposition, Buffalo, New York
Oct. 10 • Lorenzo Snow dies
U.S. President William McKinley
assassinated at Pan American
Exposition

1903
Oct. 6 • Unable to attend
Conference, hears of his call
to the Twelve from friends
Oct. 8 • Ordained an apostle
James M. Barrie publishes
Peter Pan (1904)

1909–12
Convalesces from debilitating illness
RMS Titanic sinks on
maiden voyage (1912)

1918
Nov. 19 • Joseph F. Smith dies
U.S. Government introduces
Daylight Savings Time

1919–21
President of British and
European missions
British Empire at its zenith ruling
over 600 million people (1920)

1922
May • VP National Society of
Sons of the American Revolution
May 11 • Primary Children's
Hospital opens
Switzerland hosts the first
Winter Olympics (1924)

1930
July • First president Utah Pioneer
Trails and Landmarks Association

During his life, President George Albert Smith served as president of the International Irrigation Congress, president of the International Dry Farmers Congress, and vice-president of the Sons of the American Revolution. He served on the National Executive Board of Boy Scouts of America and was a leading member of the Utah Pioneer Trails and Landmarks Association. His Church callings included service in the Southern States Mission, ward Sunday School superintendent, general president and board member of the YMMIA, European Mission president, apostle, and president of the Church. Vocationally, he was a businessman, having worked for ZCMI and the U.S. Land Office as well as serving on the boards of directors of, among others, Utah Savings and Trust, Utah-Idaho Sugar Company, Libbey Investment Company, Heber J. Grant and Company, and Western Airlines. Yet it was true to his loving spirit to take time for other's needs—people always came first with President George Albert Smith.

Bryant S. Hinckley understood this when he wrote that

Sixteen-year-old George Albert Smith, about 1886 (Church Archives)

"the deeds which will last longest and shine the brightest in the affections of those who know him best will not be his public utterances, his patriotic service, his business ability, nor the stimulating power which he imparts to all the movements and organizations with which he becomes connected, and we would not minimize any of these for they are important; but the deeds which will forever adorn his life have been done in quiet ways. His supreme work has been accomplished in unseen places and at unknown hours, and often with forgotten and neglected people."

So great was George Albert Smith's love and concern for the welfare of others that he often disregarded offenses upon him. Such was the case when a blanket was stolen from his car. Upon learning of the theft, he neither fretted about being victimized nor bellowed for revenge and justice. Instead, he earnestly replied, "If I had thought the man who took it really needed it, I would have presented it to him and he would not have become a thief."

Reflecting on his feelings about all people, President Smith wrote in April 1950, "I do not have an enemy that I

1931
Boy Scouts of America National Board member

1932
Mar. • Publishes personal "Creed" in *Improvement Era*
Franklin D. Roosevelt wins U.S. Presidency

1934
May 31 • Receives Boy Scouts of America's Silver Buffalo, the first Latter-day Saint leader to do so
First freeway (Autobahn) opens, Germany

1939
Jan 22 • Ordains and sets apart first Native American bishop, Moroni Timbimboo
First successful flight powered by a jet engine, Germany

1945
May 14 • Heber J. Grant dies
May 21 • Ordained President of the Church
June 26 • Meets with U.S. President Harry S. Truman
Sept. 23 • Dedicates Idaho Falls Temple
Oct. 18 • Decides to send relief for Saints in war-ravaged Europe
Nov. 3 • Meets with President Truman again, discusses relief efforts
Nov. 6 • First non-English temple ceremony (Spanish), Arizona Temple
U.S. detonates first Atomic bomb, New Mexico

1946
May • First President to visit members and missionaries in Mexico

1947
May 20 • Offers prayer to open U.S. Senate session, the first president to do so
July 24 • Celebrates Pioneer Centennial
Church membership exceed 1,000,000
Jackie Robinson, first African-American, plays in the major League

1948
Oct. 17 • Mormon Tabernacle Choir performs 1000th national radio broadcast
Publishes his only book, *Sharing the Gospel with Others*
United Nations votes for partition of Palestine

1949
Oct. 1–3 • KSL begins television broadcast of General Conference

1950
June 1 • Dedicates Brigham Young statue at U.S. Capital Building
Sept. 4 • First early morning seminary class organized, Southern California
Korean War begins

1951
Apr. 4 • Dies in Salt Lake City
CBS airs first color television broadcast

George Albert and Lucy Emily Woodruff Smith, about 1892
(Church Archives)

know of, and there is no one in the world that I have any enmity towards. All men and all women are my Father's children, and I have sought during my life to observe the wise direction of the Redeemer of mankind—to love my neighbor as myself."

Frail since childhood and burdened with health problems, life was never easy for George Albert Smith. As a young man, surveying for the railroad in southern Utah, his eyesight was nearly destroyed by the bright summer sun. Despite surgery, his eyes were permanently damaged. In February 1909, under the considerable stress of an apostle's schedule (his duties demanded traveling more than 30,000 miles a year), George Albert suffered

GEORGE ALBERT SMITH'S FAMILY

George Albert Smith was the son of Sarah Farr and John Henry Smith, who were the parents of eleven children (eight sons and three daughters), three of whom died in childhood. He was named for his pioneer grandfather George A. Smith, who was an apostle and counselor to Brigham Young. President Smith's maternal grandfather, Lorin Farr, was a pioneer mayor of Ogden, Utah. George Albert grew up in a religious and industrious home filled not only with love of immediate family but also with respect and love of the extended human family. His father, an apostle and counselor to Joseph F. Smith, taught that he had "never seen a child of God so deep in the gutter that I have not had the impulse to stoop down and lift him up and put him on his feet and start him again." This philosophy was exemplified throughout George Albert Smith's life.

On May 25, 1892, in the Manti Temple, George Albert wed Lucy Emily Woodruff, whom he had known since he was ten years old. Together, they were the parents of Emily (Stewart), Edith (Elliot), and George Albert Jr.

In a May 1948 letter, Emily Smith Stewart shared the following glimpse of George Albert Smith as a father:

"His wonderful sense of humor is something that really should be written about, his joking with his children and his grandchildren, has made the fun that we have enjoyed all through our lifetime; anniversaries and holidays have been great events in our family. Father always made a great deal of holidays. As a very little child I remember when we moved into our new home on West Temple, father took me very secretly upstairs to show me some lovely pictures which he had purchased for mother's birthday. He had a great surprise for her, although the birthday was still weeks away. I remember how he very carefully took them down from the top shelf, unwrapped them and showed them to me.

"Father has always been a great companion to his children. When I was very small, in fact before I was five, he took me to the ponds up north of Salt Lake and taught me to skate. He taught me to ride horse-back, to row a boat, to swim. He always felt that it was very important for children to have fun and friends and to have an open house for their friends. Father and mother's home has always been a home for those who didn't have a home of their own and who were in need of one temporarily. They have helped to educate many children besides their own. . . .

"Another phase of father's life with his home relationship I should like to emphasize is his and mother's desire to have in their home objects of art and culture, which would be an inspiration for their family. I can never remember in my lifetime when there was not an opportunity to enjoy beautiful art in our own home. Also, we have always had the benefit of a very splendid library. We have enjoyed the theater from our childhood and have been taught to appreciate the cultural things both in our own community and wherever we have traveled. We have been directed and taught to look for the cultural and expressive things of nationalities and communities. Father has always urged us to take advantage of all forms of instruction—good lectures, good magazines and good books."

George Albert Smith, about 1912 (Thomas Studio, Church Archives)

total exhaustion and "pain from head to foot." His doctor prescribed full rest and cessation of work. The next three years of incapacitation and recovery were difficult for this man of such robust mind and spirit. For the rest of his life, he carefully guarded his energy and protected his health against the ever-present potential of chronic fatigue.

With careful pacing of his vigor, he returned to a full schedule and would eventually record that "in these eighty years, I have traveled more than a million miles in the world in the interest of the gospel of Jesus Christ. I have been in many climes and in many lands and in many nations, and from my childhood people have been kind and helpful to me, members of the Church and non-members as well. Wherever I have gone, I have found noble men and women."

On May 21, 1945, George Albert Smith was ordained president of the Church. With the end of World War II, he faced the unique challenge of reestablishing the Church throughout the war-ravished world. Most important, he needed to help heal war-caused hatred, distrust, and

impoverishment. During the summer and again in the autumn of 1945, President Smith met with U.S. president Harry S. Truman in order to facilitate the Church's role in relief efforts for the Saints in Europe. Under President Smith's guidance, food and clothing were sent to Germany and other European nations, missions were reorganized, and communication between Saints of warring nations was refocused on the gospel of love and peace. Additionally, and quite in character, he visited members throughout the United States, Mexico, and Czechoslovakia.

Addressing members of the Church, he wrote, "Once again, through the goodness and mercy of our Father in heaven, we have lived to see the end of another war. . . . What a terrible thing this war has been. It seems a pity

Emily and Edith Smith, about 1901. On the reverse side one of the daughters noted, "Running to meet beloved Father, carrying their dolls. The fence is the one in front of grandparents home (23 N. W. Temple SLC) Sarah Farr and John Henry Smith. Father happened to have camera and snapped picture." (Church Archives)

George Albert Smith in the mountains in the early 1930s (Church Archives)

Joseph Fielding Smith, George Albert Smith, and Israel Smith (RLDS Church president) in George Albert Smith's office, April 1936 (Church Archives)

that intelligent people will continue, from generation to generation, to make war upon one another and destroy one another, to spread sorrow and distress and to waste their substance, just to satisfy the selfishness of a few people who want to dictate terms to the world. . . . The best evidence of gratitude at this time is to do all we can to bring happiness to this sad world. . . . let us extend kindness and consideration to all who need it, not forgetting those who are bereft."

President Smith's lifelong example and belief in secular service as well as fulfilling Church duties allowed him to befriend non-Mormons throughout the world. His genuine Christ-guided love of people helped reverse many of the negative feelings about the Church during the early twentieth century. It was a role he cherished, and he actively sought opportunities to help improve the possibilities of understanding, tolerance, and peace among people and nations.

Noble Warrum Sr., a close friend of President Smith who was not a member of the Church, summed up the feelings of many when he wrote, "He was not a poet or a great financier, nor was he as fine an orator as his father, but if ever a man walked the streets of this world who was fit to walk and talk with God, it was George Albert Smith."

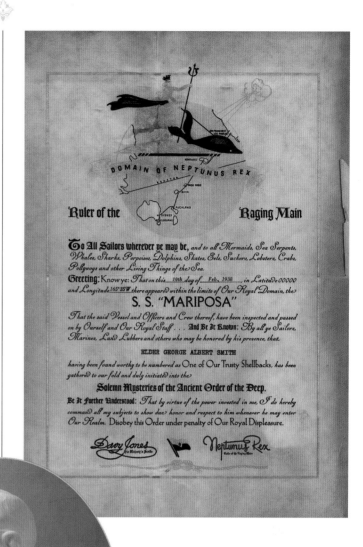

(Above) S.S. Mariposa crossing the equator; certificate dated February 10, 1938 (Church Archives)

(Left) Avard T. Fairbanks's sculpture, 1950 (MCHA)

(Below) George Albert Smith's business card (Courtesy Gregory P. and MarJane Christofferson)

GEORGE ALBERT SMITH

47 E. SOUTH TEMPLE ST.
SALT LAKE CITY, UTAH

A new president and his counselors, about 1945 (Church Archives)

President George Albert Smith speaking in Mexico, May 1946 (Church Archives)

GRATITUDE TO THE PIONEERS

Within George Albert Smith's large circle of interests was his study and promotion of Church and Utah history. The depth of his involvement is evident in his activity in the Utah Pioneer Trails and Landmarks Association. During the Pioneer Centennial in 1947, he gave the following advice on how to best honor the sacrifice of Utah's pioneers:

"I do not know when I have felt happier or more grateful for the blessings of life than I do at this time of the Centennial. We have much reason to thank our Heavenly Father.

"When I realize that our people came from a land rich agriculturally, made their way across the great plains after being driven from their comfortable homes in Nauvoo, and came into this then desert waste to build up the Church to the glory of God and to transform the desert, I know that I, for one, have much to be grateful for.

"Sometime ago in traveling over a portion of the old Pioneer trail I stood at the side of one grave containing bodies of fifteen of the members of this Church who gave their all for the cause, and passed on to their reward; hundreds of others also lie in unmarked graves.

"I have been many times on that trail over which barefoot, hungry, and weary, in the cold of winter and the heat of summer, thousands of our people made their way into this valley, buoyed up with the hope that they could here worship God according to the dictates of their consciences. Today when I think of this marvelous land in which we live, our world-famed Temple Square, our homes and farms, and our buildings that have been dedicated to the worship of our Father in heaven, it seems to me that we ought to examine ourselves and check on our lives to see whether or not we are living up to our privileges and are worthy of that which the Lord has given us. He has said: 'Not every one that saith unto me, Lord, Lord, shall enter into the kingdom of heaven; but he that doeth the will of my Father which is in heaven' (Matthew 7:21).

"It was in order that we might know what His will is toward His children that He gave Joseph Smith, the boy prophet, the latter-day revelation which resulted in the organization of the Church of Jesus Christ of Latter-day Saints. Then some of the very stalwarts of the earth were pricked in their hearts with a desire to know the truth, and the missionaries of the Church sought them among the nations, and the pilgrimage to this western world began. The community comforts that we enjoy here are the result of their faith and devotion.

"The only way we have of giving convincing evidence of our gratitude is by honoring Him and keeping His commandments. That we may so do, and in the end enjoy eternal life in the companionship of one another, under the direction of our Lord and Master, Jesus Christ, I pray with all my heart."

George Albert Smith at This Is the Place Monument dedication, July 24, 1947 (Boyart Photography, Church Archives)

TWENTY CENTS · JULY 21, 1947

TIME

THE WEEKLY NEWSMAGAZINE

MORMON LEADER SMITH
After 100 years, milk and honey in the land of the honeybee.

$6.50 A YEAR · (REG. U. S. PAT. OFF.) · VOL. L NO. 3

Time magazine cover, July 21, 1947

(Above) George Albert Smith with Czechoslovakian missionaries,
October 14, 1949 (Church Archives)

(Right) George Albert Smith at home, about 1950 (Church Archives)

(Below) George Albert Smith in Hawaii, August 1950 (Church Archives)

PRESIDENT SMITH'S CREED

In his continuous effort "to be a living example of the love of Christ," President Smith, through much thought and meditation, created a creed by which to guide his thoughts and actions:

I would be a friend to the friendless and find joy in ministering to the needs of the poor.

I would visit the sick and afflicted and inspire in them a desire for faith to be healed.

I would teach the truth to the understanding and blessing of all mankind.

I would seek out the erring one and try to win him back to a righteous and a happy life.

I would not seek to force people to live up to my ideals, but rather love them into doing the thing that is right.

I would live with the masses and help to solve their problems that their earth life may be happy.

I would avoid the publicity of high positions and discourage the flattery of thoughtless friends.

I would not knowingly wound the feeling of any, not even one who may have wronged me, but would seek to do him good and make him my friend.

I would overcome the tendency to selfishness and jealousy and rejoice in the success of all the children of my Heavenly Father.

I would not be an enemy to any living soul.

Knowing that the Redeemer of mankind has offered to the world the only plan that will fully develop us and make us really happy here and hereafter, I feel it not only a duty but a blessed privilege to disseminate this truth.

(Above) George Q. Morris, George Albert Smith, and Fred A. Turley at Sundown Ranch, Aripine, Arizona, May, 6, 1941 (Courtesy Fred A. and Wilma Turley Family)

(Below) John Giles, George Q. Morris, and George Albert Smith at Sundown Ranch, Aripine, Arizona, May 6, 1941 (Courtesy Fred A. and Wilma Turley Family)

WILMA FILLERUP TURLEY DIARY
May 1941

May 1: Went to hoe loco [locoweed] in Westover Section—rained a little, but we cleaned the loco out. Surprised the girls with a little May Day gift. Bless their hearts.

May 2, 3: Cleaning, getting ready for Sunday and friends. I baked a lemon pie and rested. Dad fixed fence.

May 4: Good Conference with Apostle George Albert Smith, Bro. George Q. Morris and John Giles, of the General YMMIA; a fine spirit.

May 5: Elder George Albert Smith and Bros. Cannon and Giles came up to our home. It is a pleasure to have them and what a good visit. They rested and seemed to enjoy everything. Our first warm day, so we had fried chicken and gingerbread for supper by the outdoor fireplace. A fine evening, I just wish Stan, Grant and Wanda were here. Bro. George Albert Smith, one of the Twelve, left his blessing on our home. He prayed with us at the end of a perfect day, and I feel we, our home and family, will be the better for having had him in our home.

May 6: We took them down to see the cows. They enjoyed it; dressing up in chaps, etc. for pictures. Made lemon pie for Bro. Morris.

State of the Church at the time of George Albert Smith's death	
Year of death	1951
Church membership	1,111,314
Stakes	184
Temples	8
Missions	42
Missionaries set apart during administration	13,769
Book of Mormon translations completed during administration	2

In Their Own Words

Joseph Smith

If I had not actually got into this work and been called of God, I would back out. But I cannot back out: I have no doubt of the truth.

Brigham Young

My mission to the people is to teach them with regard to their every-day lives. I presume there are many here who have heard me say, years and years ago, that I cared very little about what will take place after the Millennium. Elders may preach long discourses concerning what took place in the days of Adam, what occurred before the creation, and what will take place thousands of years from now, talking of things which have occurred or that will occur yet, of which they are ignorant, feeding the people on wind; but that is not my method of teaching. My desire is to teach the people what they should do now, and let the Millennium take care of itself. To teach them to serve God and to build up His Kingdom is my mission. I have taught faith, repentance, baptism for the remission of sins, and the laying on of hands for the reception of the Holy Ghost . . . . We are to be taught with regard to our every-day life in a temporal point of view.

John Taylor

I will now tell you about some of my feelings when I first came into this Church. . . . When I first heard the Gospel I was compelled to admit there was something reasonable about it. I almost hoped it was not true. "If it is true," said I, "as an honest man I shall be obliged to obey it, or else I cannot have any confidence in myself." When I had investigated the subject, and become convinced that it was true, I said, "I am in for it; I must embrace it; I cannot reject the principles of eternal truth."

Wilford Woodruff

I am overwhelmed as it were in Mormonism for it is my life, meat, and drink and I do not expect to be anything else but a Mormon either in life or death. . . . It certainly looks like a marvelous work and a wonder that an obscure unlearned miller should stand . . . at the head of ten thousand saints.

(Above oval) Brigham Young, about 1874-75 (Charles R. Savage, courtesy Kim N. Leavitt)

(Opposite oval) Harold B. Lee, about 1973 (Courtesy L. Brent Goates)

Lorenzo Snow

I have tried to submit completely to the Lord's will. I can assure you, brethren and sisters, that I had no ambition to assume the responsibility which now rests upon me. If I could have escaped it honorably I should never have been found in my present position. I have never asked for it, nor have I ever asked the assistance of any of my brethren that I might attain to this position; but the Lord revealed to me and to my brethren that this was His will, and I have no disposition to shirk any responsibility. . . . I have tried to serve Him, to overcome the weaknesses of the flesh and to bring myself with every power and faculty of my nature into complete subservience to His will.

Joseph F. Smith

I thank God for the feeling that I possess and enjoy, and for the realization that I have, that I stand not only in the presence of Almighty God, my Maker and Father, but in the presence of his Only Begotten Son in the flesh, the Savior of the world; and I stand in the presence of Peter and James (and perhaps the eyes of John are also upon us and we know it not); and I stand also in the presence of Joseph and Hyrum and Brigham and John, and Wilford, and Lorenzo, and those who have been valiant in the testimony of Jesus Christ and faithful to their mission in the world, who have gone before. When I go, I want to have the privilege of meeting them with the consciousness that I have followed their example, that I have carried out the mission in which they were engaged as they would have it carried out; that I have been as faithful in the discharge of duty, committed to me and required at my hand, as they were faithful in their time; and that when I meet them, I shall meet them as I met them here, in love, in harmony, in unison and in perfect confidence that I have done my duty as they have done theirs. I hope you will forgive me for my emotion. You would have peculiar emotions, would you not? If you felt that you stood in the presence of your Father, in the very presence of Almighty God, in the very presence of the Son of God and of holy angels? You would feel rather emotional, rather sensitive. I feel it to the very depths of my soul this moment.

Heber J. Grant

I will ask no man to be more liberal with his means, than I am with mine, in proportion to what he possesses, for the advancement of God's kingdom. I will ask no man to observe the Word of Wisdom any more closely than I will observe it. I will ask no man to be more conscientious and prompt in the payment of his tithes and his offerings than I will be. I will ask no man to be more ready and willing to come early and to go late, and to labor with full power of mind and body, than I will labor, always in humility. I hope and pray for the blessings of the Lord, acknowledging freely and frankly, that without the Lord's blessings it will be an impossibility for me to make a success of the high calling whereunto I have been called. . . . I accept the great responsibility, without fear of the consequences, knowing that God will sustain me as He has sustained all of my predecessors who have occupied this position, provided always, that I shall labor in humility and in diligence, ever seeking for the guidance of His Holy Spirit.

George Albert Smith

I wonder if anyone here feels as weak and humble as the man who stands before you. I have been coming to this house [Salt Lake Tabernacle] since my infancy. I have seen all the Presidents of the Church since that time sustained by the congregations here, as their names have been presented from this stand. I have seen the Church continue to grow in numbers, and have realized throughout all my years that the Church of Jesus Christ is what its name implies. We who are members of this Church are indeed fortunate to have found the light and to have accepted the truth.

David O. McKay

I pledge to you that I shall do my best so to live as to merit the companionship of the Holy Spirit, and pray here in your presence that my counselors and I may indeed be "partakers of the divine spirit." . . . And now to the members of the Church: we all need your help, your faith and prayers, not your adverse criticisms, but your help. You can do that in prayer if you cannot reach us in person. . . . Today you have by your [sustaining] vote placed upon us the greatest responsibility, as well as the greatest honor, that lies within your power to bestow as members of the Church of Jesus Christ of Latter-day Saints. Your doing so increases the duty of the First Presidency to render service to the people.

Joseph Fielding Smith

I desire to say that no man of himself can lead this church. It is the Church of the Lord Jesus Christ; he is at the head. The Church bears his name, has his priesthood, administers his gospel, preaches his doctrine, and does his work. . . . If this were the work of man, it would fail, but it is the work of the Lord, and he does not fail.

Harold B. Lee

I want to tell you a little sacred experience I had following the call to be the President of the Church. On the early morning thereafter with my wife I kneeled in humble prayer, and suddenly it seemed as though my mind and heart went out to over three million people in all the world. I seemed to have a love for every one of them no matter where they lived nor what their color was, whether they were rich or poor, whether they were humble or great, or educated or not. Suddenly I felt as though they all belonged to me, as though they were all my own brothers and sisters.

Spencer W. Kimball

I know this is the right program, and the Lord has arranged so that I should be in this position. I am extremely humbled. I want only one thing, and that is that the people of this Church shall have all the blessings to which they are entitled.

Ezra Taft Benson

I have not words to express my gratitude to God, the Father of our spirits, to our Lord and Savior, Jesus Christ, and to the Holy Ghost, the Testator. I wish to convey my appreciation to all those who raised their hands in a covenant to the Lord to sustain me. I have felt the expression of your hearts and your commitment to the Lord as your hands pointed heavenward. . . . I have been aware of those who preceded me in this office as President of the Church. I have felt very keenly my dependence upon the Lord and the absolute necessity of relying upon Him for His direction in the conduct of the affairs of the church as those in the past have done.

Howard W. Hunter

My greatest strength . . . has been my abiding testimony that this is the work of God and not of men. Jesus Christ is the head of this church. He leads it in word and deed. I am honored beyond expression to be called for a season to be an instrument in His hands to preside over His church. But without the knowledge that Christ is the head of the Church, neither I nor any other man could bear the weight of the calling that has come. . . . Like my Brethren before me, I receive with this calling the assurance that God will direct his prophet. I humbly accept the call to serve and declare with the Psalmist, "The Lord is my strength and my shield; my heart trusted in him, and I am helped (Psalms 28:7)."

Gordon B. Hinckley

I would hope that I might be held in remembrance as a man who tried to do some good in the world, to make the world a better place, to improve it. And as a man who walked with integrity with his associates, both those in the Church and out of the Church, with love and appreciation for the goodness that he saw in people wherever he went.

David O. McKay

V iola Eardley led her four children through the Christmas shoppers crowding Salt Lake City's downtown ZCMI. Her three older children went off on their own, but the youngest, six-year-old Sheri, stayed close to her mother, waiting in a line that was slowly making its way to the cash register. Christmas music filled the store, and Sheri was soon dancing and whirling, until she twirled into the legs of an older gentleman. Suddenly transfixed, she stopped. Later, as an adult, she wrote, "I looked up at the kindest, gentlest face I had ever seen."

"The music seemed to pause, and everyone around us stood still, watching. The white-haired man placed his hands on my head and said, 'Merry Christmas, my little child, and may the Lord always bless you.'

"I stood transfixed, watching him as he moved away. People nodded and smiled at him as he passed. When he was out of sight, I tiptoed back to my mother's side.

"'Honey, do you know who that was?' she asked me.

"'I'm not really sure, Mom, but I think it was Christ.'

"'Pretty close, dear, pretty close. That was President David O. McKay.'"

The six-foot-one-inch, straight-backed, and broad-shouldered David Oman McKay was impressively athletic looking at eighty-two years old. One could not help but notice his healthy mane of well-coifed white hair, his engaging smile, and the spring in his step. Indeed, President McKay was a pleasantly striking gentleman, both in his manner and his physical presence.

This incident, which Sheri would forever remember, was but one incident in a lifetime of kindness, consideration, and principle. Known for his grace and gentleness, President McKay was described in the February 1970 *Time* as "an affable new image of Mormonism to a world that had previously seen the Mormon leaders as dour, dark-suited figures."

In fact, President McKay often stressed, "We don't need to be long-faced and pious to be religious. We shouldn't be gloomy when we worship God; we should be happy. Sometimes I'm overwhelmed by the joy to be found everywhere."

(Left) Portrait of David O. McKay, 1964 (Alvin L. Gittins, Pioneer Memorial Theatre, University of Utah)

(Above oval) Portrait of David O. McKay (MCHA)

BORN
SEPTEMBER 8, 1873
HUNTSVILLE, UTAH

PARENTS
DAVID AND
JENNETTE EVANS MCKAY

BAPTIZED
SEPTEMBER 8, 1881
(AGE 8)

STATURE
6' 1"
195–200 POUNDS

MARRIED
JANUARY 2, 1901
TO EMMA RAY RIGGS
(AGE 27)

APOSTLE
APRIL 9, 1906
(AGE 32)

PRESIDENT
APRIL 9, 1951
(AGE 77)

DIED
JANUARY 18, 1970
SALT LAKE CITY, UTAH
(AGE 96)

Bryant S. Hinckley, president of the Liberty Stake and father of President Gordon B. Hinckley, wrote of David O. McKay's gift of leadership, "His splendid courage, his strong and flexible intellect, his idealism, his kind but chivalrous attitude toward the humblest, combine to give him that magic power which calls forth the best there is in one. It is stimulating to meet him—you go from his presence feeling a little finer, a little better than you were."

In so many ways throughout his life, President McKay exemplified the reality that "attitude is everything." Norman Vincent Peale remembered that "as President McKay mounted the platform to address a group, he tripped on the stairs. There was a gasp from the people. But he stood up and faced the audience with that irrepressible smile. 'It's awful to grow old,' he said ruefully, 'but I prefer it to the alternative.'"

Four-year-old David O. McKay stands straddled between his father's knees, 1877 (Church Archives)

This sense of humor and upbeat demeanor also expressed itself when, in his early nineties, President McKay was aided by two younger men as he struggled up a hill to inspect a possible chapel construction site. As they slowly made their way up the incline, the prophet stopped and informed his companions, "Brethren, I don't mind helping one of you climb this hill, but I can't carry you both."

Born in Huntsville, Utah, on September 8, 1873, he was the third child and first son of the ten children of David McKay and Jennette Evans McKay, immigrants from Scotland and Wales. David Oman McKay was born a year after the creation of Yellowstone National Park, a year before Sir Winston Churchill's birth, and four years after the joining of the transcontinental railroad. In 1873, the Indian Wars were approaching their zenith in the West, Brigham Young was alive, the Church's practice of plural marriage was widely misunderstood, and Victoria was in her thirty-sixth year as queen of England. President McKay's life spanned the Massacre at Wounded Knee, the Spanish-American War, World War I, the Russian Revolution, the rise of Hitler and World War II, the Korean War, the assassination of President John F. Kennedy, and the Vietnam War. During David O. McKay's last year of earthly life, 1969, Neil Armstrong walked on the moon, hippies held a music festival at Woodstock, and the supersonic Concorde took its first test flight. Playing at theaters was

1873
Sept. 8 • Born in Huntsville, Utah
Remington Firearms Company begins making typewriters

1877
Aug. 29 • Brigham Young dies

1881
Sept. 8 • Baptized in Huntsville, Utah

1887
July 25 • John Taylor dies
Lumiere brothers demonstrate the first public film show, Paris (1895)

1897
June 9 • Graduates from University of Utah

1897–99
Mission to Great Britain, labors in Scotland

1898
Sept. 2 • Wilford Woodruff dies

1899–1901
Faculty Weber Stake Academy, Ogden, Utah

1901
Jan. 2 • Marries Emma Ray Riggs
Oct. 10 • Lorenzo Snow dies
Nobel Foundation awards first prizes

1906
Apr. 9 • Ordained an apostle
Frederick Gowland establishes existence of vitamins

1917
Publishes his first book, **Ancient Apostles**

1918
Nov. 19 • Joseph F. Smith dies
World leaders establish the League of Nations

1919–21
Church commissioner of education

1920–21
Visits members and missionaries on world tour
U.S. grants women the right to vote (1920)

1922–24
President of the British and European missions
Alexander Fleming discovers penicillin (1928)

1934
Oct. 6 • Second counselor to Heber J. Grant
U.S. population: 131,669,275 (1940)

1945
May 14 • Heber J. Grant dies
May 21 • Second counselor to George Albert Smith
Bedouins shepherds discover the first Dead Sea Scrolls (1947)

1951
Apr. 4 • George Albert Smith dies
Apr. 9 • Sustained president of the Church
22nd Amendment limits U.S. presidents to two terms

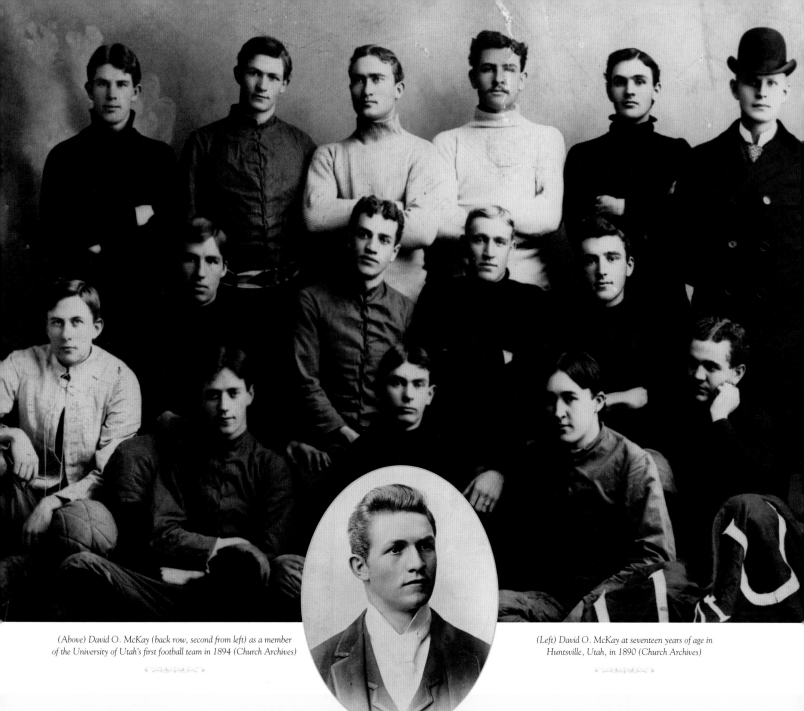

(Above) David O. McKay (back row, second from left) as a member
of the University of Utah's first football team in 1894 (Church Archives)

(Left) David O. McKay at seventeen years of age in
Huntsville, Utah, in 1890 (Church Archives)

1952
Summer • Visits European members
and missionaries
Korean War ends (1953)

1954
Visits Latin and South American
members and missionaries

1955
Jan.–Feb. • Visits South Pacific
members and missionaries
Feb. 12 • Groundbreaking for
Church College of Hawaii
Sept. 11 • Dedicates Swiss Temple

1956
Mar. 11 • Dedicates Los Angeles
Temple
Oct. 3 • Dedicates Relief Society
Building
Transatlantic telephone service begins

1958
April 20 • Dedicates New Zealand
Temple
May 18 • First stake outside United
States/Canada created, Auckland,
New Zealand
Sept. 7 • Dedicates London Temple

1960
Mar. 27 • First stake in Europe
created, Manchester, England
U.S. population: 179,823,175

1961
Sept. 30 • Establishes All-Church
Coordinating Council
*East German government erects
the Berlin Wall*

1962
Dec. 3 • First Spanish-speaking
stake created, Mexico City
Cuban Missile Crisis

1963
Church membership exceeds
2,000,000

1964
Nov. 17 • Dedicates Oakland Temple

1965
Jan. • Inaugurates Family
Home Evening program
*Canada changes national flag
to "Maple Leaf"*

1966
May 1 • First South American
stake created, Sao Paulo, Brazil

1967
Sept. 29 • Establishes regional
representatives
*Pierre Trudeau becomes
Canadian prime minister (1968)*

1969
Jan. 20 • Tabernacle Choir sings at
U.S. President Nixon's inauguration
*U.S. astronaut Neil Armstrong
walks on the moon*

1970
Jan. 18 • Dies in Salt Lake City
U.S. population: 203,302,231

DAVID O. MCKAY'S TEN RULES OF HAPPINESS

1. Develop yourself by self-discipline.

2. Joy comes through creation—sorrow through destruction. Every living thing can grow: Use the world wisely to realize soul growth.

3. Do things which are hard to do.

4. Entertain upbuilding thoughts. What you think about when you do not have to think shows what you really are.

5. Do your best this hour, and you will do better the next.

6. Be true to those who trust you.

7. Pray for wisdom, courage, and a kind heart.

8. Give heed to God's messages through inspiration. If self-indulgence, jealousy, avarice, or worry have deadened your response, pray to the Lord to wipe out these impediments.

9. True friends enrich life. If you would have friends, be one.

10. Faith is the foundation of all things–including happiness.

(Top) John Hafen's portrait of Elder David O. McKay in 1907 (MCHA)

(Above) Trowel (lower right) used by David O. McKay at the Cardston, Alberta Temple cornerstone laying on September 19, 1915 (MCHA)

(Right) Cornerstone laying ceremonies of the Cardston, Alberta Temple on September 19, 1915 (A. T. Henson, MCHA)

hog. He sent a telegram reminding the family, "Don't forget Caesar; he may be thirsty."

Although life was demanding and sometimes tragic (his two older sisters died when he was six), his parents' love and example filled their eldest son with an infectious joy-of-life manifested in his love of the outdoors, horseback riding, hiking, fishing, swimming, baseball, and football—he played guard for the University of Utah. For David O. McKay, life was infinitely interesting. His love of literature and learning was a lifelong passion, and he liked to

a movie about two men well-known in Utah during President McKay's boyhood—Butch Cassidy and the Sundance Kid.

As a child growing up on his family's Huntsville farm, David O. McKay learned the importance and satisfaction of hard work as well as reverence for the land. He discovered that shirking one's farm chores could have serious consequences. The work was constant and demanding—there were hogs to be fed, cows to be milked, hay to be cut and hauled, and irrigation ditches to be cleared, and the vegetable gardens needed endless tending. Years later, still maintaining the Huntsville property, David O. McKay's ingrained sense of responsibility was a lesson to his children. As an apostle busily preparing for the stake conference to which he was traveling by railroad, he worried about Caesar—the family's large, black

(Top left) David O. McKay's passport, 1920 (Church Archives)

(Above oval) Hugh J. Cannon and David O. McKay leaving San Francisco, March 29, 1921, during their world tour (Church Archives)

(Above) David O. McKay about 1922 (Church Archives)

(Top left) David O. McKay fishing in the Tetons in 1945 (Church Archives)
(Top right) David O. McKay reading in his library on August 26, 1957 (Church Archives)
(Below) Painting of McKay Home in Huntsville, Utah (Courtesy Al Rounds)

Traditional bobsled ride in Huntsville, December 21, 1957 (Church Archives)

remind people that "good reading is to the intellect what good food is to the body." A hallmark of his writings and speeches, throughout his life, was his affinity for quoting passages from great literature. Burns, Shakespeare, Carlisle, and Whittier were among his particular favorites.

His love of learning expanded into an enduring devotion to education. In 1899, he was hired to teach at Weber Academy (now Weber State University) and served as its principal from 1902 until 1906, when he was called to be an apostle. His role as an educator continued in the general superintendency of the Sunday School from 1906 to 1934, and as the Church's commissioner of education from 1919 to 1921. In later years he served on the boards of directors of Utah State University,

University of Utah, and Brigham Young University.

The unifying nature of President McKay's personality is well-known—but what is not always fully appreciated is that it was set on a world stage. Leaders as well as ordinary people throughout the world found him to be witty, wise, urbane, and humble. His extensive world travels and global thinking and outlook began with his 1897 mission to Great Britain, where he presided over the Scottish conference, birthplace of his father. During this time he saw a motto carved in stone: "Whate-er thou art, act well thy part." Its message gave him a lifelong sense of purpose and enlivened his understanding of the gospel's power.

In 1920, President Heber J. Grant assigned Elder David O. McKay and Liberty Stake president Hugh

(Above) Greeting children while on a trip to England in 1955 (Church Archives)

(Left) First Presidency, 1951 (Church Archives)

(Above) David O. McKay and wife Emma Ray Riggs with Cecil B. DeMille and Charlton Heston, who played the role of Moses, on the set of The Ten Commandments in 1955 (Church Archives)

(Left) Letter to the queen of the Netherlands, July 14, 1952 (Church Archives)

PROPHETS OF THE LATTER DAYS

Cannon to "make a general survey of the missions, study conditions there, gather data concerning them, and, in short, obtain general information . . . of the Pacific missions, to go on to South Africa and even to the European missions." The thirteen-month, 62,000-mile, globe-circling mission expanded Elder McKay's knowledge and sense of the Church as a worldwide fellowship transcending national boundaries and cultural differences. It also brought the Church endearingly closer to members who lived in areas never before visited by apostolic Church leaders. During his sixty-three years and nine months as apostle and president, David O. McKay traveled more extensively than any previous Church leader in these latter-days—more than two million miles during his presidency. During these travels, he befriended national and international government officials, business and union leaders, movie moguls and stars, monarchs, and heads of other religions, but most important, he spread the seeds of hope through his loving and gentle manner.

Perhaps most appreciated by members and non-members alike was the love David O. McKay and his wife, Emma Ray, shared for each other. All his life President McKay not only advocated marriage but also urged couples to actively grow ever closer through continual courtship. In a note written on their twentieth wedding anniversary, David O. McKay expressed his ever-growing love for his wife: "January second Nineteen One marked the beginning of a new year, the beginning of a new century, the beginning of a new and happy Life! I loved you that morning with the love and fire of youth. It was pure and sincere. You were my heart's treasure, no bride more sweet, and pure, and beautiful! But this

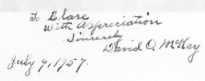

(Above) Gordon B. Hinckley presents pen sketch by
Henryk Jakubowski from the Brazilian Mission,
January 24, 1955 (Church Archives)

(Opposite page) Autographed photograph to Harold B. Lee,
April 14, 1960 (Boyard Studio, courtesy L. Brent Goates)

(Left) Autographed portrait for his secretary, July 1957
(Courtesy Gregory P. and MarJane Christofferson)

morning . . . I think I didn't know what love was when I took you as my bride. It was but as the light of a star compared with [the] glorious sunlight of Love that fills my soul to-day."

President McKay's legacy includes an endearing love of all people, concern for family, the expanding missions into new countries, increasing the number of full-time missionaries, fostering the importance of "every member a missionary," spotlighting the needs of an international Church, and building temples outside North America. Shining above all his great service to the Lord is President McKay's guiding principle on how to conduct one's life, as revealed to his son Lawrence: "I never make a decision without asking myself, 'How will I explain this to the Savior when I meet him?'"

To
Elder Harold B. Lee
Beloved brother and
associate.
with confidence and
esteem
Affectionately
David O. McKay
April 14, 1960

Quotations from President McKay's Favorite Poems

To make a happy fireside clime
 To weans and wife,
That's the true pathos and sublime
 O' human life.
 —*Robert Burns (from "Epistle to Dr. Blacklock")*

O Brother Man! Fold to thy heart thy brother;
 Where pity dwells, the peace of God is there;
To worship rightly is to love each other,
 Each smile a hymn, each kindly deed a prayer.
Follow with reverent steps the great example
 Of Him whose holy work was 'doing good';
So shall the wide earth seem our Father's temple,
 Each loving life a psalm of gratitude.
Then shall all shackles fall; the stormy clanger
 Of wild music o'er the earth shall cease;
Love shall tread out the baleful fire of anger,
 And it its ashes plant the tree of peace!
 —*John Greenleaf Whittier*

There is a destiny which makes us brothers,
 None lives to self alone;
All that we send into the lives of others,
 Comes back into our own.
 —*Edwin Markham*

No other success can compensate for failure in the home.

(Background image) David O. McKay kissing his wife Emma (Church Archives)

(Above oval) David O. McKay standing next to Emma (Church Archives)

TEN CONDITIONS WHICH CONTRIBUTE TO A HAPPY HOME

1. Ever keep in mind you begin to lay the foundation of a happy home in your pre-marital lives. While in courtship you should learn to be loyal and true to your future husband or wife. Keep yourselves clean and pure. Cherish the highest ideals of chastity and purity. Do not be deceived.

2. Choose your mate by judgment and inspiration, as well as by physical attraction. Intellect and breeding are vital and important in the human family.

3. Approach marriage with the lofty view it merits. Marriage is ordained of God. It is not something to be entered into lightly or to be dissolved at the first difficulty that arises.

4. Remember that the noblest purpose of marriage is pro-creation. Home is children's natural nursery. Happiness in the home is enhanced by having children at the fireside.

5. Let the spirit of reverence pervade the home. Have your home such that if the Savior called unexpectedly he could be invited to stay and not feel out of his element. Pray in the home.

6. Let husband or wife never speak in loud tones to each other.

7. Learn the value of self-control. We are never sorry for the word unspoken. Lack of self-control is the greatest source of unhappiness in the home. Children should be taught self-control, self-respect, and respect for others.

8. Fasten home ties by continued companionship. Companionship fosters love. Do everything to cement love for all eternity.

9. Make accessible to children proper literature and music.

10. By example and precept, encourage participation in Church activity. This is fundamental in developing a true character. Church activity should be led, not directed by parents.

—David O. McKay

DAVID O. MCKAY'S FAMILY

In an April 1964 general conference address, David O. McKay emphasized the importance of mothers and fathers, stating, "No other success can compensate for failure in the home. The poorest shack in which love prevails over a united family is of greater value to God and future humanity than any other riches."

Emma Ray Riggs and David O. McKay were married in the Salt Lake Temple on January 2, 1901. They raised six children to adulthood—David Lawrence, LouJean, Llewelyn, Emma Rae, Edward, and Robert. Sister McKay expressed her deep love and affection for President McKay when she wrote "that Shakespeare must have had someone like him in mind when he said, 'What a piece of work is man! How noble in reason! How infinite in faculties! In form and moving how express and admirable!'"

In the following account, Lawrence McKay gives a powerful example of how his loving father reacted to a son's misconduct and the worry caused to his parents.

"Father took his family to Ocean Park, California, when I was eight years old. We took the San Pedro, Los Angeles and Salt Lake Railway to Los Angeles. I remember the wooden station there. We rode in a Model T Ford through the countryside to Ocean Park. Our driver pointed out a new type of road covering to keep down the dust. You put oil on it. This empty country road is now Wilshire Boulevard. I was disappointed in my first view of the Pacific Ocean. The tide was out, and it looked like a big lake. We settled down for the night in an apartment house a few blocks from the beach. I arose early and went out for another look at the ocean. Being a parent now, I can imagine mother waking up and saying, 'Dade [President McKay's nickname], Lawrence is gone!' I am afraid that I would scold my son for going away and crossing the speedway without telling me where he was going. But, as I stood there on the beach watching the big waves coming in (the tide was in), I was suddenly conscious of my father standing by me. All he said was, 'It's beautiful, isn't it?'"

(Upper left) The McKays in Huntsville, Utah (Church Archives)

State of the Church at the time of David O. McKay's death	
Year of death	1970
Church membership	2,807,456
Stakes	500
Temples	13
Missions	92
Missionaries set apart during administration	80,975
Book of Mormon translations completed during administration	4

BAPTISMS

(Above) "Joseph Smith Baptizes Oliver Cowdery." Joseph wrote of the occasion, "[As] soon as I had been baptized by him, I also had the spirit of prophecy, when, standing up, I prophesied concerning the rise of this Church, and many other things connected with the Church, and this generation of the children of men. We were filled with the Holy Ghost, and rejoiced in the God of our salvation." (Del Parson, 1966, VRL)

Joseph Smith
Age   23 years 5 months
Date   May 15, 1829
Place   In the Susquehanna River,
        Harmony, Pennsylvania
By   Oliver Cowdery as directed
        by John the Baptist

Brigham Young
Age   30 years 10 months
Date   April 15, 1832
Place   In a millpond on his property,
        Mendon, New York
By   Eleazar Miller

John Taylor
Age   27 years 6 months
Date   May 9, 1836
Place   In a stream,
        Toronto, Canada
By   Parley P. Pratt

Wilford Woodruff
Age   26 years 10 months
Date   December 31, 1833
Place   In a stream, Richland,
        New York
By   Zera Pulsipher

"I heard a report circulated on the 29th day of Dec 1833 that there was to be a meeting held in the neighborhood by a Mormon priest. . . . [My brother and I] were anxious to attend the meeting. Accordingly, we went and found a full congregation of people. The person that was to preach was Zerah Pulsipher, an elder of the Church of Christ or of the Latter-day Saints.

. . . I felt the spirit of God to bear witness that he was the servant of God. . . . Brother Pulsipher continued laboring with us for several days and, on the 31th of Dec., I, with my brother, Azmon Woodruff . . . went forward in baptism." —Wilford Woodruff

Lorenzo Snow
Age   22 years 2 months
Date   June 3, 1836
Place   Chagrin River, Kirtland, Ohio
By   John F. Boynton

Joseph F. Smith
Age   13 years 6 months
Date   May 21, 1852
Place   City Creek,
        Salt Lake City, Utah
By   Heber C. Kimball

Heber J. Grant
Age   7 years 6 months
Date   June 2, 1864
Place   In a wooden font on
        Brigham Young's property,
        Salt Lake City, Utah
By   Thomas Higgs

George Albert Smith
Age   8 years 2 months
Date   June 6, 1878
Place   City Creek,
        Salt Lake City, Utah
By   James Moyle

David O. McKay
Age   8 years on his birthday
Date   September 8, 1881
Place   Spring Creek,
        Huntsville, Utah
By   Peter Geertsen

Joseph Fielding Smith
Age   8 years on his birthday
Date   July 19, 1884
Place   City Creek,
        Salt Lake City, Utah
By   Joseph F. Smith

Harold B. Lee
Age   8 years 2 months
Date   June 9, 1907
Place   Bybee Pond, Clifton, Idaho
By   Lester Bybee

"I was baptized a member of the Church on June 9, 1907, at Clifton, Idaho, by Lester Bybee. The place was known as 'Bybee Pond' at the old lime kiln, located on the Bybee property. This was on a Sunday morning. I was confirmed the same day by Bishop E. G. Farmer." —Harold B. Lee

Spencer W. Kimball
Age   8 years on his birthday
Date   28 March 1903
Place   Family Bathtub,
        Thatcher, Arizona
By   Andrew Kimball
Age   12 years 6 months
Date   October 5, 1907
Place   Union Canal,
        Thatcher, Arizona
By   George A. Hoopes

(Above) Spencer W. Kimball at the site of his second baptism, the Union Canal, in Thatcher, Arizona, about 1980. Because his father stood outside the family bathtub when Spencer was baptized on his eight birthday, it was thought to ensure that the ordinance was performed correctly that Spencer should be baptized again. Twelve-year-old Spencer was baptized again in the Union Canal just a block away from his home (Courtesy Edward L. Kimball)

Ezra Taft Benson
Age   8 years on his birthday
Date   August 4, 1907
Place   Logan River Canal,
        Logan, Utah
By   George Taft Benson

Howard W. Hunter
Age   12 years 5 months
Date   April 4, 1920
Place   Natatorium swimming pool,
        Boise, Idaho
By   George W. Willis

Gordon B. Hinckley
Age   8 years 10 months
Date   April 28, 1919
Place   Deseret Gym swimming pool,
        Salt Lake City, Utah
By   Bryant S. Hinckley

BISHOPS AND STAKE PRESIDENTS

Pasadena Stake presidency: Oaken Broadhead, Howard W. Hunter (stake president), Kay Berry, and Emron Jones, March 1950 (Church Archives)

President David O. McKay visiting with stake leaders in the Salt Lake Valley (Counselor Gordon B. Hinckley later served as Stake President, far right) in the early 1950s (Office of the President)

PRESIDENTS WHO SERVED AS A BISHOP OR STAKE PRESIDENT

Joseph Smith
Stake president (while serving as president of the Church)
Kirtland [Ohio] Stake

Heber J. Grant
Stake president • Tooele [Utah] Stake

Harold B. Lee
Stake president • Pioneer [Utah] Stake

Spencer W. Kimball
Stake president • Mount Graham [Arizona] Stake

Ezra Taft Benson
Stake president • Boise [Idaho] Stake • Washington, D.C. Stake

Howard W. Hunter
Bishop • El Sereno [California] Ward
Stake president • Pasadena [California] Stake

Gordon B. Hinckley
Stake president • East Millcreek [Utah] Stake

When I was first made a stake president, we had two very large and worrisome projects. The first was to build a stake center. In those days we raised 50 percent of the money and handled the contracting, architectural services, and other things ourselves. The second consuming project was a large welfare farm. I said to my first counselor, who was a builder, "You take care of the new building. This will be your responsibility. I will come and drive some nails and do what I can, but the construction of this stake center is your responsibility." He did it. He did it much better than I could have done it. That stake center is still one of the finest in the Church. To the second I said, "The stake farm is your responsibility. If I get a phone call in the middle of the night that our cows are in the neighbor's corn, I will simply ask the caller to get in touch with you and I will go back to sleep." It worked that way. These two men did the work, and I received the credit. I submit that this is good management. The good executive builds on the strengths of his colleagues.

—Gordon B. Hinckley

Known as one of the most prolific gospel writers of his day, Joseph Fielding Smith learned to love the words of the prophets and apostles, both ancient and modern. He developed a mastery of them through a lifetime of study that began when he was a very young boy. Joseph Fielding Smith recalled, "When I was a small boy, too young to hold the Aaronic Priesthood, my father placed a copy of the Book of Mormon in my hands with the request that I read it." It was not in his nature to reject his father's counsel, so he began in earnest to read from the book, and by the time he was ten years of age, he had read it twice. It set the course of his life as he drank deeply from the well of the scriptures. Even as a young man, he often hurried to finish his chores or leave a ball game early so he could spend more time with the scriptures.

Throughout adolescence, he continued to grow and mature in the things of the spirit. It was not until January 1896, however, that Joseph Fielding Smith began to understand that his love of the scriptures and the words of the prophet were given him for a greater purpose. On January 19, he received a patriarchal blessing under the hands of John Smith, the patriarch to the Church and his uncle. He was promised the "privilege to live to a good old age." He was informed that he would "become a mighty man in Israel" and that it was his duty "to sit in counsel with [his] brethren and to preside among the people." Finally, he was told, "It shall be thy duty to travel much at home and abroad, by land and water, laboring in the ministry." The blessing was a prophetic blueprint that was filled in every detail during his nearly ninety-seven years of life.

Following his mission, he began employment at the Church Historian's Office. It was during this service that he received the call to serve in the Quorum of the Twelve Apostles. It was the first and only time in Church history when two brothers served simultaneously in the Quorum of the Twelve (Joseph's brother Hyrum Mack had been ordained an apostle nine years earlier). Over the next decades, Joseph Fielding Smith served as Church historian, president of the Genealogical Society, and Salt Lake Temple president.

(Left) 1983 Shauna Clinger portrait of Joseph Fielding Smith (MCHA)

(Above oval) Joseph Fielding Smith, about 1925 (Courtesy Joseph Fielding and Brenda McConkie)

BORN
JULY 19, 1876
SALT LAKE CITY, UTAH

PARENTS
JOSEPH F. AND
JULINA LAMBSON SMITH

BAPTIZED
JULY 19, 1884
(AGE 8)

STATURE
5' 10"
165 POUNDS

MARRIED
APRIL 26, 1898
TO LOUIE EMILY
(EMYLA) SHURTLIFF
(AGE 21)

APOSTLE
APRIL 7, 1910
(AGE 33)

PRESIDENT
JANUARY 23, 1970
(AGE 93)

DIED
JULY 2, 1972
SALT LAKE CITY, UTAH
(AGE 95)

Portrait of Joseph Fielding Smith as an infant, about 1878 (Dan Weggland, MCHA)

Charles R. Savage photograph of Joseph Fielding Smith about five years of age, from the photograph section of the Joseph F. and Julina Smith family Bible (Courtesy Mary Louise Richardson Walker)

His work in the Church Historian's office yielded important benefits to himself and, eventually, to the Church in general. It was during his service there that Joseph Fielding Smith and his assistants compiled *Teachings of the Prophet Joseph Smith*, published in 1938. It was a landmark publication. He wrote at the time, "It is felt that this volume will meet a need and promote faith among the members of the Church. With this intent it is sent out on its mission as another testimony of the divine calling of the Prophet Joseph Smith." *Teachings* was not his first publication, nor was it his last. In the end, Joseph Fielding Smith published some twenty-five books on doctrine, scripture, and Church history—by far the most prolific writer among the General Authorities. Among his

1876
July 19 • Born in Salt Lake City
Philadelphia hosts the Centennial Exposition

1877
Aug. 29 • Brigham Young dies
Gunfight at the O.K. Corral (1881)

1884
July 19 • Baptized in Salt Lake City
Statue of Liberty dedicated, New York (1886)

1887
July 25 • John Taylor dies
Whitcomb Judson introduces the zipper (1891)

1896
Jan. 19 • Receives patriarchal blessing with great promises
Boston Marathon begins (1897)

1898
Apr. 26 • Marries Louie Emily Shurtliff (dies March 30, 1908)
Sept. 2 • Wilford Woodruff dies
United States obtains Philippines, Samoa, Guam, and Puerto Rico (1899)

1899–1901
Mission to Great Britain

1901
Begins employment in Church Historian's Office
Oct. 10 • Lorenzo Snow dies
Edward VII becomes king of England

1908
Nov. 2 • Marries Ethel Georgina Reynolds (dies August 26, 1937)
Gideons begin placing Bibles in hotel rooms

1910
Apr. 7 • Ordained an apostle
Panama Canal opens (1914)

1918
Nov. 19 • Joseph F. Smith dies
U.S. population: 105,710,620 (1920)

1921–70
Church historian

1922
Publishes his first book, ***Essentials in Church History***
Howard Carter discovers King Tutankhamen's tomb, Egypt

1938
Apr. 12 • Marries Jessie Evans (dies August 3, 1971)
Selects, arranges, and publishes ***Teachings of the Prophet Joseph Smith***
Hahn and Strassman demonstrate nuclear fission

1939
Directs evacuation of missionaries from Europe

1944
June 4 • Begins radio program "The Restoration of All Things"

1945
May 14 • Heber J. Grant dies
World leaders create the United Nations

"MY DARLING JOSEPH F."

Shortly after his baptism on July 19, 1884, Joseph Fielding Smith received a letter from his father, affectionately known as "Papa" by his children. Joseph F. Smith, a counselor in the First Presidency, was "underground," avoiding federal officers who were trying to arrest him for plural marriage at the time. He secretly visited Salt Lake City in July and performed this sacred ordinance for his son on his birthday in City Creek, a traditional baptism site in Salt Lake City, and then quietly left his family, returning to a hiding place from where he wrote this tender letter. In it, Joseph F. Smith provides tender counsel and direction to his young son: "You know you have been baptized and will soon be a big boy, and the greatest desire of my heart for you, my son, is that you may be a good, pure and wise man, so that if the Lord needs you for any good work in the church and kingdom of God, you will be worthy of God's pleasure and commands, and willing always to respond [to] the authority of the Priesthood, and the requirements of heaven." During the rest of Joseph F. Smith's life, he continued to provide encouragement, counsel, and direction to his son through numerous letters when they were apart from each other, especially during Joseph Fielding Smith's mission to the British Isles (1899–1901). These letters not only became a precious personal treasure but also provided timely and inspired direction from a loving father who continued to influence Joseph Fielding Smith even after his death in 1918.

(Right) Letter to Joseph Fielding Smith from his father, Joseph F. Smith dated November 13, 1884 (Courtesy Amelia Smith McConkie)

1945–49	1965	1968	1971
President of Salt Lake Temple	Oct. 29 • Counselor to David O.	Aug. 3 • Dedicates and breaks	Jan. • *Ensign, New Era,* and *Friend*
Charles "Chuck" Yeager breaks sound barrier (1947)	McKay in First Presidency	ground at several Missouri historical sites	begin publication
	1963	*Martin Luther King Jr.*	Aug. 27–29 • Presides at first area conference, Manchester, England
1951	Sept. 15 • Dedicates Liberty	*assassinated*	Church membership exceeds
Apr. 4 • George Albert Smith dies	Jail Visitors' Center		3,000,000
Edmund Hillary makes first successful climb of Mt. Everest (1953)	1965	1970	*World Population: 4,026,680,026*
	Oct. 29 • Additional counselor	Jan. 18 • David O. McKay dies	
1954	in First Presidency	Jan. 23 • Ordained president	1972
Bookcraft releases first volume	*Winston Churchill dies*	of the Church	Jan. 18 • Dedicates Ogden Temple
of *Doctrines of Salvation*		Mar. 15 • First stake in Asia	Feb. 9 • Dedicates Provo Temple
	1966	created, Tokyo, Japan	July 2 • Dies in Salt Lake City
1955	Jun. 1–2 • Accompanies President	Mar. 22 • First stake in Africa	*U.S. President Richard M. Nixon*
Aug. 25 • Dedicates Guam for	McKay on visit to historic sites	created, Transvaal, South Africa	*visits China*
the preaching of the gospel	in Missouri	*Soviet Spacecraft lands on Venus*	
Russian Cosmonaut Yuri A. Gagarin orbits earth (1961)			

published works are also the words to four hymns sung by members of the Church over the years, including one that is printed in the current Church hymnal (1985 edition), "Does the Journey Seem Long?"

His brief ministry as Church president began on January 23, 1970, just days after David O. McKay passed away. During the next twenty-nine months, Joseph Fielding Smith helped the Church prepare more adequately to deal with its international growth and the challenges of a modern age, which often had little respect for religious belief and practice. He held the first area conference (in Manchester, England, in August 1971) so that members who would never have an opportunity to gather in large numbers to worship with the Saints at general conference in Salt Lake City could have a similar experience near their homes. He officially set aside Monday evenings for Family Home Evening. He oversaw the introduction of the current English language Church publications, the *Ensign*, *New Era*, and *Friend*. And he called the first health-service missionaries, who helped to meet the needs of developing nations.

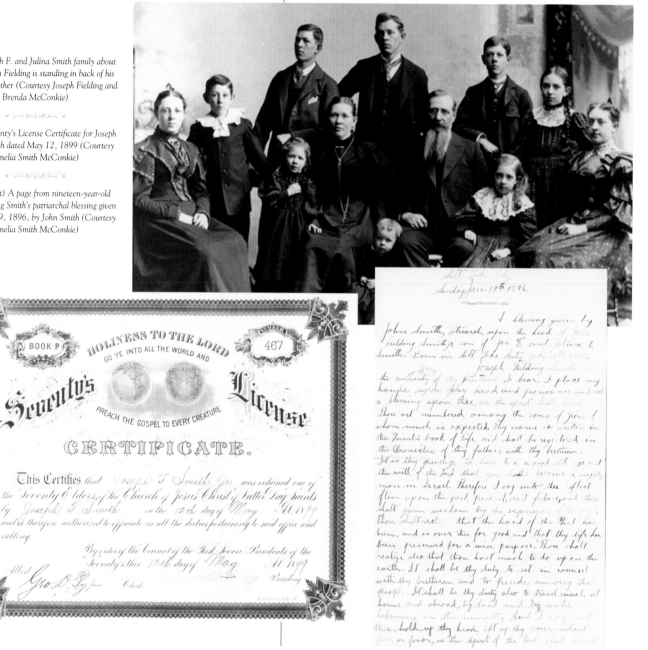

(Right) Joseph F. and Julina Smith family about 1898; Joseph Fielding is standing in back of his father and mother (Courtesy Joseph Fielding and Brenda McConkie)

(Below) Seventy's License Certificate for Joseph Fielding Smith dated May 12, 1899 (Courtesy Amelia Smith McConkie)

(Lower right) A page from nineteen-year-old Joseph Fielding Smith's patriarchal blessing given on January 19, 1896, by John Smith (Courtesy Amelia Smith McConkie)

Joseph Fielding Smith's presidency was a busy and productive period of his life. It was, however, brief. Just two days before the Fourth of July in 1972, President Smith sat in his favorite black vinyl recliner chair on a Sunday evening. The chair had been brought to his daughter Amelia Smith McConkie's home when he moved in following his wife's death almost a year earlier. Joseph Fielding Smith had attended church, visited family members, and eaten a light dinner around 7:30 P.M. He was enjoying a delightful conversation with his daughter, who was also writing a few letters at the time. Amelia left the room briefly to obtain a few addresses that she needed for her letters. Before she returned, Joseph Fielding Smith slipped away, just a few weeks short of his ninety-sixth birthday. His son-in-law, Bruce R. McConkie, who was at home at the time, described the sacred moment: "His passing was as sweet and easy, as calm and as peaceful as though he had fallen asleep, which he had. . . . Truly when the Lord took his prophet, there was no sting. President Smith did not taste of death."

Joseph F. Smith Jr. signature; he was known as Joseph F. Smith Jr. from his birth until the time of his father's death in November 1918 (Courtesy R.Q. and Susan Shupe)

Joseph Fielding Smith as a missionary in England the year after he was married, about 1899 (J. T. Hillen, courtesy Amelia Smith McConkie)

Joseph Fielding Smith a few years after his appointment to the Quorum of the Twelve in 1910 (Courtesy Alice Barratt Smith)

To my Darling Rachel from Her loving Papa and Brother

ANSWERS TO GOSPEL QUESTIONS

During his ministry, Joseph Fielding Smith received numerous letters from Church members and others. His responses became the basis for a series of articles published in a Church periodical beginning in May 1953 titled "Your Questions." Later the series became the basis of a five-volume work, *Answers to Gospel Questions*, published in 1957.

Mrs. Eva R. Ellison
1243 6 Avenue A South
Lethbridge, Alberta
November 2, 1955

RECEIVED
NOV 4 - 1955
Joseph Fielding Smith

Elder Jos. Fielding Smith
Church Offices
East South Temple Street
Salt Lake City, Utah

Dear Brother Smith:

Knowing how very busy you are, I hesitate to intrude upon your time, but I need an answer to a question, and since you have clarified so many points through your writings, I take the liberty of asking you to clear up another question.

In our Mutual class last evening, I quoted Lorenzo Snow's couplet "As man now is, God once was: As God now is, man may be". I am aware that this is not found in our Standard Works, but since it was quoted by one of our Church Presidents who said just prior to his death that nothing had ever been revealed more distinctly to him than this knowledge; and since the Prophet Joseph Smith, upon hearing it from Bro. Snow, replied: "Brother Snow, that is a true gospel doctrine, and it is a revelation from God to you", I have more or less come to consider these lines as scripture. In quoting them, I referred to them as scripture. I was immediately taken to task and told that this was not scripture. I did not make an issue of it, as I couldn't see that it was necessary. However, I would like to know if the Church considers this scripture? I have been led to believe that we have much scripture which is not contained in the Four Standard Books. Am I wrong in this also?

If I have stated something which is not correct, I should like to clear it up in our class. I am the ward Gleaner Leader and it is a real challenge to work with these alert young people and I try to be so careful not to misinterpret or teach "false doctrine". Therefore, I shall appreciate your help when you find time to give me.

With best regards to you and Sister Smith. We have many fond memories of your visits with us, and we pray for your well being.

Sincerely your sister,

Eva R. Ellison

see reverse

ANSWER:

The Lord has revealed that those who are faithful and true in the keeping of his commandments should be exalted and become his sons and his daughters and be like him. (See 1 John 3:1-3. Romans 8:13-17. John 10:35-36.)

The Prophet Joseph Smith taught, as did Paul and others including our Lord, that we may become like God by obedience to his will, thus he will give us all things pertaining to his kingdom. (D.&.C. 84:38,Rev. 21:?) Then we will be like him. We are also taught that the Father passed through a course similiar to that of Jesus Christ. So the Prophet taught us. President Snow put this doctrine into this couplet. I wish our missionaries would not use it, as they are not always able to defend it.

Sincerely,

Joseph Fielding Smith

(Above) Joseph Fielding Smith about the time of his call to serve as president of the Quorum of the Twelve (Courtesy Gregory P. and MarJane Christofferson)

(Top right) Eva R. Ellison letter to Joseph Fielding Smith, 1965 (Courtesy Gregory P. and MarJane Christofferson)

(Right) Joseph Fielding Smith's response to Eva R. Ellison's letter, typed on the back of her inquiry, 1965 (Courtesy Gregory P. and MarJane Christofferson)

(Below) Joseph Fielding Smith at his typewriter, about 1953 (Courtesy Amilia Smith McConkie)

(Lower right) Joseph Fielding Smith's typewriter and desk (MCHA)

THE CHURCH OF JESUS CHRIST OF LATTER-DAY SAINTS
OFFICE OF THE FIRST PRESIDENCY
SALT LAKE CITY, UTAH 84111
September 7, 1967

Elder Clarence F. Robison
1682 West 900 North
Provo, Utah 84601

Dear Brother Robison:

With the ever increasing growth of the Church there becomes evident a greater need to train our stake and ward leaders in the programs of the Church that they in turn might train the membership in their responsibilities before the Lord.

To assist in accomplishing this we are calling a number of brethren to serve as Regional Priesthood Representatives of the Twelve to work with the leadership of the stakes. You have been recommended by the Twelve to serve in this important capacity. We earnestly hope that you are in a position to respond to this call.

Those so called will be expected to give Church service time only, as do bishops and stake presidents. However, it will be necessary that they be released from other Church administrative responsibilities. Furthermore, it is anticipated that there will be a rotation of these assignments from time to time with no fixed term of service.

This new program will be announced at the forthcoming General Conference. Until then we ask that it not be discussed with others. A special seminar for the brethren called to this responsibility will be held September 27 and 28, 1967, in Salt Lake City. You will receive from the office of the Council of Twelve further particulars concerning these training meetings.

It is hoped that you will be able to arrange your affairs to permit your attendance on these two days preceding the conference and on the Monday following the conference when a brief summary session will be held.

Will you please indicate by return mail your willingness to respond to this call. Should your circumstances make it infeasible so to serve, we shall welcome a confidential statement concerning the circumstances.

We repose in you our confidence and extend our appreciation for your devoted service in the cause of the Master.

Sincerely yours,

THE FIRST PRESIDENCY

By *David O. McKay*

Hugh B Brown

N. Eldon Tanner

Joseph Fielding Smith

COUNSELOR IN THE FIRST PRESIDENCY

On October 29, 1965, Joseph Fielding Smith was set apart as a third counselor to David O. McKay, with Thorpe B. Isaacson being set apart as a fourth counselor. At the first meeting of the enlarged First Presidency just over a month later, President McKay said, "I welcome you as counselors in the First Presidency and acknowledge with hesitancy that I am not so well as I used to be and called you brethren as counselors in the First Presidency to help carry the work. I pray the Lord's blessing to attend us in this quorum of the First Presidency. It is nothing new in the Church. The Prophet Joseph Smith had several counselors; President Brigham Young had seven at one time, I think; and this will constitute the quorum of the First Presidency. I should like to meet regularly with you and to take up matters . . . as the occasion requires." Joseph Fielding Smith served faithfully as a counselor while continuing his responsibilities as Church historian and president of the Twelve until President McKay's death in 1970.

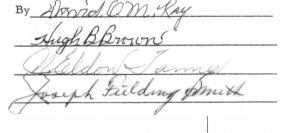

Joseph Fielding Smith was called as an additional counselor in the First Presidency on October 29, 1965. This letter, dated September 7, 1967, is signed by all members of the First Presidency, including Joseph Fielding Smith, calling Clarence Robison as a regional representative, a new administrative position announced a few weeks later to the body of the Church. (Courtesy Monita Turley Robison)

(Above) Joseph Fielding and Jesse Ella Evans Smith, June 3, 1971
(Courtesy Joseph Fielding and Brenda McConkie)

(Above right) Joseph Fielding and Jesse Ella Evans Smith with great-granddaughter
Sherrie, June 3, 1971 (Courtesy Joseph Fielding and Brenda McConkie)

(Above) View of Joseph Fielding Smith and Derek A. Cuthbert in a rose garden
in Manchester, England. President Smith was in the British Isles presiding over
the Church's first area conference in August 1971 (Church Archives)

(Right) Missionary certificate signed by Joseph Fielding Smith,
October 14, 1971 (Courtesy T. Jeffery Cottle)

ELDER T. JEFFERY COTTLE'S MISSIONARY JOURNAL

Fort Lauderdale, Florida Mission, July 3, 1972 Monday

Got up at 6:30, had personal study, ate, had study class. Went tracting and left one Family Home Evening book. A clerk at the post office told us that the Prophet Joseph Fielding Smith had died. So we went home and listened on Elder Moser's radio and confirmed he had. He was a great man. Went down to the doctor's and got Elder Moser's shot and went looking up some [copies of the Book of Mormon] that we had placed. Went home, ate, went to Mrs. Payne's home. Wanted to give her the scroll we had done for her. She wasn't home. It really started to rain and rained most of the night. I bought a paper to see about the prophet. Studied in bed.

> "I think the thing I
> like most about Christmas is
> the children," President Smith
> said, as he squeezed his
> great-granddaughter
> closer to him.

JOSEPH FIELDING SMITH'S FAMILY

Like his father before him, Joseph Fielding Smith carried the spirit of Church patriarch Hyrum Smith, his grandfather. Faithful and loyal, Hyrum was the Prophet Joseph Smith's elder brother, counselor, friend, and co-martyr at Carthage Jail. Joseph Fielding Smith's ministry was greatly influenced by Hyrum's dedication to the Restoration. Born in 1876, Joseph Fielding Smith was the son of Joseph F. and Julina Lambson Smith, the fourth of thirteen children. Brigham Young was still president of the Church, the Salt Lake Temple was nearly twenty years from completion, and America was celebrating its first hundred years. He grew up in Salt Lake City among a large extended family. He married Louie E. Shurtliff on April 26, 1898, just a little more than a year before leaving on a mission to the British Isles. The couple had two children before Louie died in March 1908. In November of that same year, Joseph married Ethel G. Reynolds. Before her death in August 1937, nine more children were added to the family. Finally, Joseph Fielding Smith married Jessie Ella Evans, known affectionately as "Aunt Jessie" by family members, in 1938. She was his constant companion until her death in 1971, just a year before Joseph Fielding Smith passed away in July 1972. His love for his children, grandchildren, and great-grandchildren was a constant source of joy, happiness, and comfort, especially during the periods of mourning following the death of each of his three wives. He was a solicitous father. As his daughter Ethel recalled, "When illness comes, the man I know watches tenderly over the afflicted one and waits upon him. It is their father for whom they cry, feeling his presence a panacea for all ills. It is his hands that bind up the wounds, his arms that give courage to the suffered." During the few occasions when correction was needed, again it was a kind and thoughtful father whose worst rebuke was to place his hands on a child's shoulders and say, "I wish my kiddies would be good."

JOSEPH FIELDING MCCONKIE

My Mission Call
June 1960

After completing my first year at BYU I returned home to Salt Lake City. My father said, "Now, son get out and get a job," and I said, "Dad, I want to go on a mission." He said, "You can't go on a mission" [at that time missionaries were not called until the age of twenty]. I protested, and said, "I want to go on a mission." Within a week I was interviewed and entered the mission home. Before I left we went to visit my Grandfather, Joseph Fielding

(Above) Joseph Fielding Smith and Joseph Fielding McConkie, June 1960 (Courtesy Joseph Fielding and Brenda McConkie)

Smith. We were going to announce that I was going on a mission. As we approached his door, my father said to me, "You be very careful what you say to your Grandfather." "Why?" I asked. "Because he doesn't approve of nineteen-year-old missionaries," was the response. We started to talk about mission work when all of a sudden Granddaddy got a real stern look on his face and everything stopped. Time stopped, people stopped breathing— the whole world stood still, and he looked at me very seriously and said, "Young man, how old are you?" I smiled and said, "Well, Granddaddy, I'm in my 20th year." (I'd learned that from reading the Joseph Smith story.) He smiled and nodded his head. The clock began to tick again, all present began to breathe again, and the world commenced again to rotate on its axis. [Elder Joseph Fielding McConkie labored in the North British Mission; shortly thereafter, the Church started calling nineteen-year-old young men to serve full-time missions].

D. Arthur Haycock spent six months trying to get a job in 1938. Finally a break came when he was hired to work in the Finance Department of the Church. One afternoon following lunch at the Lion House, he saw someone heading up the back stairs of the Church Administration Building next door. Hoping to avoid the effort to locate his keys to get into the building, he hurried up the same stairs and caught the door just before it locked shut. As he approached the elevator in the building, he discovered that it was Joseph Fielding Smith who had gone through the door and was now keeping the elevator door open long enough for him get in. As the two men rode together, young Arthur thought he would have a little fun with Elder Smith, saying, "I just followed you in the back door and caught the elevator door before it closed. I'm kind of hoping that's how it will be on the other side. If I can catch the pearly gates before they close behind someone like you, I may make it." Elder Smith did not reply immediately, but as the elevator door opened and he stepped out, he looked Arthur up and down and said, "If I were you, my brother, I wouldn't count on it." Joseph Fielding Smith winked as he replied, giving Arthur a glimpse of a man that took gospel principles very seriously but could, when occasion warranted, provide a little humor for those around him.

AN INVITATION

Joseph Fielding Smith, President of The Church of Jesus Christ of Latter-day Saints, April 1972

During his last General Conference before his death, Joseph Fielding Smith, solemnly, yet with prophetic authority, invited the world to become disciples of Jesus Christ: "There is no cure for the ills of the world except the gospel of Jesus Christ. . . . And so we invite all our Father's children, everywhere, to believe in Christ, to receive him as he is revealed by living prophets, and to join The Church of Jesus Christ of Latter-day Saints. . . . To the honest in heart in all nations we say: The Lord loves you. He wants you to receive the full blessings of the gospel."

State of the Church at the time of Joseph Fielding Smith's death	
Year of death	1972
Church membership	3,218,908
Stakes	581
Temples	15
Missions	101
Missionaries set apart during administration	16,218
Book of Mormon translations completed during administration	1

PROPHETS AT HOME

It may be hard for Church members to realize that each president of the Church has faced the challenges of raising a family and building a place called home. In some ways, the prophet and his family face the additional burden of public exposure, which often places them under a magnifying glass. The demanding duties of Church service, which include many weekends away from home, certainly affects the way they feel and interact at home. During their busy ministries, the prophets found great satisfaction in being with family members and spending time at home. Joseph Smith wrote of such an experience in 1835, "At home all this day and enjoyed myself with my family, it being Christmas day the only time I have had this privilege so satisfactorily for a long time." Each prophet has attempted to balance his prophetic responsibilities to the world and the responsibilities and enjoyment of family and home. Of course, some prophets like Joseph Smith and Brigham Young, had young children living with them during their service,

providing them with a distinctly different experience, while others were already grandparents and great-grandparents at the time of their call to lead the Church. For some the house that had been home was eventually sold as their duties in the First Presidency and age pressed upon them. President Gordon B. Hinckley recalls his feelings moving from their home to an apartment:

"We built this home [and] eleven-and-a-half years ago, I planted trees. They have now grown large. . . . We have many quaking aspens, we have shrubs of various varieties, we have three peach trees that bear fruit, four apple trees, three plums, three cherries. When we move into the apartment we will have none of these, and we will miss them. But we will not miss the hundreds of thousands of leaves that fall from them in the autumn. Still, as I walked about the place today . . . thoughts came into my mind concerning whether we are doing the right thing. . . . Only my age prompts me in this direction."

(Above) Wilford Woodruff home, known as the "Woodruff Villa," built in 1892 on 500 East near 1700 South in Salt Lake City (Church Archives)

(Left) "Families are Forever" sign from the Howard W. Hunter Home (MCHA)

(Above) Brigham Young, Lorenzo Snow, and Joseph F. Smith lived in the Beehive House, which served as the president's official residency during their ministries. These two early interior views were taken sometime during the seventeen years when Joseph F. Smith's family occupied the home. (Courtesy Miriam Taylor Meads)

(Left) George Albert Smith greeting Christmas visitors at his home, about 1948 (Church Archives)

(Lower left) Gate to the McKay Home in Huntsville, Utah. David O. and Emma Riggs McKay lived in Salt Lake City following David's call to the Quorum of the Twelve. However, the old homestead in Huntsville continued to be a gathering place for their family. (Church Archives)

(Below) "The Family: A Proclamation to the World," only the fifth such proclamation issued in this dispensation, was announced in the fall of 1995 emphasizing the importance of family and home. (Church Archives)

THE FAMILY

A PROCLAMATION TO THE WORLD

THE FIRST PRESIDENCY AND COUNCIL OF THE TWELVE APOSTLES OF THE CHURCH OF JESUS CHRIST OF LATTER-DAY SAINTS

WE, THE FIRST PRESIDENCY and the Council of the Twelve Apostles of The Church of Jesus Christ of Latter-day Saints, solemnly proclaim that marriage between a man and a woman is ordained of God and that the family is central to the Creator's plan for the eternal destiny of His children.

ALL HUMAN BEINGS—male and female—are created in the image of God. Each is a beloved spirit son or daughter of heavenly parents, and, as such, each has a divine nature and destiny. Gender is an essential characteristic of individual premortal, mortal, and eternal identity and purpose.

IN THE PREMORTAL REALM, spirit sons and daughters knew and worshiped God as their Eternal Father and accepted His plan by which His children could obtain a physical body and gain earthly experience to progress toward perfection and ultimately realize his or her divine destiny as an heir of eternal life. The divine plan of happiness enables family relationships to be perpetuated beyond the grave. Sacred ordinances and covenants available in holy temples make it possible for individuals to return to the presence of God and for families to be united eternally.

THE FIRST COMMANDMENT that God gave to Adam and Eve pertained to their potential for parenthood as husband and wife. We declare that God's commandment for His children to multiply and replenish the earth remains in force. We further declare that God has commanded that the sacred powers of procreation are to be employed only between man and woman, lawfully wedded as husband and wife.

WE DECLARE the means by which mortal life is created to be divinely appointed. We affirm the sanctity of life and of its importance in God's eternal plan.

HUSBAND AND WIFE have a solemn responsibility to love and care for each other and for their children. "Children are an heritage of the Lord" (Psalms 127:3). Parents have a sacred duty to rear their children in love and righteousness, to provide for their physical and spiritual needs, to teach them to love and serve one another, to observe the commandments of God and to be law-abiding citizens wherever they live. Husbands and wives—mothers and fathers—will be held accountable before God for the discharge of these obligations.

THE FAMILY is ordained of God. Marriage between man and woman is essential to His eternal plan. Children are entitled to birth within the bonds of matrimony, and to be reared by a father and a mother who honor marital vows with complete fidelity. Happiness in family life is most likely to be achieved when founded upon the teachings of the Lord Jesus Christ. Successful marriages and families are established and maintained on principles of faith, prayer, repentance, forgiveness, respect, love, compassion, work, and wholesome recreational activities. By divine design, fathers are to preside over their families in love and righteousness and are responsible to provide the necessities of life and protection for their families. Mothers are primarily responsible for the nurture of their children. In these sacred responsibilities, fathers and mothers are obligated to help one another as equal partners. Disability, death, or other circumstances may necessitate individual adaptation. Extended families should lend support when needed.

WE WARN that individuals who violate covenants of chastity, who abuse spouse or offspring, or who fail to fulfill family responsibilities will one day stand accountable before God. Further, we warn that the disintegration of the family will bring upon individuals, communities, and nations the calamities foretold by ancient and modern prophets.

WE CALL UPON responsible citizens and officers of government everywhere to promote those measures designed to maintain and strengthen the family as the fundamental unit of society.

This proclamation was read by President Gordon B. Hinckley as part of his message at the General Relief Society Meeting held September 23, 1995, in Salt Lake City, Utah.

Harold B. Lee

H arold B. Lee was a Salt Lake City commissioner and local stake president in April 1935. Times were hard, and people throughout the world were struggling to survive the effects of the Great Depression. The citizens of Utah had been hit hard by the economic reversals since the collapse of the U.S. stock market in 1929. There was great suffering among the Saints. Harold recalled, "We had been wrestling with this question of welfare." The situation was grave. In his stake alone, more than half the nearly eight thousand members were wholly or partially dependent for support. At this time Harold was invited to meet with the First Presidency to discuss what he had been doing in his stake to relieve the suffering. "It was Saturday morning," he recalled. "There were no calls on their calendar, and for hours in that forenoon they talked with me." Eventually, the First Presidency asked Harold to resign from the city commission and indicated that they were releasing him from being stake president since they wanted him "to head up the welfare movement to turn the tide from government relief, direct relief, and help to put the Church in a position where it could take care of its own needy."

Harold was overwhelmed by the magnitude of the assignment he received from his priesthood leader. He was a young man, only thirty-six years of age at the time, with limited experience. Born in a small town in Idaho, Harold had hardly traveled beyond the political boundaries of Utah and Idaho. When he thought about it, it was almost too much to contemplate; the Presidency wanted him "to reach out to the entire membership of the Church."

When he left the Church Administration Building that morning, Harold did what he had done many times before: he turned to the Lord for help and direction. "After that morning I rode in my car (spring was just breaking) up to the head of City Creek Canyon into what was then called Rotary Park; and there, all by myself, I offered one of the most humble prayers of my life."

He recalled with vivid detail what happened next: "There came to me on that glorious morning one of the most heavenly realizations of the power of the priesthood of God. It was as though something were saying to me, 'There is no new organization necessary to take care of the needs of this people. All that is necessary is to put the priesthood of God to work. There is nothing else that you need as a substitute.'"

(Left) Portrait of Harold B. Lee by Knud Edsberg (MCHA)

(Above oval) Portrait of Harold B. Lee by David Ahrnsbrak, 1984 (MCHA)

BORN
MARCH 28, 1899
CLIFTON, IDAHO

PARENTS
SAMUEL MARION
AND LOUISA BINGHAM LEE

BAPTIZED
JUNE 9, 1907
(AGE 8)

STATURE
5' 9"
175 POUNDS

MARRIED
NOVEMBER 14, 1923
TO FERN LUCINDA TANNER
(AGE 24)

APOSTLE
APRIL 10, 1941
(AGE 42)

PRESIDENT
JULY 7, 1972
(AGE 73)

DIED
DECEMBER 26, 1973
SALT LAKE CITY, UTAH
(AGE 74)

This was not the first time Harold demonstrated a deep spiritual nature that allowed him to receive the word of the Lord. When he was about eight years of age, his father took him to a farm some distance away from their home. Harold recalled, "While he worked I tried to busy myself with things that a young boy would. The day was hot and dusty and I played about until I was tired. Over the fence there was a broken-down shed that looked very interesting to me. In my mind I thought of this broken-down shed as a castle that I would like to explore, so I went to the fence and started to climb through to go over to that shed."

It was in that instant that a voice came to him: "Harold, don't go over there." The boy looked around to see who was speaking. He knew that his father was at the other end of the field and could not possibly have seen what he was doing. He reflected for a moment and then realized, "Someone that I could not see was warning me not to go over there." He obeyed and left immediately. He noted, "Maybe the

Harold, Clyde, and Perry Lee, 1904 (Courtesy L. Brent Goates)

timbers would fall down and crush me. Maybe there were poisonous snakes or a rusty nail that I might step on. I do not know, but someone must have known."

His sensitivity to the Spirit did not come without continued effort on his part. He reveals the struggle when reflecting on his call to the apostleship in 1941: "No sleep came that night. My wife became anxious and wanted me to take something to induce me to go to sleep. But I said, 'No, I don't want to miss any moment of the experience that I am having tonight.' It seemed as though the whole panorama of my life was passing before me that night. I think I could have told you everyone against whom I had any kind of grievance. I think I could have remembered those who may have had any grievance against me, and the thought came to me that before I could be worthy to accept the position of a member of the Twelve Apostles, I must love and forgive every soul that walked the earth."

Harold continued to develop this sensitivity to the

(Above) The Lee Family in 1941 (Courtesy L. Brent Goates)

(Left) Harold B. Lee (center) and fellow missionaries, about 1921 (Courtesy L. Brent Goates)

whisperings of the Spirit and the nearness of the Lord and his messengers. Later, he related an experience he had while traveling across-country by airplane in 1967. He was on his way home, sick and in trouble, when someone laid hands upon Harold's head. Harold looked up but saw no one. He reflected in a general conference address in 1973: "That happened again before we arrived home, again with the same experience. Who it was, by what means or what medium, I may never know, except I knew that I was receiving a blessing that I came a few hours later to know I needed most desperately."

Shortly after he arrived home, there came "massive hemorrhages which, had they occurred while we were in flight, I wouldn't be here today talking about it."

When he was called to be president of the Church he had another sacred experience: "On the early morning [after his ordination] with my wife I kneeled in humble prayer, and suddenly it seemed as though my mind and heart went out to over three million people in the entire world. I seemed to have a love for every one of them no matter where they lived nor what their color was, whether they were rich or poor, whether they were humble

1951
Apr. 4 • George Albert Smith dies
First Canadian TV stations begin broadcasting (1952)

1954
June 15 • Begins teaching CES teachers, BYU
Fall • Visits Asian members and military service personnel (Korea)
Ray Kroc founds McDonald Corporation (1955)

1958
Oct. 28–30 • Visits Holy Land

1959
Aug.–Nov. • Visits Central and South American members and missionaries
Harold Maiman invents first operable laser (1960)

1961
Directs development of correlation program

1963
June 17 • Marries Freda Joan Jensen
U.S. presidential candidate Robert F. Kennedy assassinated (1968)

1970
Jan. 18 • David O. McKay dies
Jan. 23 • First counselor to Joseph Fielding Smith

1971
Sept. 4 • Meets with Apollo 15 astronauts, Salt Lake City
Sony introduces the VCR

1972
July 2 • Joseph Fielding Smith dies
July 7 • Ordained president of the Church
July 24 • Participates in Days of '47 pioneer parade, Salt Lake City
Aug. 26–28 • Presides at Second Area Conference, Mexico City, Mexico
Sept. • Visits Europe and Holy Land, the first president to visit the Holy Land
Nov. 10 • Announces creation of Aaronic Priesthood MIA
World Population: 4,085,399,763

1973
Feb. • Sends first agricultural missionaries to South America
Mar. 8 • First mainland Asia stake created, Seoul, Korea
Apr. 7 • Announces creation of Welfare Services Department
Dec. 26 • Dies in Salt Lake City
Arab-Israeli War breaks out

Harold B. Lee at the time of his call to the apostleship in 1941 (Courtesy L. Brent Goates)

Harold B. Lee's priesthood line of authority card (Courtesy L. Brent Goates)

or great, or educated or not. Suddenly I felt as though they all belonged to me, as though they were all my own brothers and sisters."

Three months later, Harold Bingham Lee was sustained as the eleventh president of the Church on October 6, 1972. In his address to the congregation on that occasion he said, "Today is the greatest moment of my life. There has been here an overwhelming spiritual endowment, attesting no doubt, that in all likelihood we are in the presence of personages, seen and unseen, who

are in attendance. Who knows but that even our Lord and Master would be near us on such an occasion as this, for we, and the world, must never forget that this is his church, and under his almighty direction we are to serve."

In a final assessment of his life and ministry, D. Arthur Haycock observed, "He was deeply spiritual. He was so close to the other side that he often said that there was no veil." President Marion G. Romney added, "The source of his greatness was his knowledge that he lived in the shadow of the Almighty."

Harold B. Lee and Spencer W. Kimball on a Church assignment in Dallas, Texas, in January 1958, shortly after Spencer W. Kimball had throat surgery. His journal provides the setting for his first address to the Saints and the kindness and attention he received from Elder Lee. (Courtesy L. Brent Goates)

HAROLD B. LEE'S FAMILY

Harold Bingham Lee was the second of six children born to Samuel Marion and Louisa Bingham Lee. The circumstances of his birth in a humble home in Clifton, Idaho, on March 28, 1899, did not draw the attention of millions, but heaven knew and took note.

When he was twenty-four years old, he married Fern Lucinda Tanner on November 14, 1923 (they had two daughters). Following Fern's death in 1962, he married Freda Joan Jensen on June 17, 1963.

(Above left) Harold B. Lee and first wife Fern Lucinda Tanner with British Church leaders and family members in 1958. A handwritten caption on the back states: "Leaving for home on the Queen Elizabeth from Southampton on our return from So. Africa." (Courtesy L. Brent Goates)

(Above right) Harold B. Lee and Freda Joan Jensen on their wedding day, June 17, 1963 (Courtesy L. Brent Goates)

SPENCER W. KIMBALL JOURNAL

January 1958

January 21: I suppose my cold had something to do with it but I had a very difficult time getting started. I gulped and hesitated and started over and over and finally was able to speak with my limitations. They fixed a harness for me with a special mike hanging from my neck. I believe it helped a little. I tried and made almost no sound. I swallowed and gulped and tried again with the same sickening feeling. The thought came: Better quit—you can't do it—you can't impose on the people like this, but I continued to persevere and finally got my voice, not as good as I have had but they heard and I had their attention. It was hard work. I spoke Sat. night to the husbands and wives meeting and had the same difficulty starting until I nearly gave up. . . . I think I spoke less well than I have at home due to the cold. The night from Denver South I got chilled even with the extra blanket and my overcoat. . . . Then I began coughing, and I was uncomfortable all the way to Houston. . . . Then came the back ache which was like a kidney pain. It got progressively worse through Friday and Saturday until Sunday morning when we got through our interviewing at 1 A.M. I could hardly stand it. Brother Lee kept asking if I was alright even after we went to bed. We occupied the same room with twin beds. I tried till three to hide my pain and told him I was fine each time but he was too smart for me. I could find no comfortable position and as I twisted and turned it kept him awake also. I think he attributed it at first to weariness but soon came to realize it was more. He kept asking if there was anything he could do for me and I tried to cover up. I was sure it was serious and that I might be sent to the hospital with all the publicity that would bring and the consequent loss of service and long delayed assignments again. I kept hoping it would cease or that I could contain myself and not reveal my feelings. I could have done it had I had a separate room but the Trunnells have a large family and did well to give us one room. When I realized that I could not stand it longer nor hide it further I finally admitted to him when he asked: "Yes, Brother Lee, I cannot deceive you any longer. I am in terrible pain and have been for two days and nights with hardly a comfortable hour." He had some sleeping pills Dr. [LeRoy] Kimball gave to him. I took one. He came and knelt by my bed and gave me a wonderful blessing and in moments I was relieved and in a while I was asleep and slept for about three hours waking all wet with perspiration. I had had some slight chills the night before which worried me. We went to sleep about 3 A.M. and got up early to attend to the heavy duties of the Sabbath. While I knew the blessing would be efficacious, yet as my first period free from pain and distress lengthened to 6 hours and 8 and 10 and 15 without a return of the backache I came to realize that if the medicine did any good its effect had long before worn off and it was the blessing which had rid me totally of the backache. It has now been three days and two nights and no return. The Lord is so good to me and so far beyond my [deserving]. I have continued to cough considerably but less and less but my voice still is inferior.

Harold B. Lee being sustained as president
of the Church, October 6, 1972
(Courtesy L. Brent Goates)

Testimony

President Harold B. Lee • August 27, 1972

As one who has the responsibility of bearing witness to the divine mission of the Lord, I assure you, my dear faithful brothers and sisters, that I know as I know that I live, that our Lord and Master Jesus Christ, who is the head of this Church, is a living, real personality. There is on every hand evidence of his handiwork, and the nearness to him has given me the strength and the determination to follow where he leads. Again I bear you my testimony as to the divinity of this work. I know with more certainty than I have ever known before that we are engaged in the work of the Lord. Remember that the head of this Church is our Lord and Master, Jesus Christ. I am only presently the presiding authority of this Church. During the experience of these last few weeks, I have come also to know more certainly that the Savior is a real, living personality. To him should we give our loyalty, our faith, and our love. In my responsibility I will endeavor to serve you as I lend all the strength I have to see to it that the work of the Lord will be projected to the fullest extent, as you faithful saints will prepare yourselves to receive all that our Father has in store for his faithful servants.

(Left) "Book of Harold B. Lee" (Courtesy L. Brent Goates)

(Above) First Presidency and wives, Pioneer Day parade, Salt Lake City, 1973 (Courtesy L. Brent Goates)

Harold B. Lee had his secretary carefully take apart his scriptures so he could add pages on which he copied extracts from books and talks of Church leaders and scholars on specific doctrinal topics. He was well known for his gospel scholarship and his ability to answer questions asked by members of the Church, especially the missionaries.

(Left) President Harold B. Lee, about 1972 (Courtesy L. Brent Goates)

(Below) Mission call extended to Elder Neitzel, dated July 25, 1973, signed by President Harold B. Lee (Courtesy Richard Neitzel Holzapfel)

THE CHURCH OF JESUS CHRIST OF LATTER-DAY SAINTS
OFFICE OF THE FIRST PRESIDENCY
SALT LAKE CITY, UTAH 84111

July 25, 1973

Elder Richard Charles Neitzel
Portsmouth, Merrimack Stake
P. O. Box 287
York Harbor, Maine 02991

Dear Elder Neitzel:

You are hereby called to be a missionary of The Church of Jesus Christ of Latter-day Saints to labor in the Italy North Mission.

You are scheduled to enter the Mission Home in Salt Lake City at 75 East North Temple on Saturday, September 15, 1973.

Your presiding officers have recommended you as one worthy to represent the Church of our Lord as a Minister of the Gospel. It will be your duty to live righteously, to keep the commandments of the Lord, to honor the holy Priesthood which you bear, to increase your testimony of the divinity of the Restored Gospel of Jesus Christ, to be an exemplar in your life of all the Christian virtues, and so to conduct yourself as a devoted servant of the Lord that you may be an effective advocate and messenger of the Truth. We repose in you our confidence and extend to you our prayers that the Lord will help you thus to meet your responsibilities.

The Lord will reward the goodness of your life, and greater blessings and more happiness than you have yet experienced await you as you serve Him humbly and prayerfully in this labor of love among His children.

We ask that you please send your written acceptance promptly, endorsed by your presiding officer in the ward or branch where you live.

Sincerely yours,

President

In the 1960s Elder Harold B. Lee began a tradition of meeting with all departing missionaries in the Salt Lake Temple for a ninety-minute question-and-answer period between two endowment sessions. President Lee continued this tradition of speaking to the missionaries in the temple even after his call as president of the Church.

Richard Charles Neitzel Journal
September 1973

September 17: I hit the big number "19" today. This morning we went to the Salt Lake Temple. We went through an endowment session this morning. This was my second session. I had taken out my endowments September 6, 1973 in the Los Angeles Temple with my sister [Linda] and my brother-in-law [Ron Lindsey]. After the first endowment we went up stairs to the Assembly Room of the Temple to have a question and answer session with President Lee. After this session we went down again to another, more meaningful endowment session. The Temple session lasted 8 hours. The time went by too fast. What a birthday!

(Above) President Harold B. Lee and Elder Gordon B. Hinckley during their
visit to the Holy Land, September 1972 (Courtesy L. Brent Goates)

(Top right) President and Sister Lee at the Western Wall in Jerusalem,
September 20, 1972 (Courtesy L. Brent Goates)

(Right) President and Sister Lee at the Jordan River near the Sea of Galilee,
September 21, 1972 (Courtesy L. Brent Goates)

ON THE BRINK OF ETERNITY

Less than three months after being ordained prophet, seer, and revelator of the Church, Harold B. Lee embarked on a two-week tour of the Europe and the Middle East. Accompanied by his wife, Joan, and Elder Gordon B. and Marjorie Hinckley, President Lee became the first modern Church president to visit the Holy Land. After stops in England and Greece, the Lees and the Hinckleys made their way to Galilee and Jerusalem, where they spent three days retracing the steps of Christ and meeting with various government officials. On the evening of September 20, President Lee met with local members of the Church at the Garden Tomb and held a special service commemorating the resurrection of Jesus Christ. Later that night, it became apparent that the grueling pace of the trip was taking its toll on President Lee. Already beset with health problems, he felt especially weak and fatigued and was having difficulty breathing. His wife, Joan, called on Elder Hinckley and Mission President Edwin Q. Cannon to give him a blessing. Elder Hinckley recorded, "I felt the power of the Lord and as I invoked the blessing I rebuked the Destroyer. I felt confident that the Lord would heal His servant. President Lee appeared stronger the next morning, but said only that he felt better. Two days after the blessing, after we had finished breakfast, President Lee shared with us his testimony that the Lord had brought to pass a miracle in his behalf in response to the blessing given him. His health was remarkably improved, for which we were grateful. The President said 'We had to come to the land of miracles to witness a miracle within ourselves.'" In his own journal, President Lee expounded on the experience and the deep sense of responsibility it left him: "The next morning, after a severe coughing spell, I expelled two clots which seemed to be blood—one, about the size of a dime, was like dried blood, and the other one was red, as a fresh clot. Immediately my shortness of breath ceased, the weariness was diminished, and the back pains began to subside, and 24 hours later they were entirely gone. I now realize I was skirting on the brink of eternity and a miracle, in this land of ever great miracles, was extended by a merciful God who obviously was prolonging my ministry for a longer time, to give to him in whose service I am, all the strength of my heart, mind, and soul, to indicate in some measure my gratitude for his never-failing consideration to me and my loved ones."

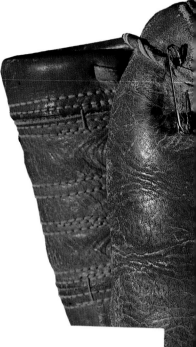

(Left) Elder and Sister Lee returning home from their South Africa mission tour, November 1958, greeted by their grandson, David B. Goates (Courtesy L. Brent Goates)

(Right) Baseball glove given to grandson David B. Goates (Courtesy David B. Goates)

THE BASEBALL MITT

David B. Goates

At nine years of age I began my first year of Little League Baseball. Grandfather Lee occasionally attended my games when his schedule permitted. In his view baseball, for me, appeared to be a blood sport played as though every pitch were a life or death proposition. On one particular evening, after a pop fly, I rounded third without slowing down even though the third-base coach signaled me to stop. I was thrown out at home. When the umpire made the call, I bounced up screaming at the top of my lungs to protest the call.

It was after this incident that my Grandfather wrote me a letter. In it he challenged me to gain control of my temper, as he himself had had to do. Along with this challenge, he proposed a deal. In exchange for my efforts he gave me this baseball mitt. The caveat was that if I lost my temper, I had to give the mitt back until I had again resolved to deal with my frustration in a better way.

As mild-mannered as I am today, those who know me well would marvel at his characterization as a "fierce competitor" in those formative years. More importantly, President Lee reveals some of his own struggle with a "fierce temper."

Perhaps much of the eventual transformation in learning to control my temper can be traced to my Grandfather, who seeing himself in his own grandson was determined to "nip it in the bud," before it became more a life-long habit with potentially serious consequences.

I accepted his "proposition" (I had to ask my Mother for the definition), the mitt went back and forth a few times that next season, but a life lesson was learned.

FORTY-SEVEN EAST
SOUTH TEMPLE STREET
SALT LAKE CITY
UTAH

HAROLD B. LEE

2-18-59.

My dear David:

As I have watched you whenever you are playing a game, I'm sure that you have a rare quality of which real champions are made in either baseball, football or basketball. You are what a sportsman would say — "a fierce competitor" — You have a determination to win.

You have another tendency, however, which, unless you are able to conquer it, you will never be a champion in any sport, and I fear in any other field. I have noticed that you are not able to take defeat in a contest without becoming very upset in your feelings, and many times angry with others whose mistakes, you think, have resulted in the defeat. In other words, you lack patience with those with whom you play. Patience with others is a quality of good sportsmanship. Everyone admires a good sport — one who can lose as well as win and see in his losses faults within himself which must be corrected or improvements in the "team" if you are playing with others, in order to be a winner next time. The ones who "lose his head" and become angry or cries when he doesn't win is called a "poor sport" or a "sore-head" and soon if he doesn't change, begins to lose his friends. Worse than that when he allows himself to become angry, he is almost always sure after that to lose because he is not able to control his mind as well as his body in order to give the best in whatever he is doing.

I know something about what I'm telling, because, all my life, I too, have had to conquer a fierce temper

Letter, dated February 18, 1959, to David B. Goates from his grandfather, Harold B. Lee, discussing David's sportsmanship (first page) (Courtesy David B. Goates)

FORTY-SEVEN EAST
SOUTH TEMPLE STREET
SALT LAKE CITY
UTAH

HAROLD B. LEE

and an impatience with others who don't quite measure up as I think he should. Anger and unhappiness is like a poison to your mind and your body. You and I must not allow ourselves to have this poison within us to destroy our usefulness. When one on our team makes a mistake or a blunder we must be the first to say: "Too bad boy. Better luck next time." When we lose, we must learn to say to our selves: "Well a better man won. I'm going to practice and work harder so that next time I can do much better."

Now about the baseball glove! I have obtained a fine full-sized fielders glove for you to replace the one you have lost, but there is one condition on which it is to be continually and permanently your own. You are to make a bargain with me that in order to own and to use this full-sized man's glove, you will hereafter act in your playing as a "man's man" or as I have explained above — will let the wearing of this glove be a constant reminder that this glove cannot be worn by a "poor sport." Should you while playing, lose your patience and be otherwise than a "good sport," then you are to return it to me until you feel you have conquered yourself and are prepared to wear again this fine-quality glove — the same fine quality of which champions are made. I want you now to write me a letter accepting my proposition and when I get your letter assuring me of your determination to be a good team-man and a gentleman in your playing hereafter, the glove is yours until you fail me. With my love, Your grandfather,
Harold B. Lee.

Second page

THE PROPHET'S FINAL COUNSEL AND BLESSING

President Harold B. Lee

October 7, 1973

I thank the Lord that I may have passed some of the tests, but maybe there will have to be more before I shall have been polished to do all that the Lord would have me do. Sometimes when the veil has been very thin, I have thought that if the struggle had been still greater that maybe then there would have been no veil. I stand by, not asking for anything more than the Lord wants to give me, but I know that he is up there and he is guiding and directing. I extend my blessings to you wonderful Saints. Go back to your homes now. Take the love of the General Authorities to your people. We extend to those who are not members of the Church the hand of fellowship. May we reach out to those who have lost their sense of direction and, before it is too late, try to win them back into the fold; because they are all God's children, and he wants us to save all of them.

Peace be with you, not the peace that comes from the legislation in the halls of congress, but the peace that comes in the way that the Master said, by overcoming all the things of the world. That God may help us so to understand and may you know that I know with a certainty that defies all doubt that this is his work, that he is guiding us and directing us today, as he has done in every dispensation of the gospel, and I say that with all the humility of my soul, in the name of the Lord, Jesus Christ. Amen.

State of the Church at the time of Harold B. Lee's death	
Year of death	1973
Church membership	3,306,658
Stakes	630
Temples	15
Missions	108
Missionaries set apart during administration	9,471
Book of Mormon translations completed during administration	0

HAROLD B. LEE

165

PROPHETS AT LEISURE

(Right) Joseph Smith showing youth how to pull sticks (Del Parson, VRL)

(Below) Wilford Woodruff in Alaska, July 1895 (Courtesy Alaska and Polar Regions Archives, Rasmuson Library, University of Alaska Fairbanks)

MEMORIES OF THE PROPHET

I have often seen the Prophet indulge in a game of checkers. He was cheerful—often wrestling with Sidney Rigdon. One time he had his pants torn badly, but had a good laugh over it. In Missouri, when mob forces oppressed the Saints, we were encamped in Adam-ondi-Ahman, mostly around campfires without tents. One night the snow fell four or five inches. The Prophet, seeing our forlorn condition, called us to form into two parties—Lyman Wight at the head of one line and he (Joseph) heading the other line—to have a sham battle. The weapons were snowballs. We set to with a will full of glee and fun.
—Edward Stevenson

WILFORD WOODRUFF'S TRIP TO ALASKA, 1895

In July of 1895, President Woodruff made this trip to Alaska seeking some relief from his health problems. During the last years of his life, activities such as fishing and gardening became increasingly difficult, so the simple pleasures of reading and visiting friends and family became his main leisurely activities. On occasion, however, nature trips such as the one to Alaska brought relaxation and diversion to the aged prophet. Of the trip, the Deseret News reported that the beauty of the Alaskan wilderness "aroused feelings of admiration and praise for the creator who had raised such monuments to his greatness and power." In his journal, President Woodruff made several comments about the sights. Regarding a trip to the Mina Glacier, he wrote, "The whole ocean was covered with ice bergs, from very large ones down to small ones. The sea was covered in this way as far as the eye could see. We stayed three hours at the glacier. . . . I felt that I had seen in the wonderful glacier one of the finest sights of my life." It was on the outing to this glacier that this photograph of the First Presidency (Joseph F. Smith, and George Q. Cannon stand behind and to the left of President Woodruff who is seated) on board the *Willapa* was most likely taken.

L ife offers people seasons of childhood, young adulthood, and the mature years of adult responsibilities. From the time he received the plates from the angel Moroni in 1827, Joseph Smith found it difficult to find private time for leisure and recreation. Yet the energetic young prophet did cultivate recreation and leisure and expanded the Saints' understanding of its place in their lives. It was a time when many Christians in the United States debated what, if any, recreation was appropriate. Nauvoo saw a great expansion of feelings and activities, especially as it related to dance, music, and drama through his example and teachings. Brigham Young followed in Joseph's footsteps when he established the Saints in the Rocky Mountains. There he enlarged upon Joseph's teachings, indicating that "there is no music in hell, for all good music belongs to heaven." He lamented that Utah had only four annual holidays, New Year's, Independence Day, Pioneer Day, and Christmas; he wanted more. Brother Brigham not only encouraged reading, dancing, theater, and other physical activities to

(Above left) Joseph F. Smith swimming in California, about 1900 (MLUU)

(Above) Heber J. Grant golfing, about 1940 (Church Archives)

(Left) David O. McKay on his horse "Sunnyboy" (Church Archives)

*(Below) Gordon B. Hinckley fishing in Alaska in June 1995
(Lowell R. Hardy, Office of the President)*

enliven the soul, but he also participated himself and supported financially to the establishment of such activities. Wilford Woodruff loved to fish, read, and garden. Lorenzo Snow may have been the first president of the Church to ride in an automobile. Joseph F. Smith picked up golf late in his life. President Heber J. Grant, who had been an avid sportsman from the time he was a young man, remained physically active throughout his long life. Sometimes age affects the activities prophets can engage in during their presidencies. Joseph Fielding Smith, for example no longer played handball, a sport he excelled in, but substituted other activities such as reading, singing, and traveling for the more physically demanding activities usually associated with twentieth-century sports. The prophetic mantle places upon him whom the Lord has called great emotional, physical, and spiritual pressures. That the prophets would seek time to relax and rejuvenate is only natural. Even the Lord rested on the seventh day (see Genesis 2:2).

"MEDICINE FOR THE SOUL"

In June of 1995, after presiding at a regional conference in Anchorage Alaska, President and Sister Hinckley spent three days vacationing in Alaska's Glacier Bay National Park. Of the experience President Hinckley wrote, "We dressed in casual clothes, which was a great relief. . . . We had come to rest, to take time to reflect beneath the stars, to fish, and to see the marvelous handiwork of the Creator. . . . I felt inspired by the beauty of the scenery—the surrounding mountains thickly covered with timber that is virgin, never having seen the woodman's saw or axe. I reflected on the wonders of nature, these great glacial waters, icy cold, and brilliant in the sunlight." Near the end of the trip, President Hinckley wrote, "Being out like this is medicine for the soul."

A postle Spencer W. Kimball stood before an attentive April 1954 general conference audience packing the historic Salt Lake Tabernacle. Clearly and with emphasis he proclaimed, "O intolerance, thou art an ugly creature! What crimes have been committed under thy influence, what injustices under thy Satanic spell! . . . What a monster is prejudice! It means pre-judging. How many of us are guilty of it? Often we think ourselves free of its destructive force, but we need only to test ourselves. Our expressions, our voice tones, our movements, our thoughts betray us. We are often so willing that others make the contacts, do the proselyting, have the associations. Until we project ourselves into the very situation, we little realize our bias and our prejudice. Why will we, the prospered, the blessed, hiss? When, oh, when, will we cease to spurn?"

He was speaking in behalf of minorities, making particular mention "of Japanese and Chinese brothers and sisters; of Hawaiians and other Islanders; of Indians, Mexicans, Spanish-Americans and others." On this occasion, his concern was sparked by an anonymously written letter to him complaining, "I never dreamed I would live to see the day when the Church would invite . . . an Indian buck appointed a bishop—an Indian squaw to talk in the Ogden Tabernacle—Indians to go through the Salt Lake Temple."

In answer, Elder Kimball asked: "When the Lord has made of all flesh equal; when He has accepted both the Gentiles and Israel; when He finds no difference between them, who are we to find a difference and exclude from the Church and its activities and blessings of the . . . Indian? . . . I love the Lamanites, the Indians, and all their cousins. . . . May God bless the Lamanite-Nephite peoples, stir their hearts."

These emphatic words flowed from an apostle whose patriarchal blessing promised he would "preach the Gospel to many people, but more especially to the Lamanites." As a boy growing up in rural southeast Arizona, Spencer W. Kimball had, in the words of his son Edward, "watched the freight trains carry Indians through Thatcher. In return for rights to build across the San Carlos Reservation the railroad had agreed to let Apaches ride free for forty years, but not inside the passenger cars; so they rode the tops, the braves with long hair,

(Left) Spencer W. Kimball portrait (Judith Mehre, 1983, MCHA)

(Above oval) Spencer W. Kimball, about 1985 (Church Archives)

BORN
MARCH 28, 1895
SALT LAKE CITY, UTAH

PARENTS
ANDREW AND
OLIVE WOOLLEY KIMBALL

BAPTIZED
MARCH 28, 1903
(AGE 8)

STATURE
5' 6"
165 POUNDS

MARRIED
NOVEMBER 16, 1917
TO CAMILLA EYRING
(AGE 22)

APOSTLE
OCTOBER 7, 1943
(AGE 48)

PRESIDENT
DECEMBER 30, 1973
(AGE 78)

DIED
NOVEMBER 5, 1985
SALT LAKE CITY, UTAH
(AGE 90)

the women in bright calico, carrying their babies, a colorful sight steaming across the hot desert." It was a picture that stayed with him—it was an image that brought questions to his mind and heart. Young Spencer's sensitivity to the plight of Lamanites was further enhanced by his father Andrew's photographs and stories of teaching the gospel in the Indian Territory Mission.

In 1946, President George Albert Smith assigned Elder Kimball the responsibility of working with the Indians. For the rest of his life, Spencer W. Kimball spotlighted the multiple problems of the Indians, helped establish the Indian Student Placement Services, and worked closely with individuals as well as tribal leaders. He passionately battled against prejudice and all racial bigotry.

His empathy and concern for the plight of the disenfranchised was hard earned. His daughter, Olive Beth Mack, stated, "Dad has had a great deal of sorrow and sickness and many difficulties to overcome. These have only served to make him a stronger person, and have given him much empathy for

Gordon, Spencer, and Dell, November 1906
(William's Gallery, courtesy Edward L. Kimball)

others." During his childhood he nearly drowned; he suffered facial paralysis and survived typhoid fever, and three of his sisters and his mother died. After he was called to be an apostle, Spencer W. Kimball suffered a series of heart attacks and survived throat cancer and removal of part of his vocal cords. In 1972 open-heart surgery replaced a blocked artery and a defective valve. "An undefeatable personality," Spencer W. Kimball not merely survived but also overcame and impressively grew from personal adversity.

Present Kimball's love was not an abstract philosophy but a call for positive personal conduct. At a dinner celebrating President Kimball's eighty-fifth birthday, Norman Vincent Peale recited a story of the prophet's excellent example of compassionate action. It is an oft-quoted story that warrants repeating for its example of pure, Christ-like love. During a wild midwestern snowstorm, thousands of airline passengers were stranded at Chicago's O'Hare Airport while flights were frantically rescheduled and rerouted. Among these thousands was a pregnant woman

---

1895
Mar. 28 • Born in Salt Lake City
Wihelm Röntgen discovers X-rays

1898
Family moves to Arizona
Sept. 2 • Wilford Woodruff dies
U.S. population: 75,994,575

1901
Oct. 10 • Lorenzo Snow dies

1903
Mar. 28 • Baptized in Thatcher, Arizona
Arizona becomes 48th state (1912)

1914
Graduates from Gila Academy
African American Garrett A. Morgan invents gas mask

1914–16
Mission to Central States

1917
Nov. 1 • Marries Camilla Eyring

1918
Nov. 19 • Joseph F. Smith dies
First shortwave radio experiments (1919)

1938–43
President of Mount Graham (Arizona) Stake

1943
Oct. 7 • Ordained an apostle
U.S. President Franklin D. Roosevelt wins unprecedented fourth term (1944)

1945
May 14 • Heber J. Grant dies

1946
Chairman of Church Indian Committee
United Nations issues Universal Declaration of Human Rights (1948)

1951
Apr. 4 • George Albert Smith

1957
Portion of vocal chords removed due to cancer
Soviet Union launches first human-made satellite

1969
Publishes first book, **Miracle of Forgiveness**

1970
Jan. 18 • David O. McKay dies
Intel develops first silicon chip microprocessor (1971)

1972
July 2 • Joseph Fielding Smith dies

1973
Dec. 26 • Harold B. Lee dies
Dec. 30 • Ordained president of the Church
World population: 4,144,811,837

1974
Jan. 14 • Name of stakes changed to reflect geographic location
Nov. 19 • Dedicates Washington, D.C., Temple

and her two-year-old child. "The woman was in one line after another trying to buy a ticket to a Michigan point. People were criticizing her because she would reach forward with her foot to push the child up in the line as the line moved forward—she was under doctor's orders to not carry the child.

"She was in anguish when a man approached her with a kindly smile." He said to her, "'Young lady it appears to me that you need help!' He took the dirty, little two-year-old child in his arms and loved it, patted it on the back, gave it a stick of chewing gum. Then he went to the people in the line and he told them about the woman—how she had to get a flight out to Michigan. They agreed, under the influence of his spirit, to let her go ahead of them. He took her to the flight and got her started on her way."

Dr. Peale ended his story with this question: "Now that's a simple story, but how many people would do it?" Quite simply, it is what a man of action and purity would do—Spencer W. Kimball.

On December 30, 1973, after the untimely death of

Elder Spencer W. Kimball in St. Louis, Missouri, May 23, 1915
(Courtesy Edward L. Kimball)

Harold B. Lee, Spencer W. Kimball was ordained president of The Church of Jesus Christ of Latter-day Saints. During the April 1974 general conference, President Kimball reassured the Saints, "This, then, is our program: to reaffirm and boldly carry forward the work of God in cleanliness, uprightness, and to take that gospel of truth to that world that needs so much that godly life. Eternal life is our goal. It can be reached only by following the path our Lord has marked out for us. I know this is true and right. I love our Heavenly Father, and I love his Son, and I am proud to be even a weak vessel to push forward their great eternal work."

During Spencer W. Kimball's administration, 1974–85, the Church added two visions received by Joseph Smith and Joseph F. Smith to the Doctrine and Covenants, reorganized the First Quorum of Seventy, began holding area conferences throughout the world, inaugurated the genealogical name extraction program, and successfully opposed the Equal Rights Amendment and the U.S. government's MX missile program. Sunday church meetings were consolidated into a

1975
July 24 • Dedicates Church Office Building
Oct. 3 • Organizes First Quorum of Seventy
Vietnam War ends

1976
Apr. 3 • Church adopts two revelations (D&C 137 and 138)
James Earl Carter wins U.S. Presidency

1978
June 1 • Receives revelation on priesthood (Official Declaration 2)
Oct. 30 • Dedicates Sao Paulo Temple
Church membership exceeds 4,000,000

1979
Feb. 18 • 1000th stake created, Nauvoo, Illinois
Sept. 29 • New edition of Bible published
Margaret Thatcher becomes British prime minister

1980
Mar. 2 • Announces meeting consolidation in U.S. and Canada
Apr. 6 • Celebrates 150th anniversary of the Church
U.S. population: 226,545,805

1981
Satellite dishes installed at stake centers
Sept. 26 • New edition of Triple Combination published
Nov. 16 • Dedicates Jordan River Temple
Center for Disease Control in Atlanta identifies AIDS

1982
Oct. 3 • Church announces the Book of Mormon subtitle, "Another Testament of Jesus Christ"
Church membership exceeds 5,000,000
British relinquishes the last vestiges of control in Canada

1983
Aug. 5–9 • Church dedicates two temples within a week's time, Samoa and Tonga
Sony introduces the compact disc

1984
June 24 • Establishes area presidencies
Oct. 28 • 1500th stake created, Mexico Yaqui Stake

1985
June 29 • Freiberg (East Germany) Temple dedicated
Nov. 5 • Dies in Salt Lake City
World population: 4,929,461,483

Shortly after his ordination to the apostleship on October 7, 1943, Elder Spencer W. Kimball preformed a sealing in the Salt Lake Temple. His journal reveals his humility and the attending emotions relating to the sealing keys he now held.

attended the reception at the BeeHive house for Sister Ruth May Fox on her 90th anniversary. He had ten living children in the reception line and many of her 198 direct descendents were there

WEDNESDAY Nov. 17th.1943.

I reached the office about 8 A.M. It was still darkened and I think I was, as usual, about the first of all the folks at the office. I interviewed for a Temple Recommend Sister Barbara Beth Tidwell of Glendale East Ward Die of the San Fernando Ward. Brother Cannon of the Beneficial sales staff came in to get acquainted.

My first Temple Wedding for TIME AND ETERNITY!!! Brother Harold B. Lee assisted me to show me how the work is done. We entered the front of the temple and found the couple and the friends soon ready. It was my pleasure and privilege to perform my first ceremony uniting Thurmon Moody and Eva Dell Pace for TIME AND ETERNITY. I think I was as much stirred emotionally as was the young gouple whom I united. The mother of the groom was a member of the St Louis branch as a young girl when I was in the mission. She now has 12 children. She married Marvin Moody.

I practised the organ for an half hour. I met with Bro. Widtsoe and the Presidency of the Ogden Stake regarding the division and reorganization of the two stakes.

THURSDAY Nov. 18 1943.

Today was our regular weekly meeting and since no meeting was held the previous Thursday there was much to do. I enjoyed the meetings very much though there was still much sadness over

ON THE BANKS OF THE SUSQUEHANNA

During a mission tour, Spencer W. Kimball and family visited members, missionaries, and Church history sites in the eastern United States. He noted in his journal regarding a baptismal service in Harmony, Pennsylvania, "We determined [we were] at least in the near vicinity of the place where 116 yrs ago today John the Baptist restored the Aaronic Priesthood and where Joseph and Oliver were baptized—there were 35 present for the meeting which was held a few feet from the water's edge. The river was high in spring flood, the trees in leaf and the grass green and violets in bloom in profusion. The birds sang sweetly overhead as we sang 'Praise to the Man' with our heads bared. . . . It was a glorious hour."

(Above) Spencer W. Kimball and Roy W. Doxey, May 15, 1945 (Courtesy Edward L. Kimball)

(Above left) Spencer W. Kimball's Journal, November 17, 1943 (Courtesy Edward L. Kimball)

Reading the wording on the monuments of
WILLIAM and ANN HENDRICKS
good Cherokees who were kind to my Father
when he was on his missions 1885 to 1897
M E N A R D   O K L A.
INDIAN TERRITORY

The graves of those good people are won a
small dfenced plot at the top of the rise
of a little hill in the middle of the field
I paid the renter to clean up the plot and lift up a
and straighten up the monuments. NOV 1951

(Above) Spencer W. Kimball and grandchild, about 1972 (Courtesy Edward L. Kimball)

(Left) Photograph and thought from Spencer W. Kimball's journal, November 1951 (Courtesy Edward L. Kimball)

three-hour block, the number of missionaries increased, and the number of temples grew from fifteen to thirty-six.

In a letter of June 8, 1978, formally addressed to Church general and local priesthood leaders, President Kimball and his counselors (N. Eldon Tanner and Marion G. Romney) announced: "We have pleaded long and earnestly in behalf of these, our faithful brethren, spending many hours in the Upper Room of the Temple supplicating the Lord for divine guidance. He has heard our prayers, and by revelation has confirmed that the long-promised day has come when every faithful, worthy man in the Church may receive the holy priesthood, with power to exercise its divine authority, and enjoy with his loved ones every blessing that flows therefrom, including the blessings of the temple. Accordingly, all worthy male members of the Church may be ordained to the priesthood without regard for race or color." This revelation was unanimously sustained as the word and will of the Lord on September 30, 1978. It was a time of joy, celebration, and fulfillment. The revelation was an answer to fervent,

heartfelt questions and prayers—words from the Lord spoken through his prophet who was the most loving of men.

Some fifty-nine years before he became president of the Church, a discouraged young missionary, Spencer W. Kimball of the Central States Mission, received a letter from his father, Andrew Kimball. It is a touching, beautifully encouraging note in which a loving father predicts the man his son will become: "I am pleased with your game spirit. You will make good, Spencer. You are small in stature—so was your sweet mother—but big natured and whole souled. You will make good, my boy. Your hard experiences will enable you to know just a little of what it costs to be a Latter-day Saint and something of what your father and grandfather waded through. Keep up a good, courageous spirit, but don't get to think it is too much for you to bear. It will all come out well and you will have something to tell your posterity. . . . God bless my sweet boy."

Spencer W. Kimball following a dinner program in Page, Arizona, October 27, 1972 (Courtesy Edward L. Kimball)

Spencer W. Kimball and Carole Kiozumi at the Sapporo Japan mission home, August 19, 1975 (Courtesy Edward L. Kimball)

Spencer W. Kimball, January 6, 1974 (Church Archives)

"UP CITY CREEK CANYON"

In January of 1974, two French photographers from a notable magazine in Paris came to Salt Lake City to do a story on the Church. President Kimball was very accommodating, even to the point of allowing these gentlemen into his home to photograph a simulated family home evening. After a Sunday morning Tabernacle Choir performance, he recorded in his journal that he went with these men "up City Creek Canyon and found a quiet place where they had me walk quietly, as in meditation, and they took my picture."

(Above) Spencer W. Kimball greeting the Saints in the mid-1970s
(Courtesy Edward L. Kimball)

(Top right) Camilla and Spencer W. Kimball signing autographs
on Temple Square, about 1975 (Courtesy Louise Kimball Clark)

(Below left and right) President Kimball attempted to respond to
inquiries from church members; most of his letters were quite long.
(Courtesy Greg P. and MarJane Christofferson)

THE CHURCH OF JESUS CHRIST OF LATTER-DAY SAINTS
47 EAST SOUTH TEMPLE STREET
SALT LAKE CITY, UTAH 84111

SPENCER W. KIMBALL, PRESIDENT   March 25, 1976

Mr. Eddie Sousa
27914 Capetown Avenue
Hayward, California 94545

Dear Brother Sousa:

    Thank you for your letter of March 22.

    I appreciated learning something of your life, and was
sorry indeed to know that you are ill and not able to participate in your usual activities.

    As you requested, I am sending an autographed photo-
graph and also a booklet about our temples which I hope
you will find of interest.

    With kindest wishes,

                              Faithfully yours,

                              Spencer W Kimball
                              President

(Above) Camilla and Spencer W. Kimball with Church leaders at the dedication of Poland for the preaching of the gospel, August 24, 1977 (Courtesy Edward L. Kimball)

(Above right) Spencer W. Kimball speaking at the 151st annual general conference, April 1981 (Don Grayston, courtesy Edward L. Kimball)

(Right) Kimball family at Long Beach, California, August 1939 (Courtesy Edward L. Kimball)

SUMMER TRIPS TO LONG BEACH

Just before my third birthday I came down with polio. For half a dozen years after that I spent part of each summer in Los Angeles at the Children's Orthopedic Hospital having a series of surgeries on my weakened legs. The annual trip to California served also as a family vacation. Before checking me into the hospital, the family would rent a cheap apartment in Long Beach and spend time at the beach and especially at the Pike, an amusement pier located there. Because walking was difficult for me, when I got tired my father was quick to carry me on his back. He never treated it as a burden.

—Edward L. Kimball

Spencer W. Kimball's Family

Spencer W. Kimball was born in Salt Lake City on March 28, 1895. He was the sixth child and third son of eleven children (four died in childhood) born to Olive Woolley and Andrew Kimball. On the Kimball side, his grandfather Heber C. Kimball was an apostle, pioneer, and counselor to Brigham Young. Spencer's grandfather Edwin D. Woolley managed Brigham Young's business affairs and was the bishop of Salt Lake City's 13th Ward for forty years.

In 1898, when Spencer was three years old, the Andrew Kimball family was called by the First Presidency to move to Thatcher, Arizona. The energetic and faithful Andrew Kimball was the president of the St. Joseph Stake for more than twenty-six years while working as a farmer and a traveling dry-goods salesman. Olive Kimball, who tragically died when Spencer was eleven, provided her children with a home filled with gospel faith, intellectual and cultural curiosity, and a sense of family responsibility and love.

Growing up in the hard-bit country of southeastern Arizona's Gila Valley provided Spencer Kimball ample opportunity to learn the importance of frugality and the necessity of diligence in tending to chores. The economics of frontier farming was tenuous at best, and any shirking of duties—cow-milking, fence-mending, weeding, painting, pig-feeding—could have serious consequences. From an early age Spencer Kimball strove for excellence in his chores, school, and church. However, he also found time for fun—pranks, parties, music, and sports.

On November 16, 1917 Spencer W. Kimball married school-teacher Camilla Eyring—an intelligent and forthright woman. They parented four children: Spencer L., Olive Beth, Andrew E., and Edward L.

Daughter Olive Beth Mack remembered her parents in this way: "Our parents always [shown] a great deal of love and concern for us children. They've guided rather than pushed us into the paths that they wanted us to go. This love has been extended to us all of our lives and reaches out to all members of our family. . . . One of the wonderful memories that I have of my childhood is of our yearly vacations. Many times Dad would wake me early in the morning to go on a walk with him. I'm sure I learned a great many things as we were walking on the beach, or through the city, or in the mountains hand in hand. As an only daughter, I feel very privileged to have had such a close association with him."

In tribute to the great affection he shared with his wife, Camilla, Spencer W. Kimball penned the following poem, entitled "When I Look Back":

Spencer and Camilla Kimball, November 1977
(B. Duncan Photography, courtesy Edward L. Kimball)

When I look back across our mingled years,
I know it is not just the joys we shared
That made our lives one pattern, but the tears
We shed together, and the rough, wild seas we fared.
Through all the disappointments we have faced,
Through this world's faults and failures, we have come
To heights of understanding that are based
More on the sorrows than the joys of home.
Young love is beautiful to contemplate
But old love is the finished tapestry
Stretched out from oaken floors to heaven's gate.
We wove on earth for all eternity
With threads made stronger by the steady beat
Of hearts that suffered but knew no defeat.

THE BRAZIL NORTH MISSION

In November 1967, Elder Spencer W. Kimball visited Brazil while on a tour of the South American missions. The Brethren were considering closing portions of the northern Brazil to missionary work because of priesthood restrictions in place at the time. My mission president assigned me to visit the branches in northern Brazil ahead of time and then brief Elder Kimball on the state of affairs in these areas. During Elder Kimball's visit we discussed what I felt were the major challenges facing northern Brazil at the time. Upon completing my mission, Elder Kimball invited me to meet him at his office. During that visit Elder Kimball told me that the Brethren had decided not only to leave northern Brazil open for missionary work, but to divide the Brazilian mission and form the Brazilian North mission in an effort to expand our presence in Brazil. The public announcement [of the change] followed soon after and I have since marveled about his kindness in taking the time from his busy schedule to tell me personally about something with which I had been deeply involved. The Brazilian North Mission was organized on July 7, 1968, and within a decade Spencer W. Kimball announced the revelation extending temple blessings to all worthy members of the Church—both decisions have blessed countless lives in northern Brazil.

—Gregory P. Christofferson

Camilla and Spencer W. Kimball on a tour of Brazil with mission president
W. Grant Bangerter, February 1959 (Courtesy Edward L. Kimball)

Spencer W. Kimball meeting with a young couple in his office (Courtesy Edward L. Kimball)

(Above) Spencer W. Kimball and Gregory P. Christofferson (a missionary)
in Recife, Brazil, November 25, 1967 (Courtesy Gregory P. and MarJane Christofferson)

"LENGTHEN OUR STRIDE" AND "DO IT!"

As president, Spencer W. Kimball told Church leaders and members that we must "lengthen our stride." He also urged members to strive for their best, admonishing them with his personal motto: "Do It!" In the statements below he explains the thought behind the sayings:

Lengthen Our Stride

"When I think of the concept of 'lengthening our stride,' I, of course, apply it to myself as well as urging it upon the Church. The 'lengthening of our stride' suggests urgency instead of hesitancy, 'now' instead of tomorrow; it suggests not only an acceleration, but efficiency. It suggests, too, that the whole body of the Church move forward in unison with a quickened pace and pulse, doing our duty with all our heart, instead of halfheartedly. It means, therefore, mobilizing and stretching all our muscles and drawing on all our resources. It suggests also that we stride with pride and with a sense of anticipation as we meet the challenges facing the kingdom. Out of all this will come a momentum that will be sobering and exhilarating at the same time.

"Brothers and sisters, we cannot improve on the doctrines or the basic organization of the Church. . . . But we can improve on ourselves, and we can improve the way in which we do our individual duties, the way we keep in step with the progress. We are not suggesting in the 'lengthening of our stride' that we try to move faster than we are able, or than would be wise, but rather a mobilization of our potential in order to move the kingdom forward for the more rapid and deeper benefit of our fellow men everywhere.

"The idea of 'lengthening our stride' or 'stretching our muscles' or 'reaching our highest' has an interesting scriptural base. The second verse in the fifty-fourth chapter of Isaiah proclaims: 'Enlarge the place of thy tent, and let them stretch forth the curtains of thine habitations: spare not, lengthen thy cords, and strengthen thy stakes.'"

Do It!

"In my office at home in Salt Lake City, I have a little sign . . . and it says on it, 'Do it!' I keep it handy so that if I get a little careless in my attitudes, I may remember, 'Do it!' And so I would like to say to you today, you have sat patiently through many sessions of conference [Honolulu Hawaii Area Conference] and dedication, and the Lord has blessed you. The brethren have spoken to you, and we sincerely hope their thoughts have fallen on ears that were listening. And so we say again, 'Go home and Do it!' . . . That is the answer. "Do it!' Do not just talk about it and think about it and accept it, but 'Do it!'"

PLEASURE VS. JOY

Much of the world seeks satisfying joy; unfortunately, many people mistakenly pursue shallow, empty gratification—the meaning and measure of the two are often confused. One leads to Christ-like happiness and peace, while the other leads to hollow, disquieting consequences. In the following words, President Kimball succinctly directs us to the proper life-path:

"The abundant life noted in the scriptures is the spiritual sum that is arrived at by the multiplying of our service to others and by investing our talents in service to God and to man. Jesus said, you will recall, that on the first two commandments hang all the law and the prophets, and those two commandments involve developing our love of God, of self, of our neighbors, and of all men. There can be no real abundance in life that is not connected with the keeping and the carrying out of those two great commandments.

"Unless the way we live draws us closer to our Heavenly Father and to our fellow men, there will be an enormous emptiness in our lives. It is frightening for me to see, for instance, how the life-style of so many today causes them to disengage from their families and their friends and their peers toward a heedless pursuit of pleasure or materialism. So often loyalty to family, to community, and to country is pushed aside in favor of other pursuits that are wrongly thought to be productive of happiness when, in fact, they often produce only questionable pleasure that passes quickly.

"One of the differences between true joy and mere pleasure is that certain pleasures are realized only at the cost of someone else's pain. Joy, on the other hand, springs out of selflessness and service, and it benefits rather than hurts others."

(Above) Embroidered "Do It" sign that hung in Spencer W. Kimball's home office (Courtesy Edward L. Kimball)

State of the Church at the time of Spencer W. Kimball's death	
Year of death	1985
Church membership	5,919,483
Stakes	1,570
Temples	36
Missions	188 (1985)
Missionaries set apart during administration	196,916
Book of Mormon translations completed during administration	43

PROPHETS ON JOSEPH

Lewis A. Ramsey painting of Joseph Smith, 1910 (MCHA)

JOSEPH SMITH

"I AM LIKE A HUGE, ROUGH STONE ROLLING DOWN FROM A HIGH MOUNTAIN; AND THE ONLY POLISHING I GET IS WHEN SOME CORNER GETS RUBBED OFF BY COMING IN CONTACT WITH SOMETHING ELSE, . . . ALL HELL KNOCKING OFF A CORNER HERE AND A CORNER THERE. THUS WILL I BECOME A SMOOTH AND POLISHED SHAFT IN THE QUIVER OF THE ALMIGHTY."

BRIGHAM YOUNG

"When I saw Joseph Smith, he took heaven, figuratively speaking, and brought it down to earth; and he took the earth, brought it up, and opened up, in plainness and simplicity, the things of God; and that is the beauty of his mission."

JOHN TAYLOR

"I testify that I was acquainted with Joseph Smith for years. . . . I testify before God, angels, and men, that he was a good, honorable, virtuous man . . . that his private and public character was unimpeachable—and that he lived and died as a man of God and a gentleman. This is my testimony."

WILFORD WOODRUFF

"Joseph Smith was what he professed to be, a prophet of God, a seer and revelator. He laid the foundation of this church and kingdom, and lived long enough to deliver the keys of the kingdom to the elders of Israel, unto the twelve apostles."

LORENZO SNOW

"I know that Joseph Smith was a Prophet of God; I know that he was an honorable man, a moral man, and that he had the respect of those who were acquainted with him. The Lord has shown me most clearly and completely that he was a Prophet of God."

JOSEPH F. SMITH

"I bear my testimony to you and to the world, that Joseph Smith was raised up by the power of God to lay the foundations of this great Latter-day work, to reveal the fulness of the gospel to the world in this dispensation. . . . I bear my testimony to it; I know that it is true."

HEBER J. GRANT

"Joseph Smith has been ridiculed and characterized as 'old Joe Smith.' I stand before you today a mere boy (39 years old), and yet Joseph Smith was martyred when he was a year younger than I am. . . . When we contemplate what he did, considering the opportunities of education that he had, it is indeed a marvel and wonder."

GEORGE ALBERT SMITH

"I wonder if that great man, Joseph Smith, who gave his life that the Church might be organized and carried on as the Lord intended, could see the Church as it exists today, with its branches established in all parts of the world, and realize that each day since he was martyred . . . the Church has become stronger than the day before?"

DAVID O. MCKAY

"When Joseph Smith taught a doctrine, he taught it authoritatively. . . . As we look through the vista of over one hundred years, we have a good opportunity of judging of the virtue of his teachings, and of concluding as to the source of his instruction."

JOSEPH FIELDING SMITH

"Since this is the anniversary of the birth of the Prophet Joseph Smith, I feel inclined to say a word about him, about his mission. As one of the greatest of all the prophets, he presides over the last dispensation."

HAROLD B. LEE

"Joseph Smith was the one whom the Lord raised up from boyhood and endowed with divine authority and taught the things necessary for him to know and to obtain the priesthood and to lay the foundation for God's kingdom in these latter days."

SPENCER W. KIMBALL

"I now add my personal and solemn testimony that God, the Eternal Father, and the risen Lord, Jesus Christ, appeared to the boy Joseph Smith."

EZRA TAFT BENSON

"I bear testimony that Joseph Smith was a prophet of the living God, one of the greatest prophets that has ever lived on the earth. He was the instrument in God's hand in ushering in the present gospel dispensation, the greatest of all, and the last of all in preparation for the second coming of the Master."

HOWARD W. HUNTER

"Joseph Smith was not only a great man, but he was an inspired servant of the Lord, a prophet of God. His greatness consists in one thing: the truthfulness of his declaration that he saw the Father and the Son and that he responded to the reality of that divine revelation."

GORDON B. HINCKLEY

"I worship the God of heaven, who is my Eternal Father. I worship the Lord Jesus Christ, who is my Savior and my Redeemer. I do not worship Joseph Smith, but I reverence and love this great seer through whom the miracle of this gospel has been restored."

George T. Benson Jr. and Sarah Sophia Dunkley left the small cluster of farms just above the Idaho-Utah state line for Logan, Utah. In the beautiful temple that overlooked the city, George and Sarah knelt at an altar and were sealed for time and all eternity on October 19, 1898. Following the ceremony, the young couple made their way north again, retracing their steps back to Whitney, Idaho. Here they began a happy life together among family and friends. Of the three hundred people living in the area, only one was not a member of the Church (and he was later baptized). It was a good place to raise a family. It was a tight-knit community where George's father had served as bishop for as long as anyone could remember. In fact, the bishop had named the city in honor of his friend Orson F. Whitney.

Nearly ten months later, Sarah was in her last weeks of pregnancy, ready to deliver her first child (there would be a total of eleven). On Friday, August 4, 1899, Sarah went into labor. George gave her a blessing and then immediately called Dr. Allan Cutler to come to their home. Additionally, George called his mother (Louisa Alexandrine Ballif Benson) and his mother-in-law (Margaret Wright Dunkley) to come. Soon the house was a beehive of activity with caring people helping out, but things were not going well. The labor was protracted, and it seemed that not only the life of the large baby (he would be eleven and three-quarter pounds) was in jeopardy, but the life of the mother as well. At the end of a long and painful struggle, the baby was finally born, but he was not breathing. Dr. Cutler said, "There's no hope for the child, but I believe we can save the mother." Leaving the seemingly dead infant on a sideboard, the good doctor turned his attention to Sarah. Instantaneously, George, his mother, and mother-in-law knelt down and asked the Lord's help. They then got to work and took the child into the next room. As was common for the day, both had had numerous opportunities to be involved in delivering children, including their own (Margaret and Louisa each had thirteen children themselves). These pioneer women, full of faith, immediately began trying to save their grandson. First, they filled two tubs with water, one cold and the other warm. Then they dipped the infant into one and then into the other. Apparently the shock caused the baby to let out a "husky yell, to the joy of all." Soon the wiggly baby

(Left) Portrait of Ezra Taft Benson, 1989 (Knud Edsberg, MCHA)

(Above oval) Portrait of Ezra Taft Benson (Judith Mehr, MCHA)

BORN
AUGUST 4, 1899
WHITNEY, IDAHO

PARENTS
GEORGE T. AND
SARAH DUNKLEY BENSON

BAPTIZED
AUGUST 4, 1907
(AGE 8)

STATURE
6' 1"
200–220 POUNDS

MARRIED
SEPTEMBER 10, 1926
TO FLORA SMITH AMUSSEN
(AGE 27)

APOSTLE
OCTOBER 7, 1943
(AGE 44)

PRESIDENT
NOVEMBER 10, 1985
(AGE 86)

DIED
MAY 30, 1994
SALT LAKE CITY, UTAH
(AGE 94)

boy was near his mother, who had also been saved by the effort of the good doctor and the prayers of the family. In the end, Sarah came to believe that her son had been preserved by the Lord because he had some important mission to perform. Since the baby boy was the first great-grandson of Ezra T. Benson (1811–69), who had been called by Brigham Young to serve in the Quorum of the Twelve Apostles in 1846, the child was named Ezra Taft Benson, known as "T" by his family and closest friends for much of his life.

Despite a difficult birth, Ezra grew to be a strong, healthy, and hardy young man. His life in Whitney tied him to the land. By the time he was four, he was already driving a team; at seven he was thinning sugar beets; and at fourteen he worked a team of horses. Time was spent pitching hay, picking and canning fruit, milking cows, feeding chickens, splitting firewood, and other such necessary activities associated with farm life. Every day was filled with work. However, for the Bensons, there was always time to pray, read, sing, swim, play games, and participate in family

Ezra Taft Benson at about three months of age, November 1899
(Thomas and Odell Photographers, Church Archives)

picnics with all the foods one would expect, such as homemade ice cream, pies, potato salad, and fried chicken. The Benson calendar was punctuated with special days important to the family—Independence Day, Pioneer Day (July 24), Christmas, Easter, birthdays, ex-tended family gatherings, and the Sabbath.

When Ezra was nearly thirteen, his father received a letter from "Box B" in Salt Lake City. The children noticed that their parents had been crying, but they did not know what it could mean. When the seven children were gathered, George and Sarah told their children that mission calls were mailed from "Box B" and that their tears were of gratitude and joy that George had been called to serve the Lord on a mission to the midwestern United States. It was not an easy call to receive, as Sarah was expecting her eighth child at the time, and farming was a challenging occupation. Nevertheless, the couple felt that the Lord would watch over George and bless Sarah and the children during his absence. It was during this time, while George was away, that Ezra, the oldest child,

---

1899
Aug. 4 • Born in Whitney, Idaho
Oscar Wilde publishes
Importance of Being Ernest

1901
Oct. 10 • Lorenzo Snow dies
William Kellogg introduces
Corn Flakes (1906)

1907
Aug. 4 • Baptized in Logan, Utah
International Paper Company
launches paper cups (1908)

1918
Nov. 19 • Joseph F. Smith dies

1921–23
Mission to Great Britain
British Government establishes the
BBC (1922)

1926
June 2 • Earns B.S. degree
from Brigham Young University
Sept. 10 • Marries Flora Smith
Amussen (dies Aug. 14, 1992)

1927
June 13 • Earns M.S. degree
from Iowa State College
Charles A. Lindbergh flies solo
across the Atlantic

1929
Mar. 4 • Works as University of
Idaho extension service agent
Academy of Motion Picture Arts and
Sciences holds first Academy Awards

1938
Nov. 27 • President of
Boise Idaho Stake

1939
Apr. 15 • Executive secretary of
National Council of Farmer
Cooperatives
Du Pont introduces nylon stockings
at the New York World's Fair

1940
June 30 • President of
Washington, D.C., Stake

1943
Oct. 7 • Ordained an apostle

1945
May 14 • Heber J. Grant dies

1945–1946
President of British and
European missions
Mohandas K. Gandhi assassinated
(1948)

1951
April 4 • George Albert Smith dies
Dwight D. Eisenhower wins
U.S. presidency (1952)

1953–1961
U.S. secretary of agriculture
U.S. astronaut John Glenn
orbits earth (1962)

1966
Nov. 10 • Dedicates Italy for
the preaching of the gospel

1970
Jan. 18 • David O. McKay dies

1972
July 2 • Joseph Fielding Smith dies
U.S. and U.S.S.R. sign SALT I treaty,
limiting nuclear weapons

began to demonstrate the strong characteristics that set him apart from others throughout the rest of his life. He recalled those days: "We had great spiritual moments in our home, many of them after Father left for his mission. In our prayers at night [Mother] would pray and pray and pray that Father would be successful, that he wouldn't worry about home. She'd pray that our work might go well in the fields, that we'd be kind to each other. . . . When your mother prays with such fervor, night after night, you think twice before you do something to disappoint her."

As noted earlier, she felt that Ezra had been preserved for a purpose and certainly expected him to successfully complete a full-time mission (1923) and to marry worthily in the House of the Lord (1926). She was probably not surprised that he excelled in his educational pursuits, completing a B.A. degree (1926) and an M.A. degree (1927).

Sadly, she did not live along enough to see his myriad of other accomplishments. In 1933, at the age of fifty-four years, Sarah died from cancer (her husband died a year later) before Ezra was called

Ezra Taft Benson as a schoolboy, about 1907
(Church Archives)

and ordained an apostle (1943), appointed to a high government position (secretary of agriculture) in one of the most powerful nations on earth (1953–61), and sustained as the thirteenth president of The Church of Jesus Christ of Latter-day Saints (1986). And though she was not able to witness these important milestones in her son's life, she seemed to have known that the Lord had been preparing and protecting Ezra all along to be a noble and great patriarch, prophet, and patriot.

THE BEST ADVICE I EVER HAD

Those picking up the November 1954 edition of *Reader's Digest* found this bit of wisdom that Ezra Taft Benson received from his father: "Remember that whatever you do or wherever you are, you are never alone. Our Heavenly Father is always near. You can reach out and receive his aid through prayer."

1973
Dec. 26 • Harold B. Lee dies
IBM introduces the personal computer—PC (1981)

1976
July 4 • Celebrates the U.S. Bicentennial

1985
Nov. 5 • Spencer W. Kimball dies
Nov. 10 • Ordained as president of the Church

1986
Apr. 5 • Begins a series of talks for specific Church groups
Oct. 4 • Stake seventies quorums discontinued

1986 *cont.*
Oct. 24 • Dedicates Denver Colorado Temple
Church membership exceeds 6,000,000
Space Shuttle Challenger explodes

1987
Aug. 28 • Dedicates Frankfurt Germany Temple

1988
June 1 • Communist Hungary officially recognizes Church
Aug. • Church completes 100 million endowments for the dead
Sept. 17 • Church joins VISN, interfaith television network

1988 *cont.*
Oct. 1 • Urges members to flood the earth with the Book of Mormon
Nov. 12 • Communist East Germany accepts missionaries
George H. W. Bush wins U.S. presidency

1989
Jan. 19 • Mormon Tabernacle Choir performs at George Bush's inauguration
Apr. 1 • Organizes Second Quorum of Seventy
Nov. 25 • Ward and stake assessments end in U.S. and Canada
Church membership exceeds 7,000,000
Germans tear down Berlin Wall

1990
Sept. 13 • Soviet Union approves "registration" of Leningrad Branch
Nov. 26 • Church announces equalization of missionary contributions in U.S. and Canada

1991
Dec. 1 • New York publisher Macmillian releases the *Encyclopedia of Mormonism*
Church membership exceeds 8,000,000
Operation Desert Storm frees Kuwait

1994
May 30 • Dies in Salt Lake City
World population: 5,613,919,443

(Above) Elder Jones (Salt Lake City), Elder Benson (Whitney, Idaho), Elder Speierman (Logan, Utah), President Palmer (Morgan, Utah), and Elder Black (Montpelier, Idaho); Ezra noted on the back of the photograph found in his missionary photo album, "The happy five that attended the Carlisle Branch Conference, October 1, 1922" (Courtesy Reed A. Benson)

Elder Benson and British missionaries with whom he served, 1921–23 (Church Archives)

ELDER CHARLES WALLACE SPEIERMAN JOURNAL
September/October 1922

September 30, 1922, Saturday: Arose early studied all the morning wrote home to Mabelle then went down town to meet the Elders Pres. Palmer, Elder Black and Elder Benson. We all had dinner then we all went visiting. Elder Benson and I went to Weightmans Forsythe Sowerby then to Burton where we all had a wonderful time I beat him twice in chess we all stayed late.

October 1, Sunday: Arose and prepared for the day as it was our branch conference we all made ready for the day, we had a very fine Sunday school and I preached a sermon on virtue and chastity then we had tea with T. Carlyle. [We] held the evening session and it was very fine after which visited Sister Gill had a very good time returned and retired

October 2, Monday: Arose early had break and all the Elders went out visiting Elder Benson and I went to Baxter's then to sister Fyfe while there we blessed her baby. I blessed Joan Margaret Fyfe and Elder Benson the older one . . . returned and had dinner saw the Elders off studied and received a letter from Mother visited Sister Gill had a good time there then returned and studied went to bed.

This photograph was taken at the time of Ezra Taft Benson's call to the Quorum of the Twelve Apostles. He was ordained by Heber J. Grant on October 7, 1943, just after Spencer W. Kimball (born March 28, 1895) was ordained an apostle. Church policy and tradition stipulates that apostles ordained on the same day are done so based on age, and because Ezra Taft Benson was born on August 4, 1899, he was ordained immediately following the older Spencer W. Kimball.

(Above) Spencer W. Kimball and Ezra Taft Benson, October 7, 1943 (Church Archives)

(Right) Ezra Taft and Flora Smith Amussen Benson family, December 1944 (Reprinted from Church News (December 22, 1944)

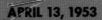

APRIL 13, 1953

ATLANTIC EDITION

TIME

THE WEEKLY NEWSMAGAZINE

AGRICULTURE SECRETARY BENSON
"No real American wants to be subsidized."

AUSTRIA	.5 schilling	FINLAND	60 finmarks	IRELAND	1/6	SOUTH AFRICA	2/–
BELGIUM	12 francs	FRANCE	80 francs	ISRAEL	.200 prutot	SPAIN	10 pesetas
BRITISH ISLES	1/6	FRENCH POSSESSIONS	85 francs	ITALY	.150 lire	SWEDEN	1 krona 25 öre
BRITISH POSSESSIONS	2/–	GERMANY	1 deutschmark	LEBANON & SYRIA	.100 piastres	SWITZERLAND	1.10 francs
CYPRUS	1 shilling 6 piastres	GREECE	.4000 drachmai	NETHERLANDS	.90 cent	TURKEY	85 kurus
DENMARK	1 krone 50 øre	IRAN	25 rials	NORWAY	1 krone 50 øre	YUGOSLAVIA	.90 dinars
EGYPT	10 piastres	IRAQ	100 fils	PORTUGAL	.7 escudos	U. S. ARMED FORCES	.20 cents

Time *magazine cover, April 13, 1953; while serving as U.S. president Dwight D. Eisenhower's secretary of agriculture from 1953 through 1961,
Ezra Taft Benson appeared on the cover of U.S.* News & World Report, Time *(twice)*, Newsweek, *and* Business Week

(Above) *Ezra Taft Benson and J. Willard Marriot riding horseback at the Marriot ranch in Virginia, 1953 (Church Archives)*

* ˜̃ ̃̃ *

(Below) *Ezra Taft Benson walking through a dustbowl, 1955 (Church Archives)*

(Above) *J. Willard Marriott, Dwight D. Eisenhower, and Ezra Taft Benson, 1954; as U.S. secretary of agriculture under President Dwight D. Eisenhower (1953–1961), Ezra Taft Benson traveled extensively throughout the United States and the world, visiting farms, farmers, and government officials (Church Archives)*

* ˜̃ ̃̃ *

(Below) *"Photo Report" from U.S. News & World Report (October 26, 1959), highlighting Secretary Benson's visit to a Church in Moscow*

PHOTO REPORT
—FROM MOSCOW

A CHURCH SERVICE IN SOVIET RUSSIA

An office memo from Grant Salisbury and Warren K. Leffler, the writer-photographer team for "U. S. News & World Report" that accompanied Secretary of Agriculture Ezra T. Benson to Russia:

THE NIGHT we left Moscow to fly down to Kiev, Secretary Benson literally took us to church.

Many of the reporters laughed about it on the way, because Mr. Benson, who is a leading Mormon, had arranged for us earlier to attend a service at the Latter-Day Saints Church in West Berlin, but all the newsmen found one excuse or another for not going. In Moscow, we had no choice because the cars picked us up at the hotel and stopped at the church on the way to the airport. It was around 7:30 o'clock on the chill, rainy evening of October 1.

As the cavalcade of cars arrived at the Central Baptist Church, on a narrow side street not far from Red Square, somebody wisecracked, "Well, boys, you're going to get to church whether you like it or not."

It turned out to be one of the most moving experiences in the lifetime of many of us. One newsman, a former marine, ranked it with the sight of the American flag rising over the old American compound in Tientsin, China, at the end of World War II.

The small church was packed, with people standing wherever they could find room.

Secretary Benson and his family were ushered to the rostrum. After a hymn, sung beautifully by the congregation, Mr. Benson began to talk, drawing on his experiences as one of the leaders of the Mormon Church in America. Watching the Russian congregation, you could see tears welling up in the eyes of people as the Secretary's words were relayed to them through a translator.

"It was very kind of your minister to ask me to extend greetings to you," Mr. Benson began. "I bring you greetings from the millions and millions of church people in America and around the world."

A soft, fervent "amen" came from the congregation. The Secretary continued, "Our Heavenly Father is not far away. He can be very close to us. I know that God lives. He is our Father. Jesus Christ, the Redeemer of the World, watches over this earth. He will direct all things. Be unafraid, keep His commandments, love

one another, pray for peace and all will be well."

By now there was scarcely a dry eye in the church. Even the few young people were weeping openly.

"This life is only a part of eternity," Mr. Benson went on. "We lived before we came here as spiritual children of God. We will live again after we leave this life. Christ broke the bonds of death and was resurrected. We will all be resurrected."

At the mention of the promise of life hereafter, muffled sobs could be heard in the small church. These people, after all, were sacrificing their chances of participating in the gains of the Communist society of Russia. Though worshiping God no longer is forbidden in the Soviet Union, those who do so usually find themselves cut off from advancement.

Communism in Russia remains avowedly atheistic. In Moscow there is one other Baptist church; there are 23 Greek Orthodox churches, two synagogues and one Moslem temple. In a city of 5.4 million people, it's a comparatively tiny crack in the godless society. The dedicated Communists, when talking to visitors about religion, usually claim that those Russians who do go to the few churches in the city do so out of curiosity—much as they would visit a museum—and not because of their devotion.

"I leave you my witness as a church servant for many years that the truth will endure," Mr. Benson concluded. "Time is always on our side. God bless you and keep you all the days of your life, I pray in the name of Jesus Christ."

As the Secretary returned to his seat, the congregation broke into the familiar hymn, "God Be With You Till We Meet Again." They were still singing and waving their handkerchiefs as we followed Mr. Benson out of the church. All the way along the crowded aisle, hands were outstretched to shake our hands.

On the drive to the airport one of the interpreters—a young Russian girl who has never known any life save that under Communism—said, "I felt like crying."

—USN&WR Photos

It was as a fellow Christian that Secretary of Agriculture Ezra Taft Benson, a high official of the Mormon Church, spoke to Russian Christians at services in Moscow's Central Baptist Church. You see him here in the plain wood pulpit.

Close-up of a "profound revolution" under way in Russia, page 96.

□ U. S. NEWS & WORLD REPORT, Oct. 26, 1959

(Reprinted from U.S. NEWS & WORLD REPORT, an independent weekly news magazine published at Washington. Further reproduction...

(Far left) Ezra Taft Benson playing with grandchild, about 1980 (Church Archives)

(Left) Ezra Taft Benson greeting Spencer W. Kimball at general conference, October 1985 (Church Archives)

(Below) U.S. President Ronald Reagan and Ezra Taft Benson, July 10, 1984 (Church Archives)

(Right) A series of images capturing Ezra Taft Benson in his office in Salt Lake City, about 1978 (Church Archives)

To Ezra Taft Benson
With best wishes,
Ronald Reagan

COME LISTEN TO A PROPHET'S VOICE

During his presidency, Ezra Taft Benson spoke often to groups of Latter-day Saints around the world. He placed renewed emphasis on reading, studying, pondering and applying the teachings of the Book of Mormon: "The Book of Mormon is the instrument that God designed to 'sweep the earth as with a flood, to gather out [His] elect' (Moses 7:62). This sacred volume of scripture needs to become more central in our preaching, our teaching, and our missionary work. . . . Indeed, I have a vision of flooding the earth with the Book of Mormon."

On April 5, 1986, President Benson addressed the young men of the Church. It was the first in a series of eight talks addressed to specific age groups or interests. Published as separate pamphlets, they enjoyed a wide distribution and represent prophetic and inspired direction from the Lord's mouthpiece to the generation who heard and read them.

- To the Young Men of the Priesthood (April 5, 1986)
- To the Young Women of the Church (September 27, 1986)
- To the Mothers in Zion (February 22, 1987)
- To the Fathers in Israel (October 3, 1987)
- To the Single Adult Brethren of the Church (April 2, 1988)
- To the Single Adult Sisters of the Church (September 24, 1988)
- To the Children of the Church (April 2, 1989)
- To the Elderly in the Church (September 30, 1989)

(Above) Ezra Taft Benson shortly after being called as president of the Church in 1986 (Public Communication Department, The Church of Jesus Christ of Latter-day Saints)

(Right) Ezra Taft Benson reading from the Book of Mormon, about 1986 (Don Busath, courtesy Busath Photography)

(Above) Ezra Taft Benson speaking in a priesthood session of general conference, October 1987 (Church Archives)

(Right) Missionary certificate signed by Ezra Taft Benson (Courtesy Kimberli Ann Nageli)

EZRA TAFT BENSON'S FAMILY

Ezra Taft Benson was the eldest of eleven children born to George T. Benson Jr. and Sarah Sophia Dunkley Benson. He always demonstrated respect and gratitude for his parents and those who came before him. He said on one occasion, "I thank the Lord for my heritage, for my parents, my grandparents, and my great-grandparents who have seen fit to give their all to help in the establishment of this the Kingdom of God upon the earth." While honoring the past, Ezra also looked to the future, and at twenty-seven years of age he started his own family when he married Flora Smith Amussen in the Salt Lake Temple (they had six children) on September 10, 1926. His love for Flora could not be measured—it was as constant as it was deep. That love flowed naturally to his children. When he was asked by President George Albert Smith to fulfill a special assignment in war-torn Europe following the ending of hostilities there in 1945, he realized that he would be separated from his loved ones for an indefinite time. Ezra recalled, "This unexpected development affected greatly our preparations for Christmas and created an unusually sentimental and loving atmosphere in our home. Flora and I realized we would be separated for a period of time, and our feelings were tender at the prospect. How grateful I was for her support, and for the knowledge we had that this was the Lord's will for our family at this time. As the Christmas season drew to a close, I recorded in my journal: 'The next year will no doubt be spent, in large measure and possibly in its entirety, abroad. It will mean some sacrifice of material comforts. I will miss my wife and sweet children. . . . I go, however, with no fear whatsoever, knowing that this is the Lord's work and that He will sustain me. I am grateful for the opportunity and deeply grateful that my wife, who is always most loyal, feels the same way. God bless them while I am away.'" The return home the following year, just before Christmas 1946, was sweet and tender, a manifestation of the Ezra's feelings. At his death in 1994, their six children had given them thirty-four grandchildren and sixty-seven great-grandchildren. He reminded his family when he could, that he wanted "no empty chairs" in the eternities.

(Above left) Ezra Taft and Flora Benson dancing, about 1987 (Church Archives)

(Above) President Ezra Taft Benson and President Thomas S. Monson at general conference, April 1989 (Church Archives)

State of the Church at the time of Ezra Taft Benson's death	
Year of death	1994
Church membership	8,9688,511
Stakes	1, 980
Temples	45
Missions	303
Missionaries set apart during administration	234,590
Book of Mormon translations completed during administration	18

PROPHETS AND WORLD LEADERS

Harry S. Truman, George Albert Smith, and Utah Governor Herbert B. Maw, June 26, 1945 (Church Archives)

George Albert Smith meeting with Manuel Avila Camcho, May 1946, from left: George Albert Smith, Joseph Anderson, Harold Brown, Gustavo T. Serrano, Arwell L. Pierce, Manuel Avila Camacho (Church Archives)

John F. Kennedy and David O. McKay having lunch together in President McKay's apartment, September 26, 1963 (Church Archives)

W hen the Church was organized in April 1830 Andrew Jackson was president of the United States. It was not until 1839, when Joseph Smith visited U.S. president Martin Van Buren in Washington, D.C., that a prophet met a national leader. Later, during Brigham Young's ministry, national leaders in the United States, Europe and other nations, including the emperor of Brazil, interacted with the president of the Church and other Church leaders. Brigham Young himself met U.S. president Ulysses S. Grant during a U.S. presidential tour of the West in 1875. In 1880, just weeks before he was sustained

David O. McKay, Emma McKay, and Lyndon B. Johnson at the Hotel Utah, September 17, 1964 (Church Archives)

A SURPRISE VISIT ON A THURSDAY AFTERNOON

U.S. Secretary of the Interior, Stewart Udall recalled, "[President Lyndon B. Johnson] decided that he wanted to stop off [in Salt Lake City] to see David O. McKay. . . . This was all put together in a matter of a few hours, which really made him scramble. But he said, 'I'd like to see him, let's stop.' It just came to his mind and it was done." A local reporter noted, "Before leaving, the President said to President McKay, 'I always feel better for having been in your presence.'"

Richard Nixon speaking in front of the Church Administration Building, July 24, 1972, from left: Harold B. Lee, Joseph Fielding Smith, Richard M. Nixon, N. Eldon Tanner (Courtesy L. Brent Goates)

Spencer W. Kimball presenting a statue to Jimmy Carter in the Salt Lake Tabernacle, November 27, 1978 (Church Archives)

David M. Kennedy, Spencer W. Kimball, and Philippines president Ferdinand Marcus, October 18, 1980 (Church Archives)

Kofi Annan and Gordon B. Hinckley, February 2002 (Intellectual Reserve, Inc.)

Gordon B. Hinckley, George W. Bush, and Laura Bush in the White House, February 8, 2002 (Intellectual Reserve, Inc.)

as president of the Church, John Taylor met briefly with U.S. president Rutherford B. Hayes at Ogden in September 1880. The next decade was a difficult period for the Church in the United States and in many places in the world. Eventually, Wilford Woodruff entertained U.S. President Benjamin Harrison in 1891 in Salt Lake City during the period of reconciliation with the U.S. government. As the environment continued to improve, President Theodore Roosevelt spoke in the Salt Lake Tabernacle in the presence of the First Presidency in 1903, signaling a change of attitude about the Church by a prominent national leader. Both U.S. presidents Taft and Wilson visited Salt Lake City, taking time to visit Joseph F. Smith and Heber J. Grant, respectively. President Harding played golf with Heber J. Grant in 1923 during his visit to Utah, and U.S. president Harry Truman met with George Albert Smith and

David O. McKay. In 1946 George Albert Smith took the opportunity to meet Mexican president Manuel Avila Camacho in Mexico City during a visit with the local Saints.

From the 1960s onward, Salt Lake City has been an important stopover for U.S. presidents and world leaders. As Church presidents expanded their own travel schedules throughout the world during this same period, contacts with leaders of nations increased, indicating the growing number and importance of Latter-day Saints in various countries.

Events during the beginning of the new millennium, including the 2001 Olympics held in Salt Lake City, provided world leaders numerous opportunities to meet with the prophet, seek his counsel and advice, and learn about the Church's activities in their own nations and throughout the world.

PROPHETS AND WORLD LEADERS

Howard W. Hunter

BORN
NOVEMBER 14, 1907
BOISE, IDAHO

PARENTS
JOHN WILLIAM "WILL"
AND NELLIE MARIE
RASMUSSEN HUNTER

BAPTIZED
APRIL 4, 1920
(AGE 12)

STATURE
6' 0"
185 POUNDS

MARRIED
JUNE 10, 1931
TO CLAIRE "CLARA" MAY JEFFS
(AGE 23)

APOSTLE
OCTOBER 15, 1959
(AGE 51)

PRESIDENT
JUNE 5, 1994
(AGE 86)

DIED
MARCH 3, 1995
SALT LAKE CITY, UTAH
(AGE 87)

I n a 1992 conversation with Elder James E. Faust, Dorothy Rasmussen remembered that her brother "Howard always wanted to do good and be good. A wonderful brother, he looked out for me. He was kind to our mother and father. Howard loved animals and regularly brought home strays."

As a young lad in Boise, Idaho, he came upon a group of neighborhood boys throwing a kitten into an irrigation canal. Over and over again the terrorized creature would crawl out of the water, only to be recaptured and then flung back into the canal.

His sister wrote, "Howard came by and picked [the kitten] up; it was lying almost dead, and he brought it home. Mother was afraid it was dead, but they wrapped it in a blanket and put it near the warm oven and nursed it." The cat indeed lived and became a member of the Hunter household.

This incident was but one of many early examples of Howard W. Hunter's outward focus—an active attitude that he maintained throughout his life. His healing and compassionate personality was revealed in the thoughts he shared when he became president of the Church in 1995, inviting "all members of the Church to live with ever more attention to the life and example of the Lord Jesus Christ, especially the love and hope and compassion He displayed. I pray we might treat each other with more kindness, more courtesy, more humility and patience and forgiveness. . . . To those who have transgressed or been offended, we say, come back. To those who are hurt and struggling and afraid, we say, let us stand with you and dry your tears. . . . Come back. Stand with us. Carry on. Be believing."

His journey from an unassuming boy saving a kitten in Boise to a prophet standing before the world was a mixture of joy and melancholy. Like many of the latter-day prophets before him, Howard W. Hunter was all too familiar with adversity and suffering. Physically, he suffered a heart attack, had a benign tumor removed, underwent a quadruple coronary bypass, had surgery for a bleeding ulcer, underwent a gall-bladder operation, broke three ribs after losing his balance and falling backward at the Tabernacle pulpit, and endured major back surgery. However, rather than feeling sorry for himself, he instead turned his thoughts to others, noting that "adversity touches many, many lives. What makes the difference is how we accept it. It's important to know it's all within the purposes of the

(Left) Portrait of Howard W. Hunter (William Whitaker, MCHA)

(Above oval) Portrait of Howard W. Hunter (Grant W. Clawson, MCHA)

Lord. . . . If we can submit ourselves to that, we can go forward in faith and understanding."

Howard Hunter's suffering was not limited to the physical. As a young married couple, he and his beloved wife, Claire, were grief-stricken by the October 1934 death of their six-month-old first child, Howard William (Billy) Hunter Jr. For the lively Claire and Howard, it was a sudden, numbing shock.

In October 1983, tragedy struck at Elder Hunter's very core when his wife, Claire, died. More than ten years earlier, Claire had begun experiencing headaches coupled with disorienting memory loss. After a variety of medical tests, procedures, and diagnoses—which included hardening of the arteries, blood clots, partial lung collapse, surgical placement of a pressure-relieving shunt in the brain, and adult-onset diabetes—doctors were unable to quiet her pain or slow her physical deterioration. Throughout it all, Elder Hunter was at her side, caring for her. During the day and when he was away on Church duties, a live-in companion aided her, but at nights he would forego sleep to see to her needs. In 1982,

Howard W. Hunter at eight months of age, 1908 (Church Archives)

after strokes further debilitated Claire, Howard was forlornly forced to place her in the care of a nursing facility. He visited her twice a day, and when away he called to check on her condition. Howard felt physically and emotionally exhausted as he watched the once vibrant love of his life slip away in pain. During this stressful time Elder Hunter suffered a heart attack. Yet his daughter-in-law Louine Hunter noted that "to the very end he did what few—if any—men have been called upon to do, to combine the endless duties and travels of an apostle with the constant care of his wife. It was a remarkable love story." On May 3, 1983, he wrote in his journal, "Each day I have the hope that she will be better, but the progress is slow. Most of the time her eyes are closed, and she doesn't recognize me." Five months later, on October 9, Claire passed away.

President Gordon B. Hinckley noted, "Much has been said about his suffering. I believe that it went on longer and was more sharp and deep than any of us really knew. He developed a high tolerance for pain and did not complain about it. That he lived so long is a miracle in and of itself. His suffering has comforted and mitigated the pain of many others who suffer. They know that he understood the heaviness of their burdens."

However, President Hunter's life was also filled with joy, and he was known for his quick wit and ready smile. He was a man of varied interests and talents—and remarkably, of great energy. As a child he took on a variety of summer and after-school jobs, including caddying, picking fruit and vegetables, making and serving ice-cream sodas, working as a busboy and bellman at the swank Idanha Hotel, cutting mats and building frames at an art store, delivering prescriptions for a drugstore, and writing newspaper advertisements.

An early interest in music was encouraged through piano and violin lessons. After teaching himself to play the marimbas he won from a music store, he then added the clarinet, drums, saxophone, and trumpet to his repertoire. In 1924, he founded "Hunter's Croonaders," a soon-to-be popular local dance band. After his June 1926 graduation from Boise High School, he and his Croonaders were invited to provide music for a two-month cruise aboard the S.S. President Jackson. During the January through February 1927 cruise, the band members visited Hong Kong, Tokyo, Shanghai, and the Philippines.

After returning from the cruise, Howard decided to move to southern California, where he found employment with the Bank of Italy. More important, he met and married, in 1931, Claire "Clara" May Jeffs. The Great Depression taught the couple the importance of staying

Two-year-old Howard W. Hunter (Church Archives)

Young Howard W. Hunter, about 1918, when he joined a Boy Scout troop sponsored by the Church in Boise, Idaho (Church Archives)

As a boy, Howard W. Hunter was actively involved in the Scouting program, attaining the rank of Eagle, about 1923 (Church Archives)

Howard W. Hunter's band, "Hunter's Croonaders," played on the S.S. President Jackson on its two-month cruise to the Orient; Howard is standing center, about 1927 (Church Archives)

out of debt. The bank he worked for shut down in 1932, forcing Howard to look for a new job. During this time he worked a variety of jobs until the Los Angeles County Flood Control District hired him in 1934. At this time, he studied law at night at the Southwestern University School of Law. He graduated cum laude in June 1939 and practiced law in California for twenty years until, unexpectedly to him, he was called to the Quorum of the Twelve Apostles in October 1959.

When called to the Twelve, Howard W. Hunter, who was president of the Pasadena Stake at the time, wrote in his journal, "President McKay greeted me with a pleasant smile and warm handshake and then said to me, 'Sit down, President Hunter, I want to talk with you. The Lord has spoken. You are called to be one of his special witnesses, and tomorrow you will be sustained as a member of the Council of the Twelve.' . . . I cannot attempt to explain the feeling that came over me. Tears came to my eyes and I could not speak. I have never felt so completely humbled as when I sat in the presence of this great, sweet, kindly man— the prophet of the Lord."

This humble, polite, and compassionate servant of the Lord, while enduring much, served in a variety of responsibilities, often traveling far distances throughout the world. Among his many duties as an apostle, he served as chairman of advisors for the New World Archaeological Foundation from 1961 to 1985, president of the Genealogical Society of Utah from 1964 to 1972, president and chairman of the board of directors of the Polynesian Cultural Center from 1965 to 1976, Church Historian from 1970 to 1972, director of the Orson Hyde

Howard W. Hunter and Claire "Clara" May Jeffs during their courtship, about 1929 (Church Archives)

Memorial Garden from 1972 to 1979, and director of the BYU-Jerusalem Center project from 1979 to 1989.

Howard W. Hunter taught, "The brotherhood of man is literal. We are all of one blood and the literal sprit offspring of our eternal Heavenly Father." This belief and faith guided him as he worked throughout the late 1970s and 1980s to establish the BYU Jerusalem Center. Working with both Israeli religious and government officials and Arab-Palestinian leaders, he successfully negotiated "the extremely sensitive . . . verbal minefields in his discussions." David Galbraith, former BYU Jerusalem Center director, saw Elder Hunter "carefully walk the political tightrope between protagonists. . . . At the same time, he made it clear to all concerned that he was very much aware of the issues involved." His efforts made many friends for the Church and saw fruition when he dedicated the center in May 1989.

When President Hunter passed away in March 1995, his counselor Gordon B. Hinckley paid beautiful tribute to the man with whom he had served for many years: "A majestic tree in the forest has fallen, leaving a place of emptiness. A great and quiet strength has departed from our midst. . . . Much has been said about his kindness, his thoughtfulness, his courtesy to others. It is all true. He surrendered himself to the pattern of the Lord whom he loved. He was a quiet and thoughtful man."

President Thomas Monson affirmed through personal experience that "President Howard W. Hunter lived as he taught, after the pattern of the Savior whom he served. . . . He was truly a prophet, a seer, and revelator for our time."

(Above) Howard W. Hunter in his backyard with his collie,
Duchess, and turtle, Peep, about 1950 (Church Archives)

(Left) The Hunter family at Thanksgiving in 1945
(Howard, Claire, John, and Richard) (Church Archives)

(Below) Howard and Claire Hunter's son John's wedding reception on December 27, 1958,
shortly before Howard W. Hunter's call to the Quorum of the Twelve (Howard and Claire
Hunter and the new in-laws, A. Kay and Beth Berry) (Church Archives)

(Above) Howard W. Hunter was ordained an apostle on
October 15, 1959, by David O. McKay at the age of
fifty-one; this composition was taken in his office in Salt
Lake City sometime after his appointment to the Twelve
(Church Archives)

(Above right) Howard W. Hunter carving the Christmas
turkey for family dinner in Ojai, California in 1983
(Courtesy Richard and Nan Hunter)

(Right) Howard W. Hunter (with Mary Holland,
Ruth Faust, John Hunter, James E. Faust,
Patricia T. Holland, and Jeffrey R. Holland)
at the Garden Tomb in Jerusalem, May 1985
(Church Archives)

Official Church Public Communications Department photograph of Howard W. Hunter at the time of his appointment to serve as president of the Quorum of the Twelve Apostles, June 2, 1988 (Church Archives)

A Nose is A Nose

A FAMILY TRADITION

When the children were growing up we did lots of performing at the Ward Talent show. One of the funnier acts we learned was the song from Saturday's Warrior, 'A Nose is A Nose.' Everyone performed, Richard, Nan, and the eight children. We were very funny and the audience loved seeing this dignified and reserved father and local church leader, with his children and his theatrical wife. So in 1988, when our first child married, we all thought that as part of the program we should perform our most amusing talent for our family and friends. Thus began a tradition. Grandpa Hunter, who knew how to have fun and how to be a good sport, donned this nose with his granddaughter, Merrily, and her friend Martha Berg at the wedding of Merrily's brother, David, in 1992.

—Nan Hunter

HOWARD W. HUNTER'S FAMILY

Howard W. Hunter was born in Boise, Idaho, on November 14, 1907. He was the first of two children born to Nellie Marie and John William Hunter. He and his sister, Dorothy, grew up in a love-filled, close-knit, and nurturing home. Although Howard's father was not a member of the Church, he was supportive of his wife's interest and activity in the Church. However, he felt his children should wait to be baptized until they were old enough to make their own decision. Howard was baptized, with his father's approval, on April 4, 1920, when he was 12 years old.

Two family events brought particular joy to Howard Hunter. The first was the early 1927 baptism of his father, of which Howard learned upon returning home after playing with his dance band for two months aboard a cruise ship. The second event took place during a special Pasadena Stake excursion to the Arizona Temple on November 14, 1953. He wrote in his journal, "While I was speaking to the congregation, my father and mother came into the chapel dressed in white. I had no idea my father was prepared for his temple blessings. . . . I was so overcome with emotion that I was unable to continue to speak. . . . On that day they were endowed and I had the privilege of witnessing their sealing, following which I was sealed to them."

In 1931, Howard Hunter and Clara May Jeffs were married in the Salt Lake Temple. They had two sons—John and Richard—and eighteen grandchildren. Clara died in 1983, leaving a void in the apostle's life.

On April 12, 1990, widower Howard Hunter married the vivacious Inis Egan. Elder Boyd K. Packer credited Inis Hunter with bringing "a sparkle back into President Hunter's life."

(Above) Howard W. Hunter and Inis Egan Hunter shortly after their marriage on April 10, 1990 (Elayne Stanton Allebest, courtesy Elayne Stanton Allebest)

(Top of page) Howard W. and Claire Hunter's family on the day he was sustained fourteenth president of The Church of Jesus Christ of Latter-day Saints, June 5, 1994 (Courtesy Richard and Nan Hunter)

grandpa and me.

When I gave grandpa this picture in a frame, he was all excited. It was a gift for his 87th birthday. Upon giving it to him, several members of the quorum of the twelve noticed how much we looked alike. Elder Faust in particular, and continued to call me the twin granddaughter.

"What would Jesus do?"

Howard W. Hunter's life was an example of following the teachings of Christ. A major theme of his nine months as president of The Church of Jesus Christ of Latter-day Saints was his invitation for members to draw close to the Savior and live by His example. In these times of less-than-stalwart models vying for our attention, Howard W. Hunter pointed to the one we should follow:

"The world is full of people who are willing to tell us, 'Do as I say.' Surely we have no lack of advice givers on about every subject. But we have so few who are prepared to say, 'Do as I do.' And, of course, only One in human history could rightfully and properly make that declaration. History provides many examples of good men and women, but even the best of mortals are flawed in some way or another. None could serve as a perfect model nor as an infallible pattern to follow, however well-intentioned they might be.

"Only Christ can be our ideal, our 'bright and morning star.' (Rev. 22:16) Only He can say without any reservation, 'Follow me, learn of me, do the things you have seen me do. Drink of my water and eat of my bread. I am the way, the truth, and the life. I am the law, and the light. Look unto me and ye shall live. Love one another as I have loved you' (See Matt. 11:29; John 4:13–14; 6:35, 51;7:37; 13:34; 14:6; 3 Nephi 15:9; 27:21).

"My, what a clear and resonant call! What certainty and example in a day of uncertainty and absence of example. . . . Let us follow the Son of God in all ways and in all walks of life. Let us make him our exemplar and our guide. We should at every opportunity ask ourselves, 'What would Jesus do?' and then be more courageous to act upon the answer. We must follow Christ, in the best sense of that word."

(Above) Howard W. Hunter and his granddaughter Julia in 1994 (Courtesy Julia Hunter)

(Above left) Howard W. Hunter at pulpit (Church Archives)

State of the Church at the time of Howard W. Hunter's death	
Year of death	1995
Church membership	9,025,914
Stakes	2,029
Temples	47
Missions	307
Missionaries set apart during administration	29,214
Book of Mormon translations completed during administration	2

TO BE A LATTER-DAY SAINT

Joseph F. Smith, about 1900
(Charles R. Savage, Church Archives)

We all need patience, forbearance, forgiveness, humility, charity, love unfeigned, devotion to the truth, abhorrence of sin, wickedness, and rebellion and disobedience to the requirements of the gospel. These are the qualifications requisite to Latter-day Saints, and to becoming Latter-day Saints, members in good standing in the Church of Jesus Christ, heirs of God, and joint heirs with Jesus Christ. No member in good standing in the Church will be drunken, riotous, profane, or will take advantage of his brother or his neighbor, or will violate the principle of virtue, honor, and

General conference crowd, Temple Square, Salt Lake City, Utah, April 6, 1906 (Church Archives)

righteousness. Members of the Church of Jesus Christ of Latter-day Saints in good standing will never be chargeable with such offenses as these, because they will avoid these evils and they will live above them. Then we have a mission in the world, each man, each woman, each child, who has grown to understanding or to the years of accountability—all ought to be examples to the world, ought not only to be qualified to preach the truth, to bear testimony of the truth, but they ought to live so that the very life they live, the very words they speak, their every action in life, will be sermons to the unwary and to the ignorant, teaching them goodness, purity, uprightness, faith in God and love for the human family.

—Joseph F. Smith

In a world that seems to be growing darker and more cynical, President Gordon B. Hinckley shines forth as a beacon of optimism and positive action. In a 1998 interview with the Houston Chronicle, he shared his belief in the goodness of people: "I feel tremendously optimistic about the future. We are in a world of all kinds of problems, as we all know. We see it on all sides—gangs, families gone, children killing children, single mothers, illegitimate births, drugs, the whole thing, but with all of that I believe there is a great residual of goodness in people. I believe that there are millions who are prayerful, faithful, strong people who are doing their best to rear their families in truth and righteousness, to live as citizens with honesty and integrity and to make a contribution of their lives."

President Hinckley's optimism has blossomed from the fertile power of his faith, knowing and teaching that "faith is not a theological platitude. It is a fact of life. Faith can become the very wellspring of purposeful living. There is no more compelling motivation to worthwhile endeavor than the knowledge that we are children of God. . . . I mean it [faith] as a living, vital force with recognition of God as our Father and Jesus Christ as our Savior."

President Hinckley believes positive lessons can be learned from the faith of those who came before us. He told a *New York Times* reporter, "We have every reason to be optimistic in this world. Tragedy is around, yes. Problems everywhere, yes. But look at Nauvoo. Look at what they built here in seven years and then left. But what did they do? Did they lie down and die? No! They went to work! They moved halfway across this continent and turned the soil of a desert and made it blossom as the rose. On that foundation this church has grown into a great worldwide organization affecting for good the lives of people in more than 140 nations. You can't, you don't, build out of pessimism or cynicism. You look with optimism, work with faith, and things happen."

His goal of positive action on behalf of the Church's effort to improve society and the lives of individuals was articulated in an interview with Salt Lake City reporter Phil Riesen: "I have only one desire, and that is to bring about an increased measure of happiness in the lives of people. We have a scripture which says that 'wickedness never was happiness.' People are happy when they are living

(Left) Portrait of Gordon B. Hinckley (Judith Mehr, MCHA)

(Above oval) Portrait of Gordon B. Hinckley (Grant Romney Clawson, 1998, MCHA)

BORN
JUNE 23, 1910
SALT LAKE CITY, UTAH

PARENTS
BRYANT STRINGHAM AND
ADA BITNER HINCKLEY

BAPTIZED
APRIL 28, 1919
(AGE 8)

STATURE
5' 10"
175 POUNDS

MARRIED
APRIL 29, 1937
TO MARJORIE PAY
(AGE 26)

APOSTLE
OCTOBER 5, 1961
(AGE 51)

PRESIDENT
MARCH 12, 1995
(AGE 84)

Gordon B. Hinckley with his father Bryant and brother Sherman during a family vacation to Yellowstone National Park (Office of the President)

right, when they are doing the right things. That is my desire, to increase that through the teachings of the gospel of Jesus Christ . . . whose name is carried in the name of this church."

This desire was a lifelong standard that began to see mature action as Gordon B. Hinckley served a mission in England (1933–35). Young, inexperienced, and far from the comforting mountains of Utah, Elder Hinckley was discouraged, wondering if he was wasting his time and his family's hard-earned resources. In a letter, Elder Hinckley's father, Bryant S. Hinckley, gave him advice he has followed ever since: "Dear Gordon, I have your recent letter. I have only one suggestion: forget yourself and go to work." Elder Hinckley read his father's words, retired to his bedroom, got on his knees, and poured out his thoughts and feelings to the Lord. It was a life-defining moment. Years later he wrote, "That July day in 1933 was my day of decision. A new light came into my life and a new joy into my heart. The fog of England seemed to lift, and I saw the sunlight. Everything good that has happened to me since then I can trace back to the decision I made that day in Preston."

Upon returning to Salt Lake City in 1935, Gordon B. Hinckley was hired to work for the Church's Radio, Publicity, and Mission Literature Committee. That job was the beginning, with the exception of two years during World War II, of sixty-six years dedicated to working for the Church in various positions, as a General Authority, and now as the prophet.

In April 1958, President David O. McKay called him to serve as an assistant to the Twelve, and then in 1961 he was ordained an apostle. Twenty years later, he was called to be a special counselor to Spencer W. Kimball. On December 2, 1982, he was made President Kimball's second counselor. He also served as first counselor to both President Ezra Taft Benson and President Howard W. Hunter.

Elder Neal A. Maxwell has observed, "President Hinckley's unusually rich experience in Church administration combines history and memory in a remarkable way. His knowledge of things 'as they were' and now 'as they are' has prepared him to contribute to 'things as they will be.'"

It is an interesting historical point that nine of the fourteen latter-day prophets preceding Gordon B. Hinckley were alive during his lifetime. Of these nine men, President Hinckley has, in some capacity, worked with eight of them. Put another way—only six presidents preceded his lifetime.

In this vein, Elder Jeffery R. Holland noted, in 1995, that "perhaps no man has ever come to the Presidency of the Church who has been so well prepared for the responsibility. Through sixty years of Church administration he has known personally, been taught by, and in one capacity or other served with every president of the Church from Heber J. Grant to Howard W. Hunter." He also added, "As one of his associates says, 'No man in the history of the Church has traveled so far to so many places

Gordon B. Hinckley speaking at an open-air meeting in London's Hyde Park while serving as a missionary in England, 1933–35 (Office of the President)

1995
Mar. 3 • Howard W. Hunter dies
Mar. 12 • Ordained as president of the Church
Apr. 1 • Establishes Area Authority Seventies
Sept. 23 • Delivers "Proclamation on the Family"
Church membership exceeds 9,000,000
Bomb destroys Oklahoma City federal building

1996
Feb. 28 • Members outside United States outnumber those within United States
Apr. 7 • Appears on *60 Minutes*, interviewed by Mike Wallace

1997
Apr. 5 • Organizes Third, Fourth, and Fifth Quorum of Seventies
Nov. 22 • 2500th stake created, Santiago, Chile
Church membership exceeds 10,000,000

1998
Sept. 8 • Appears on *Larry King Live*
World population: 5,947,910,100

1999
May 24 • Family history website launched: www.familysearch.org

2000
Jan. 1 • Releases "The Living Christ: The Testimony of the Apostles"
Feb. • Church announces the printing of the 100 millionth copy of the Book of Mormon
Oct. 8 • Dedicates Conference Center
Publishes *Standing for Something*
Church membership exceeds 11,000,000
Dedicates 21 temples during year

2001
Mar. 31 • Establishes Perpetual Education Fund
Sept. 14 • During National Prayer Day appears again on *Larry King Live*
Oct. 1 • Dedicates Boston Temple, 100th temple
Terrorists destroy World Trade Center buildings, New York City

2002
Feb. 22 • Appears on NBC during Olympics, interviewed by Tom Brokaw
Publishes *Way to Be*
June 27 • Dedicates Nauvoo Temple
Salt Lake City hosts the Winter Olympics

2003
Apr. 6 • Longest period without a change in First Presidency and Quorum of the Twelve, 8 years
May 18 • Dedicates historic buildings in Kirtland, Ohio
Iraq War breaks out

in the world with such a single purpose in mind—to preach the gospel, to bless and lift up the Saints, and to foster the redemption of the dead.'"

After the loving funeral services for President Howard Hunter came to an end, Gordon B. Hinckley sought solitude in the temple to prepare for the considerable weight of the mantle of the prophet. He secured himself in the room where the First Presidency and the Twelve meet. He read from the scriptures and reflected upon the paintings depicting the calling of the Twelve, the crucifixion, and the resurrection. He pondered the portraits of Joseph and Hyrum Smith and the paintings of all the latter-day prophets from Brigham Young to Howard W. Hunter. His journal, dated March 9, 1995, reads: "I walked around in front of these portraits and looked into the eyes of the men there represented. I felt almost as if I could speak with them. I felt almost as if they were speaking to me and giving me reassurance. . . . I sat down in the chair which I have occupied as first counselor to the president. I spent a good deal of time looking at those portraits. . . . Their eyes seemed to be upon me. I felt that they were encouraging me and pledging their support. . . . that I had no need to fear, that I would be blessed and sustained in my ministry. I got on my knees and pleaded with the Lord. I spoke with Him at length in prayer." Since his ordination on March 12, 1995, President Gordon B. Hinckley has set a considerable pace. Elder Holland wrote, "By the estimation of all who know him—or have to keep up with him—President Hinckley is the youngest 84-year-old anyone can remember. The brisk bounce in his step, the unrestrained buoyancy of his spirit, and his consuming appetite for hard work and long hours would be admired in a man half his age." It is a pace that has not slowed.

In a very public April 2000 address, this prophet of the Lord spoke to the Latter-day Saints as he shared some of his innermost thoughts: "If I may speak personally for a little while, I think no man has been blessed so richly as I have been blessed. I cannot understand it. I so much appreciate your many expressions of kindness and love.

Gordon B. Hinckley vacationing with his children, Virginia, Clark, Dick, and Kathy
(Office of the President)

GORDON B. HINCKLEY'S FAMILY

Gordon Bitner Hinckley was born in Salt Lake City on June 23, 1910. He was the first child of two sons and three daughters born to Ada Bitner and Bryant S. Hinckley. In his own words, he grew up "here in Salt Lake City, a very ordinary kind of freckle-faced boy. I had a good father and mother. My father was a man of education and talent . . . respected in the community. He had a love for the Church and its leaders. . . . My mother was a gifted and wonderful woman. She was an educator; but when she married, she left her employment to become a housewife and mother. In our minds she was a great success. . . . We knew that our father loved our mother. That was another of the great lessons of my boyhood. I have no recollection of ever hearing him speak unkindly to her or of her. . . . We looked upon them as equals, companions who worked together and loved and appreciated one another as they loved us."

Gordon B. Hinkley married Marjorie Pay on April 29, 1937, in the Salt Lake Temple. President Hinckley emphasized, "Marjorie [whom he had known since childhood] had grown into a wonderful young woman, and I had the good sense to marry her. . . . She was beautiful and I was bewitched."

They are the parents of five children: Clark, Kathy, Jane, Richard, and Virginia. Together they nurtured a home of trusting guidance. Daughter Jane remembered growing up in a home where her parents "could laugh at themselves and find humor in what happened. Somehow they avoided overreacting to all of our little daily crises."

(Above) Gordon B. Hinckley working with a film reel; he was involved
in writing and producing some of the Church's first film-related materials
(Church Archives)

❦

(Below) Council of the Twelve in 1958, shortly after Gordon B. Hinckley's
call to the Twelve (standing far right) (Church Archives)

❦

(Above) President David O. McKay introducing Gordon B. Hinckley as an assistant
to the Twelve on April 6, 1958 (J. Malan Heslop, Office of the President)

❦

. . . Thank you, brothers and sisters, for your prayers. Thank you for your support in the great work we are all trying to accomplish. Thank you for your obedience to the commandments of God. He is pleased and loves you. Thank you for your faithfulness in carrying forward the great responsibilities which you have. Thank you for your ready response to every call which is made upon you. Thank you for bringing up your children in the way of light and truth. Thank your for the unfailing testimonies which you carry in your hearts concerning God our Eternal Father and His Beloved Son, the Lord Jesus Christ."

Indeed, President Hinckley has brightened the world, leading the Church and teaching all who will listen how to "look with optimism, work with faith," and strive in the worthy effort to increase goodness and kindness in this world.

Gordon B. Hinckley and President Harold B. Lee departing on a European tour with their wives, Marjorie Pay and Freda Joan (Courtesy L. Brent Goates)

Gordon B. Hinckley with wife, Marjorie, cutting cake at the Primary's Centennial Commemorative Dinner Celebration, August 11, 1978 (Church Archives)

Gordon B. Hinckley reading a proclamation from the First Presidency and the Quorum of the Twelve from the Peter Whitmer farm home in Fayette, New York, during a session of the April 1980 general conference (Office of the President)

To President Hinckley
With best wishes, & Warm Regard
Ronald Reagan

(Above) Signed photograph from President Ronald Reagan to Gordon B. Hinckley,
then second counselor in the First Presidency, September 1984
(Office of the President)

(Below) Gordon B. Hinckley in San Carlos de Bariloche,
Argentina, November 1988 (Church Archives)

(Top right) Gordon B. Hinckley
baptizing the first member of the
Church in Burma, September 1987
(Office of the President)

(Above) Gordon B. and Marjorie
Hinckley inspecting the growth of new
trees in the aftermath of a devastating
fire in Yellowstone National Park
(Office of the President)

MY REDEEMER LIVES

(*Hymns,* no. 135)

I know that my Redeemer lives,
Triumphant Savior, Son of God,
Victorious over pain and death,
My King, my Leader, and my Lord.
He lives, my one sure rock of faith,
The one bright hope of men on earth,
The beacon to a better way,
The light beyond the veil of death.
Oh, give me thy sweet Spirit still,
The peace that comes alone from thee,
The faith to walk the lonely road
That leads to thine eternity.
　　　　　—Gordon B. Hinckley

(Above) Gordon B. Hinckley shortly after his call to be president of the Church, 1995 (Church Archives)

(Left) The First Presidency, Thomas S. Monson, Gordon B. Hinckley, and James E. Faust, 1995 (VRL)

Gordon B. and Marjorie Hinckley at Albert Dock in Liverpool, England,
August 31, 1995; thousands of Latter-day Saints immigrated to the United States
from this dock in the early days of the Church (Office of the President)

President Hinckley showing veteran news reporter
Mike Wallace around Temple Square in December 1995
(Don Grayston, Office of the President)

(Below) Gordon B. Hinckley relaxing with Marjorie on a trip to the Philippines,
May 30, 1996 (Lowell R. Hardy, Office of the President)

In an April 1997 article celebrating President and Sister Hinckley's sixtieth wedding anniversary, the *Church News* listed the couple's advice for a successful marriage:

1. Live the gospel.
2. Love, appreciate each other.
3. Develop self-discipline.
4. Curb temper and tongue.
5. Look on the bright side of things.
6. Develop, maintain respect for one another.
7. Give a soft answer.
8. Speak quietly.
9. Don't be selfish.
10. Look after one another.
11. Develop talents, opportunities of companion.
12. Recognize differences.
13. Pay tithing, stay out of debt.
14. Develop ability to communicate with each other.

FAMILYSEARCH.

INTERNET GENEALOGY SERVICE

MAY 24, 1999
SALT LAKE CITY, UTAH

A IGREJA DE
JESUS CRISTO
DOS SANTOS
DOS ÚLTIMOS DIAS

Certificamos que o portador, Élder

David Mathew Shumway

membro fiel e ativo de A Igreja de Jesus Cris
dos Santos dos Últimos Dias, é um ministro
evangelho devidamente ordenado e, como ta
possui autoridade para pregar os princípios d
evangelho e administrar suas ordenanças.

Convidamos todas as pessoas para ouvirem su
mensagem.

_____
Presidente

Salt Lake City, Utah **03 Jan. 2001**
Data

_____
Assinatura do missionário

03 Jan. 2003
Validade

(Missionary Ministerial Certificate—Elder, Portuguese). 3/95. (3/95) 21008

(Top left) Gordon B. Hinckley greeting Latter-day Saints
while on a trip to Africa (Intellectual Reserve, Inc.)

❦

(Top right) President and Sister Hinckley are welcomed in Suva, Fiji,
on October 15, 1998; during this eight-day trip in October, President and
Sister Hinckley visited eight islands (Intellectual Reserve, Inc.)

❦

(Above) President Hinckley announcing the commencement of the Church's FamilySearch
Internet Genealogy Service on May 24, 1999; the Web site made the Church's vast
genealogical records easily accessible to the world free of charge (Intellectual Reserve, Inc.)

❦

(Right) A Spanish missionary certificate signed by President Hinckley,
January 3, 2001 (Courtesy David Mathew Shumway)

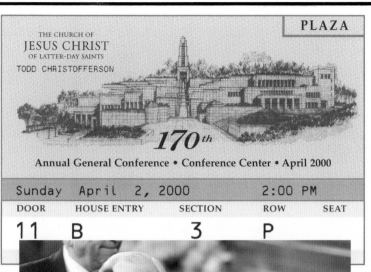

THE NINE BE'S

In a November 2000 worldwide broadcast, President Hinckley presented a list of six attributes to help guide and focus Church members' lives. Rather than an enumeration of "don't do this or that," the prophet superbly pointed out the positive, practical way to happiness in life. Although his talk was directed to the youth, its counsel benefits all people. With the 2002 publication of President Hinckley's book *Way to Be!* the list of six attributes was expanded to nine:

Be grateful

Be smart

Be involved

Be clean

Be true

Be positive

Be humble

Be still

Be prayerful

(Top right) Gordon B. Hinckley kissing Paralympic torch bearer Carrie Snoddy of Park City, Utah, March 7, 2002 (Intellectual Reserve, Inc.)

(Top left) Ticket to the 170th annual general conference in the newly completed Conference Center, April 2, 2000 (Courtesy Gregory P. and MarJane Christofferson)

(Above) Gordon B. Hinckley waving his cane at a general conference session, 2002 (Deseret News)

Current President	2003
Church membership (as of December 2002)	11,721,548
Stakes (as of December 2002)	2,602
Temples (as of May 2002)	115
Missions (as of December 2002)	335
Missionaries set apart during administration (as of December 2002)	241,913
Book of Mormon translations completed during administration (as of May 2002)	15

THE CHURCH ROLLS FORTH

From his birth on December 23, 1805, in the quiet hills of Vermont until the early spring of 1820, Joseph Smith Jr. did not attract much notice. It was only after the Smith family moved westward, seeking a new beginning in upstate New York, that young Joseph witnessed a spiritual sunrise unexpected by anyone on earth but long part of the Lord's plan. When Joseph knelt in a wooded area near his log home to offer a sincere prayer, the courts of heaven listened, knowing it was time for a new day's dawn—a new dispensation. The rolling forth of the kingdom of God began with this fervent prayer and the subsequent visitation of the Father and the Son to the young boy. Photographer George Edward Anderson captured the mood in this now-famous view of the traditional site of the First Vision in New York on August 13, 1907. BYU professor John Telford produced this beautiful print from the original glass-plate negative housed in the Church Archives and printed it as Anderson would have done originally— hence the wonderful, rich golden color.

(Above) The Sacred Grove, August 13, 1907
(George Edward Anderson, Church Archives)

(Left) An early view of Nauvoo, 1859, Johann Schroder, MCHA

In the last years of his life, while living on the banks of the Mississippi, Joseph Smith provided the Saints some of the most precious and sacred doctrines of the Restoration. In Nauvoo, the Lord expanded his gift of temple blessings by providing for the first time the saving doctrines of baptism for the dead and of eternal marriage. These truths and opportunities caused the Prophet to almost shout through his pen as he wrote to the members in Nauvoo regarding the glorious events of the Restoration: "Now, what do we hear in the gospel which we have received? A voice of gladness! A voice of mercy from heaven; and a voice of truth out of the earth; glad tidings for the dead; a voice of gladness for the living and the dead; glad tiding of great joy. . . . Let your hearts rejoice, and be exceedingly glad. Let the earth break forth into singing. Let the dead speak forth anthems of eternal praise to the King Immanuel, who hath ordained, before the world was, that which would enable us to redeem them out of their prison; for the prisoners shall go free. . . . And again I say, how glorious is the voice we hear from heaven, proclaiming in our ears, glory, and salvation, and honor, and immortality, and eternal life; kingdoms, principalities, and powers!" (D&C 128:19, 22–23)

On February 14, 1901, Lorenzo Snow announced plans to open Japan to missionary work, an important first step in expanding the foreign missions of the Church. Less than seven months later, on a wooded hill south of Yokohama, Japan, Elder Heber J. Grant dedicated the land of Japan for the preaching of the gospel (he is depicted here the next year at the dedication site). Alma O. Taylor said of this event, "His tongue was loosed and the spirit rested mightily upon him; so much that we felt the angels of God were near for our hearts burned within us as the words fell from his lips."

(Above) Centennial celebration at the Salt Lake Tabernacle, April 6, 1930, MLUU

Church membership stood at 670,017 when the Saints gathered in the historic Tabernacle (decked with special curtains for the events of the celebration) on Temple Square in honor of the Church's centennial on April 6, 1930. Thousands packed the historic building and participated in a special solemn assembly where Church members sustained their leaders and participated in an impressive hosanna shout. B. H. Roberts recalled, "It seemed, as the mighty shout was given, to vibrate waves of emotion which were sustained by the choir's rendition, at this point, of Handel's ever glorious and joyous chorus, 'Hallelujah,' from 'The Messiah.'" Other events included the illumination of the Salt Lake Temple by giant floodlights; a centennial pageant, "the Message of the Ages"; and the publication of the monumental six-volume *Comprehensive History of The Church of Jesus Christ of Latter-day Saints* by Elder Roberts.

Heber J. Grant and missionaries at the site of the dedication of Japan, February 19, 1902 (Church Archives)

David O. McKay led the Church during an unprecedented period of growth and recognition; his warmth and strong personality symbolized for many what a modern prophet looked and acted like. Here, he is at Joseph Smith Building dedication at Brigham Young University, October 16, 1941.

(Left) David O. McKay, 1941 (BYU)

(Below) Baptism of Saints in West Africa
(Courtesy Gladys Stum)

Following the revelation on priesthood in June 1978 (Official Declaration–2), the Church expanded rapidly in several areas of the world, including Africa; Robert Wilson Stum "froze" a moment in time during this exciting period of Church history when he captured a baptismal ceremony in West Africa about 1985.

(Above) At the 150th anniversary of the Church, Spencer W. Kimball presided over the historic conference from the reconstructed Peter Whitmer farm home in Fayette, New York, April 6, 1980 (Church Archives)

(Below) First Presidency Christmas Devotional, 2001 (John Luke, Intellectual Reserve, Inc.)

Each year the First Presidency speaks to the Church and the world at an annual Christmas Devotional. President Hinckley noted on December 2, 2001, "Praise be to the Almighty and to His Only Begotten Son, the Redeemer of all mankind. Every one of us is better, our lives are richer, our faith is more certain because of Jesus Christ, the living Son of the living God, our Redeemer and our King, whose birth in Bethlehem of Judea we honor at this time."

(Above) Gordon B. Hinckley appearing on the CNN talk show Larry King Live, September 8, 1998; President Hinckley, during his time as prophet, has been one of the most accessible Church presidents (Intellectual Reserve, Inc.)

(Below) The Second Coming, by Harry Anderson (MCHA)

Hearken, and lo, a voice as of one sent down from on high, who is mighty and powerful, whose going forth is unto the ends of the earth, yea, whose voice is unto men—Prepare ye the way of the Lord, make his paths straight.

The keys of the kingdom of God are committed unto man on the earth, and from thence shall the gospel roll forth unto the ends of the earth, as the stone which is cut out of the mountain without hands shall roll forth, until it has filled the whole earth.

—D&C 65:1–2

ACKNOWLEDGMENTS

We acknowledge the work of our colleagues and friends who have produced important articles and books on Church history that have assisted us in preparing this work.

Many people helped move this project along from research through publication. We appreciate the efforts of Jana Erickson, Jack M. Lyon (our editor), and Thomas E. Hewitson (our art director), at Deseret Book Company.

Our wives, Jeni Broberg Holzapfel and Sheri E. Slaughter, read drafts, provided insights and suggestions, and looked at more photographs than anyone should have to in a lifetime, all of which improved our final manuscript.

Marc Alain Bohn and Karyn Hunter Heath, two student assistants at Brigham Young University, provided help that went beyond their regular responsibilities, including early morning, late evening, and Saturday efforts. Of particular note was Marc's sustained and significant contribution on every aspect of this book.

We would like to thank our friends and associates at the Church Archives and Church History Library. In particular, we express our gratitude to April Williamsen for her diligent professionalism. Ronald O. Barney shared his considerable knowledge and provided friendly encouragement. Additionally, Mel Bashore, Jay Burrup, W. Randall Dixon, Chad Foulger, Matt Heiss, Mike Landon, Alan Morrell, Kathyrn Phillips, Brian Sokolowsky, Mike VanWagenen, and Ronald G. Watt each contributed to the final look and feel of the book.

Don Staheli and Patricia R. Fought (Office of the President), J. Scott Knudsen (Church Magazines), Christopher Lino (Pioneer Memorial Theater, University of Utah), Bruce A. Pearson (Visual Resource Library, The Church of Jesus Christ of Latter-day Saints), Ronald W. Read (Museum of Church History and Art, The Church of Jesus Christ of Latter-day Saints) and Ronald E. Romig (Church Archives, Community of Christ) provided timely and professional help in augmenting the images contained herein.

We also appreciate those librarians and archivists who efficiently and anonymously made our research possible at the following institutions: Alaska and Polar Regions Archives, Rasmuson Library, University of Alaska Fairbanks; Church Archives and Church History Library, The Church of Jesus Christ of Latter-day Saints; Daughters of the Utah Pioneers; J. Marriott Library, University of Utah; L. Tom Perry Special Collections, Harold B. Lee Library, Brigham Young University; Public Communications Department, The Church of Jesus Christ of Latter-day Saints; Special Collections and Archives, Merrill Library, Utah State University; Springville Museum of Art; and Utah State Historical Society.

Several individuals at Brigham Young University answered questions and read portions of the manuscript, in particular we want to thank: Thomas G. Alexander, Alexander L. Baugh, Richard E. Bennett, R. Devan Jensen, Paul H. Peterson, Charlotte A. Pollard, Larry C. Porter, Ted D. Stoddard, and Ronald W. Walker.

Others who helped along the way include Don Busath (Busath Photography), Ralph Chubb (Imageworks Photography, Santa Rosa, California), William Duncan (Duncan Photography, Salt Lake City, Utah), Corey Perrine (BYU Newsnet), Mark Philbrick (BYU), R. Clark Salisbury (Salisbury Photography, Logan, Utah), Jim Frankoski and Charlotte Stewart (Borge B. Anderson and Associates, Salt Lake City, Utah), Sherry Tingley (Deseret News, Salt Lake City, Utah), and John Telford (Brigham Young University, Provo, Utah).

Extra help came from the bright and talented student assistants at Brigham Young University who performed a myriad of tasks during the research and writing of this book: David M. Boren, Emily Durrant, Keri Lynn Karpowitz, James S. Lambert, Rebecca Lyn McConkie, Caroline Elizabeth Pike, and Robert F. Schwartz.

Many individuals shared from their private collections images and stories that appear here, some for the first time in print. Specifically, we would like to thank Elayne Stanton Allebest, Brent F. Ashworth, Reed A. Benson, Gary L. and Carol B. Bunker, Gregory P. and MarJane Christofferson, Leah Jeanne Swenson Christofferson, John W. Clawson, Truman F. Clawson, T. Jeffrey Cottle, Mary M. Donoho, Gary and Carolynn Ellsworth, Jack and Merrily Evans, David B. Goates, L. Brent Goates, Bailey York Holzapfel, Warren Vincent and Lou Jean Willis Huber, Julia Hunter, Richard and Nan Hunter, Scott T. Jackson, Edward L. Kimball, Carol Call King, Susannah Speierman Langenheim, Kim N. Leavitt, Karen Scalley Maxfield, Neal A. and Colleen Hinckley Maxwell, Amelia Smith McConkie, Joseph Fielding and Brenda McConkie, Mark L. McConkie, Miriam Taylor Meads, Annetta Sharp Mower, Kimberli Ann Nageli, Ann Alice Smith Nebeker, Elaine Cannon Nichols, Virginia H. Pearce, Monita Robison, Al Rounds, R. Q. and Susan Shupe, Alice Barratt Smith, Rita C. Smith, Wanda Smith, Karen Stoddard, Gladys Stum, J. Lewis Taylor, Michael D. Taylor, Fred A. and Wilma Turley Family, Mary Louise Richardson Walker, Bertram C. and Christine Willis, and Richard M. Young.

We thank Mark and Chris Thomas for listening and for their friendship. Thank you, Mark, for your insights. We also appreciate the thoughts and encouragement of Connie Disney, Lee Groberg, Charles Haws, Dale Heaps, John Keahey, Bill Larkin, Alan Morrel, Chad Orton, Heidi Swinton, Mike VanWagenen, and Fred Woods.

Last, but not least, we thank Ed and Bunkie Griffith for making this book possible through their continued support and interest.

While those above helped us along our way, we are the only ones responsible for omissions and for errors of fact and interpretation. We appreciate any suggestions or corrections as we continue our quest to better document the Restoration through words and images of the people, places, and events that have shaped this remarkable story.